CLOSING THE GAP

Liberal education and vocational preparation

RICHARD A. PRING

Professor of Educational Studies in the
University of Oxford

Consulting Editor:

DENIS LAWTON

Professor of Curriculum Studies,
University of London Institute of Education

MARINO INSTITUTE OF EDUCATION

Hodder & Stoughton

A MEMBER OF THE HODDER HEADLINE GROUP

To Sally

British Library Cataloguing in Publication Data

Pring, Richard
  Closing the Gap:Liberal Education and Vocational Preparation
  I. Title
  370.113

ISBN 0 340 64409 5

First published 1995
Impression number 10 9 8 7 6 5 4 3 2 1
Year   1999 1998 1997 1996 1995
Copyright © 1995 Richard A. Pring

Typeset by Multiplex Techniques Ltd, Orpington, Kent.
Printed in Great Britain for Hodder & Stoughton Educational, a division of Hodder Headline Plc, 338 Euston Road, London NW1 3BH, by Athenaeum Press, Gateshead, Tyne & Wear.

Contents

Part III Philosophy

Conclusion

Introduction

The period since the mid-1980s has seen the most dramatic changes in secondary education since the 1944 Education Act. A big claim perhaps, but true. Even the introduction of comprehensive schooling affected very little the kind of curriculum that children experienced or how they were assessed; the aims of education remained largely unquestioned, as did the means through which they were to be attained.

The changes I write about in this book focus on courses and curriculum, certainly, but they go further – to the purpose and method of assessment, to the policies for changing the institutions teachers work in, and to the very control of education so that these changes can be brought about. Such an account will, I hope, be of help to the growing number of people who have a role in the educational service – governors of schools and colleges; employers who, as well as being members of governing bodies, have educational and training responsibilities through Training and Enterprise Councils or through the schools / industry compacts; parents who, though given more choice in theory, feel bewildered in practice by the new courses (and new acronyms) which bear little relation to what they were familiar with at school; and heads and classroom teachers who, caught up in the details of curriculum change, may not have had the opportunity for deeper reflection upon the implications of those changes. But the book goes further than that. It seeks to tease out and to examine critically the aims and values that underpin these changes. Indeed, it sees many of these changes to be but reflections of the perennial battles between liberal education and vocational training – a deeply rooted but unnecessary dichotomy that the following arguments seek to understand but nonetheless rebut.

The book is divided into three parts. The first sets out the context in which these changes are taking place – the changing relation between school and the world of work, the distrust that many have of schools' capacity to 'prepare the future generation for life', the different demands made upon the personal resources of young people as they face an unpredictable future, the increasing intervention by government in what is taught, and the wider political framework of changed funding and privatisation of education and training.

The second part describes the new courses that have arisen within this context and the overall framework within which they exist. The scene is puzzling. On the one hand, there is a shift to more practical and experiential modes of learning with a vocational and technical focus, with an insistence upon more equal opportunities, with a greater stress upon personal development, and with a system of assessment commensurate with this emphasis. On the other hand, a National Curriculum has been introduced, which, with subject-based attainment targets at ages 7, 11, 14 and 16, seems to contradict this more integrated and student centred, practical and vocationally oriented approach to learning.

The third part looks critically at these developments. Whatever their surface appearances, the many aspects described in Parts I and II are held loosely together by sets of ideas. These ideas, in turn, reflect particular educational values, particular views about the nature and organisation of knowledge, and particular social philosophies about the relation of schools to the wider community. And yet, despite the frequent reference in curriculum proposals to personal development and responsibility, to the development of knowledge and understanding, and to the efficient organisation of education, these ideas are rarely made explicit and thus rarely opened up to the critical examination they need. It is this, the more philosophical part, which is the main focus of the book.

It is my argument that the emerging secondary school curriculum, particularly between the ages of 14 and 18, can be interpreted in different ways and in different traditions, and that, in the absence of philosophical scrutiny, the more recent stress upon 'preparation for life' will leave the future generation short-changed. Indeed, as we were told long ago, the unexamined life is not worth living, and certainly the unexamined 'preparation for life' is likely to be a preparation for nothing of value.

In the conclusion, therefore, I return to the idea of 'liberal education' so often contrasted with 'vocational training' or with preparation for usefulness in the everyday business of living. The distinction is, of course, an important one, but distinctions do not entail contradictions as is so often supposed. The nature of the distinction, therefore, is re-examined, in the light of the practical considerations and the more philosophical arguments of the book.

CONTEXT

1

Background to Educational Change

Secondary education is undergoing the most radical transformation since the 1944 Education Act. A bold claim, but one that this book will, I hope, demonstrate.

Why is this?

There is a feeling – widespread and deeply rooted – that the educational system is not succeeding. This is reflected in the belief that schools and colleges are not preparing young people adequately for the world of work; that they have failed to instil the social values necessary for a well-ordered society; that students are ill-prepared psychologically as well as economically for an unpredictable future; and that standards are too low.

Such beliefs are held by different people – employers who say that schools are not teaching basic skills and attitudes required by industry; parents who demonstrate dissatisfaction through the purchase of private education; politicians who point to 'falling standards'; and students themselves who often leave full-time education as soon as possible. So many dissatisfied people at the receiving end of education add up to a strong pressure for reform. And the changes presently taking place might be explained as a response to these doubts and criticisms.

Nonetheless, it is important to examine the background to these changes and to see what exactly is being claimed. This is not easy. In these claims and counter-claims, and in the different ways the system is responding, established values are threatened and liberal interpretations of education challenged. Perhaps, too, employers and politicians are wrong about standards in school or about the relation of school to work. That we shall have to explore so that, in the final part of the book, the more philosophical examination of what is happening might be developed. In this first part, I simply try to make sense of the background.

Political context

I use the word 'political' in a wide sense, namely, all those pressures, either from government or upon government, to develop policy in a particular way.

The widespread feeling that the system was failing was reflected twenty-five years ago in the 'Black Papers' (Cox and Dyson 1969a and 1969b, Cox and Boyson 1977). The message was that standards in schools were falling and that there was a need to return to the values closely connected with grammar and public school traditions. These values were widely understood to be the measure, the 'gold standard', against which performance as a whole might be assessed. There developed pressure groups, to the 'right' in political terms, which were critical of comprehensive schools and of the values (such as equal access to the same broad cultural education) which underpinned that system. The Black Papers represented one kind of traditional value – values located in the subject traditions of the sciences, arts, and humanities, and in a relatively didactic way of transmitting these. 'Relevance' was irrelevant and standards were protected in well-established subjects, performance in which would be assessed by formal examinations.

A different influence was that of employers, representing commerce and industry. These were critical of the educational system, including its academically successful products. Other measures of success were appealed to, and 'relevance' (especially to the world of work) was regarded as a virtue. 'Utility' should have a place in schools, and what is taught should relate more closely to economic needs, as these are defined by employers. Often the voice of employers was confused, especially as it emerged during the 'great debate' that followed the publication of the DES 1977 Green Paper, *Education in Schools: a Consultative Document*. But one point did become clear, namely, that employers, and the industrial and commercial worlds they represented, were not so enamoured with the academic values as one would have expected. More value was attached to qualities of personal development such as 'confidence', 'responsibility', 'readiness to learn', 'flexibility', 'co-operation', 'economic awareness', and 'enterprise'. 'Standards', other than those of basic literacy and numeracy, were defined in relation to progression through vocational routes.

The government response to these different voices was given by the

Prime Minister, James Callaghan, at Ruskin College, Oxford, in October 1976. Indeed, many of the major changes in secondary education since then might be seen as a footnote to that speech. 'Preparing future generations for life' was the theme and he pointed to the need for greater relevance in education on four fronts:

- the acquisition by school leavers of basic skills which they lacked but which industry needed;
- the development of more positive attitudes to industry and to the economic needs of society;
- greater technological know-how so that they might live effectively in a technological society;
- the development of personal qualities for coping with an unpredictable future.

Subsequent White Papers and ministerial speeches developed this theme, requiring greater integration of education with training, more vocational relevance, explicit statements of standards to be achieved, emphasis on basic skills and personal effectiveness. The DES 1991a White Paper *Education and Training for the 21st Century* outlined the government's plans to introduce the General National Vocational Qualification (GNVQ), which is a major attempt to bridge the academic/vocational divide. To underline the closer links between education and training, several of the most significant government papers were produced either jointly by the Department of Employment (DE) and the Department of Education and Science (DES) – *Training for Jobs* in 1984, *Education and Training for Young People* in 1985, and *Working together: Education and Training* in 1985 – or solely by the Department of Employment (the last one being *Competitiveness: Helping Business to Win* in 1994) or the Department of Trade and Industry (DTI). Indeed, it was the DE's 1981 White Paper *A New Training Initiative: A Programme for Action* which set the agenda for subsequent developments in education and training. The programme for action contained:

- guarantee of youth training for all;
- establishment of recognised standards in post-16 vocational courses;
- better preparation for working life in initial full-time education;
- collaboration over training and education between public and private providers.

The flavour of things to come was reflected in the paragraph on compulsory education:

❝ The last two years of compulsory schooling are particularly important in forming an approach to the world of work... The Government is seeking to ensure that the school curriculum develops the personal skills and qualities as well as the knowledge needed for working life, and that links between schools and employers help pupils and teachers to gain a closer understanding of the industrial, commercial and economic base of our society. (para.12)

It was the role of the Manpower Services Commission (MSC), later renamed the Training Agency and then the Training Enterprise and Education Department (TEED), to turn these proposals into practice. The DTI, on the other hand, came relatively late into the educational field but did, in its 1988 White Paper, propose that all students would have work experience before leaving school, 10% of all teachers in any one year should have experience of industry, and teacher training should adjust to the new relationship between schools and industry.

At the same time, a broader perspective of educational needs was provided in the DES 1985 White Paper *Better Schools* which announced new measures to raise standards at all levels of ability and to ensure the best possible return from resources invested in education. These measures followed, and reflected, the criticism of the Secretary of State at the 1984 North of England Conference, that the standard of pupil performance was too low, and that we compared unfavourably with our economic competitors. Sir Keith Joseph referred to the need to convince 'those whom we serve – parents, employers and the public, all of whom pay rates and taxes'. In order to obtain their conviction, he indicated the way forward for education:

- clearly defined standards of performance to meet agreed learning objectives;
- higher levels of performance, against those standards, across the ability range;
- a curriculum for all reflecting breadth, relevance, differentiation, and balance;
- concentration on practical capabilities and preparation for life and the world of work;
- reform of 16+ examinations towards more criterion-referenced assessments;
- central validation of teacher training to ensure preparation for these reforms.

Some of these proposals shaped the Education Act of 1988, which was the most radical reform of the management of education since 1944. Indeed, the Secretary of State, at the second reading of the Bill in the House of Commons, felt able to say,

❢ Our education system has operated over the past 40 years on the basis of the framework laid down by Rab Butler's 1944 Education Act, which in turn built on the Balfour Act of 1902. We need to inject a new vitality into that system. It has become producer-dominated. It has not proved sensitive to the demands for change that have become ever more urgent over the past ten years. This bill will create a new framework which will raise standards, extend choice and produce a better educated Britain. (Hansard 1987-8.)

However, that Act failed to address criticisms concerned with vocational and economic relevance. Hence, the need for subsequent legislation – and the failure to reconcile academic and vocational traditions.

These different initiatives I shall describe later. It is sufficient here to note the way in which dissatisfactions with education and training have entered government policy and of how this provides a political back-cloth to educational changes taking place in schools and colleges. The watchwords are 'standards' and 'preparation for work' – although, as this book will show, such words are open to different interpretations. There is no single tradition of liberal education or vocational training. Nonetheless, the government would claim to be reflecting a widespread concern, first, about educational standards and, second, about the relevance of education to adult and working life. This emerged in the 1970s – as though blame for declining academic and behavioural standards and for industrial ills could be laid at the doors of our schools and colleges.

It is important, therefore, to look more closely at the relation between school and work and between a tradition of liberal education, on the one hand (once the preserve of the middle class few, but now extended to all), and a tradition of vocational training on the other (once the preserve of the working class majority, but now regarded as relevant to all). In so doing, we are having to explore new forms of examination, new courses and curricula, and new ways of controlling and financing schools and colleges.

The situation is complicated by other factors that affect the political climate of education, for example, greater accountability to parents, students, employers, and greater financial control by Government over public expenditure. Nonetheless, there are to be detected, within these different political pressures and within the developing government pro-gramme, conflicting messages at a more philosophical level about edu-cational aims to be pursued, the nature of the knowledge to be learnt, the relation of liberal traditions of education to utilitarian ones of train-ing, and the relation of educational institutions to the wider community. On the one hand, there is a shift to more central control to meet the political pressures. On the other, there is emphasis upon local partici-pation. On the one hand, the curriculum needs to be more vocationally relevant. On the other, concern about standards leads to an emphasis upon traditional subject-based teaching. The details of these different and countervailing forces I shall describe in the next chapter, but postpone the more philosophical examination to Part III.

Economic context

It was assumed in the Ruskin speech that there must be a close connection between what is taught and what the economy and society need. This may seem obvious but it is not universally accepted. Indeed, lack of economic utility is frequently seen as a hallmark of a liberal education. These concepts need closer scrutiny later. Here I give a brief account of the economic background to this way of thinking.

First, there is the view that the country's poor economic performance since the war, relative to that of other competing nations, is due largely to the poor training and inadequate skills of the workforce from management downwards. In commenting upon Britain's relatively poor performance, Finegold and Soskice (1988), in an influential paper, point to it as:

> ❢ ... trapped in a low-skill equilibrium, in which the majority of enterprises staffed by poorly trained managers and workers produce low quality goods and services. (p.22)

This could be seen as the fault of employers who have failed to invest in training, choosing instead either to poach those who have been trained elsewhere or to place responsibility upon people with inadequate preparation. Hence, recent documents by the Confederation of British Industry (CBI, 1989 and 1993) have emphasised the need for employers to take much more seriously their responsibilities in training. But the CBI and others also point to the reforms required in education if industry is to have the right people to give the job-specific training to. The 1985 White Paper *Education and Training for Young People* explained:

> ❢ The results of our lagging so far behind our competitors are serious: British employers have to recruit from a population which at age 18 and over includes a higher proportion of people with no formal qualifications or with very limited occupational or academic attainments; young people in the United Kingdom are not provided with as good a foundation for the continuing education and training in adult life which must be an increasingly important feature of modern economies.

The conclusions are that there should be closer links between further education and training courses and the skill needs of industry and that the secondary school curriculum should provide a better foundation for subsequent vocational training.

Second, a more sophisticated and flexible workforce will be required in future. One million unskilled jobs have been lost from the economy in the last ten years; a further one million will disappear in the next ten. There is, therefore, unemployment amongst the young, but that falls heavily and disproportionately amongst the poorly educated and the unskilled. According to the Winter 1992 Labour Force Survey, the unemployment rate amongst 16 to 17 year olds was over 17% but for some minority ethnic groups it was nearly 40%. Meanwhile, there are job vacancies, but they are often at the technician and the technology levels of occupation for which not enough people have been prepared. Conclusions are drawn therefore about the role of the schools in producing this more sophisticated workforce – better able to communicate with each other, more flexible in attitudes to new roles and working methods, 'literate' in technological matters (especially information technology), ready and able to learn without too much dependence on an instructor, and imaginative in solving problems as they arise. Critics such as Bowles and Gintis (1976) who once saw the educational system as 'reproducing' the capitalist means of production, namely, an army of unquestioning and relatively unskilled workers performing repetitive jobs in large factories, now face the prospect of a different schooling that 'reproduces' a different sort of system, one that is more characterised by smaller firms requiring a wider and more responsible involvement of the workforce in the daily running of the industry.

Third, the industrial base is rapidly changing, requiring different skills and qualities. The main growth of jobs is in the service industries (finance, retail, social services, information – albeit often with a base in technology), not in manufacturing. And the manufacturing industries are themselves shifting from being craft to technician based. There are significant shifts from manufacture to service, from manual to non-manual, from full time to part time, and from lower to higher skilled work, requiring a modernisation of occupational training on a scale never previously recognised (see Table 1).

As the National Commission for Education (1993) argued:

> Forty years ago people doing knowledge work and skilled service work (the latter being a lesser form of knowledge work) were still less than one-third of the workforce but by now they already account for three-quarters, if not four-fifths, of the workforce in all developed countries.

What then does this mean for educational provision – the extinction of old industries and skills, the rapid growth in alternative technologies with less opportunities for the craftsman or unskilled worker, the dominance of administrative and personal services, the shift in gender roles that such massive changes are bringing in their wake, the destruction of tightly-knit communities built around the place of work, the

Table 1: *Projected changes in occupational employment 1991–2000 (National Commission 1993, p.36)*

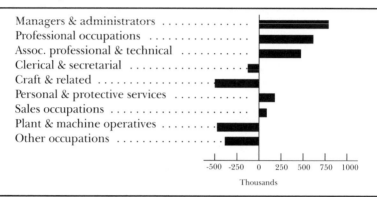

termination of the long-established apprenticeships which for many symbolised the transition from school to work and from adolescence to adulthood?

Fourth, it has been argued by, for example, Wiener (1985) in *English Culture and the Decline of the Industrial Spirit* and Barnett (1986) in *The Audit of War* that a major reason for Britain's poor economic performance has been a disdain for the practical, for commerce (apart from banking and finance) and for manufacture. This disdain is rooted in our culture and reflected in education at every level. Engineering never had the status of pure physics or mathematics. We are told, therefore, that, to be competitive, we must develop a more positive attitude to industry and to the entrepreneurial spirit.

This, then, becomes the economic backcloth to what is happening in education: changing patterns of employment, different levels of skill, criticism of prevailing values and attitudes, the demand for greater versatility and resourcefulness, the lack of adequate training. For these reasons, Finegold and Soskice (1988) conclude:

❛ The education and training system has delivered badly educated and minimally trained sixteen-year-old school leavers to an economy which has been geared to operate with a relatively unskilled labour force.

One might quarrel with such analyses of the economic scene. But the correctness of the analysis does not matter for my purpose. These are the ideas which, whether correct or not, form the debate about the shape and content of education and they raise questions about its aims and values – in particular about the relation of education to the world of work, and of the prevailing conception of liberal education to the increasing demands for vocational preparation.

A major criticism of the 1988 Education Act is that, despite the widespread acceptance of these points, it virtually ignored the many initiatives that had been started in schools – partly by MSC projects, but often through partnerships established between schools and local industry. The new legislation failed to get to grips with the changing relationship between liberal education and vocational training that schools were seeking to define in their own distinctive ways.

Social context

Anxiety over the educational system extends further than the inadequate preparation of young people for work. Preparing young people for adult life was what the Prime Minister's speech referred to and has been repeated on many occasions. That future lies partly in living the life of a citizen, a political and family life, a life that contains social responsibilities and obligations. There are values, too, which as a society we have undertaken to promote: respect for all people irrespective of race, religion or gender.

Therefore, schools are required to prepare young people for a multicultural society, to encourage tolerance between different ethnic groups, to promote social responsibility, to encourage respect for the law and democratic institutions, to develop sensibilities towards the disadvantaged, and to ensure girls enjoy equal opportunities with boys. Indeed, it is impossible to read a major document without hearing these messages explicitly. Shortly after the Ruskin address, the 1977 HMI report *Curriculum 11 to 16* argued that:

> the educational system is charged by society ... with equipping young people to take their place as citizens and workers in adult life ... Secondly there is the responsibility for educating the 'autonomous citizen', a person able to think and act for herself or himself, to resist exploitation, to innovate and to be vigilant in the defence of liberty. (DES / HMI 1977, p.9)

The same concern was expressed in *A Framework for the School Curriculum* (1979), *The School Curriculum* (1981) and *Better Schools* (1985). And schools responded with programmes of social education, citizenship, and parenthood. Moreover, they often did this in practical ways such as organising community projects. It is not surprising, therefore, that the National Curriculum Council recognised, belatedly, citizenship as a 'cross-curriculum theme' in the National Curriculum.

However, we need to be clear about the nature of that social context, for schools may be called upon as agents of social engineering in different ways. We spoke of the economic need for a well-trained and a well-educated workforce. But the social needs to which schools are asked to respond are more difficult to analyse because they are dependent upon social values within society. The distinction between education and social engineering becomes very fine, indeed – the use of schools, under the guise of education, to promote specific moral values and to train future citizens in social skills which people in power think appropriate. Despite what is said in the HMI and government documents about the importance of social and political education, there are few examples of the practical and experiential approach to learning which is strongly advocated elsewhere on the curriculum, and it was clear from Ranson's research into the views and attitudes of top civil servants that, in their view, the wider social context might require a social education geared more to helping children know their place than to developing personal autonomy. In education:

❢ there has to be selection because we are beginning to create aspirations which increasingly society cannot match. In some ways this points to the success of education in contrast to the public mythology which has been created. (Ranson 1984, p.241)

and:

❢ if we have a highly educated and idle population we may possibly anticipate more serious social conflict. People must be educated once more to know their place. (ibid)

Hence, the background to current changes might partly be explained as responses to pressures put upon schools to prepare young people for the future. That future must be seen in economic and employment terms certainly. But it is also being argued that schools have an obligation to contribute to the reshaping of society in the face of emerging moral attitudes and also in face of fears about social unrest and disharmony. There are critics of this quite explicit advocacy of social reshaping – not compatible, so it is argued, with development of personal autonomy, the hallmark of a liberal education. And certainly we shall need to examine carefully this apparent contradiction between the competing educational aims of autonomy, on the one hand, and of social and moral training, on the other. But for the moment I want simply to build up the rather complex picture as it is painted by those who are endeavouring to change the system. And already we can see some interesting contradictions emerging.

It would be wrong of course to identify this socialising role of the school with the content of the curriculum. The social messages received by students arise as much from the context in which learning takes place as they do from explicit programmes of instruction. Hargreaves (1982) in *The Challenge for the Comprehensive School* argues:

❛ our present school system, largely through the hidden curriculum, exerts on many pupils, particularly but by no means exclusively from the working class, a destruction of their dignity which is so massive and pervasive that few subsequently recover from it. (p.17)

Moreover, that context includes the range of institutions, through which young people progress and receive instruction – through which they are separated and directed along different routes, often with different status and possibilities attached to them. The gradual privatisation of education, with its consequent hierarchy of institutions, has for too long been neglected in the assessment of school effectiveness. And yet those hierarchical divisions are central to our understanding of the liberal/vocational divide.

Personal context   MARINO INSTITUTE OF EDUCATION

There are three aspects of the personal context that we must pay attention to.

First, the rapidly changing social and economic scene affects profoundly what students need from school. They need to be prepared psychologically as well as economically for what is seen by them to be an unpredictable future. Gone for many are clearly understood routes into employment, into financial security, and thus into adulthood which would normally be characterised by the transition from school to work. As a result, there are schemes to help the transition by providing induction into the world of work through experience, counselling, guidance, simulation and visits. There is something a little phoney in such programmes. Young people have for generations transferred from school to work without such a self-conscious approach – simply by going to work and learning through 'doing'. Nonetheless, given the prospects of unemployment, and the variety of further training opportunities, there is a problem of transition into the post-school stage, and schools are left to make educational sense of the situation thus created.

Second, changed economic conditions have, paradoxically, stimulated a more student-centred approach to education, reminiscent of the interest-based curriculum advocated by the Newsom (1963) and Plowden (1967) Reports, and so roundly condemned by politicians who want a return to 'traditional standards' (see Hartley 1987). What that means will need to be unravelled later. But reference is made to *negotiation* between teacher and student; there is stress upon the *relevance* of what is taught to the needs of young people as *they* have identified them. Why is this? On the surface it would seem that the economic conditions would suggest a less student-centred approach and a much more directed and controlled curriculum serving the needs of the economy. However, it is argued that what is required by industry is increased *personal effectiveness* and maturity arising from being given more responsibility and from the social and life skills which enable young people to cope effectively with their problems. Indeed, it is commonly pointed out that what employers want of school-leavers (apart from 'basic skills') are personal qualities such as the readiness to learn, a sense of responsibility, and the capacity to work co-operatively with others. All this of course will need to be examined closely – there is often more rhetoric than reality in this overt concern for personal development. Nonetheless, this re-assertion of the primacy of personal development (rather than, say, the transmission of a given subject matter) is a significant part of the background context to the changes we are considering.

Third, concern for 'personal relevance' emerges also as a response to the perceived failure of the curriculum to engage the interest of many young people, as is reflected in early leaving, truancy, and various forms of deviant behaviour. This is not a recent problem and was recognised in the Schools Council (1968) Enquiry:

❢ at worst the raising of the leaving age could mean little more than the extension of a struggle between pupils who feel that school has little to offer them and teachers who feel that they meet little other than boredom and resistance. (p.iii)

'Relevance' was seen to be crucial, but the enquiry revealed different understandings of relevance on the parts of teachers, parents and pupils. Both parents and pupils (but not teachers) put utility and relevance to working life high on their lists. Parents (but not pupils and teachers) emphasised discipline; pupils wanted the more relaxed set of relationships appropriate to their approaching adult status. Hence, there is a rejection of school, and what it is seen to stand for, by many pupils. This was picked out by the Hargreaves report for the Inner London Education Authority (ILEA 1979). A very large proportion displayed disaffection with school, partly because of the mismatch between the objectives and values of the youngsters themselves and those of the school as the students saw them. Students do not always share the values of the school and of a liberal tradition which it represents, namely, that cultural pursuits are worthwhile in themselves and that intellectual ability is all important. Furthermore, in not sharing those values, the pupils resent being assessed as failures on matters which to them seem unimportant. What they find useful and fulfilling is often outside the school. Similarly, the Elton Report (1991), which looked at problems of discipline in schools, argued that a lot of misbehaviour is to be explained in terms of a curriculum that is not seen to be practically relevant.

Therefore, preparation for life, personal effectiveness, and relevance are what are appealed to on the personal level to explain and to justify the need for curriculum change. But the concepts are not clear, as we shall come to see.

Standards

It was pointed out earlier that the need for educational change arises partly from a concern about academic standards. The Black Papers 1969–1975 criticised schools for what the authors saw to be a decline in standards, due to the abolition of the grammar school and to the promotion of 'progressive' approaches to teaching. Indeed, many of the changes that are now taking place – the restriction of the curriculum to centrally agreed subjects with approved programmes of work, the introduction of national testing, and the encroachment upon the professional control of teachers over what is taught – can be traced to these and even earlier critics (see Lawton 1992). The feeling of decline was reinforced by statements of employer representatives. According to the CBI (1989), Britain's workforce is under-educated, under-trained and under-qualified.

It should be noted, however, that criticism of schools for poor and falling standards has always been a feature of education – as the Cockcroft Report (1982) on the teaching of mathematics and the Bullock Report (1974) on the teaching of English demonstrated by quoting documents going back a century. The Cockcroft Report refers, for instance, to the statement in the Mathematical Association Report of 1954:

> Experience shows that a large proportion of entrants (to trade courses) have forgotten how to deal with simple vulgar and decimal fractions, have very hazy ideas on some easy arithmetic processes and retain no trace of knowledge of algebra, graphs or geometry, if in fact they ever did possess any.

- not too dissimilar from what some employers say today. However, such an observation entails, not complacency over accusations of declining standards, but caution over accusations of continual decline from a time when the majority of the population was both illiterate and innumerate! There is a need to look at the evidence very carefully.

These criticisms of standards are pitched at different levels.

First, with regard to literacy and numeracy, a report from the Adult Literacy and Basic Skills Unit (ALBSU) (1993) sums up the general concern:

> A major survey into the attainment of a representative group of 21 year olds has revealed that almost 15% have limited literacy skills and 20% have only very limited competence with basic maths. A further larger group will need some additional help because the skills they have are not likely to be good enough to cope with changing requirements and demands... Screening of 10,000 students in further education colleges revealed that almost four in ten would need some additional help with basic skills if they were to get a qualification at NVQ Level 2.

Second, there are international comparisons which give weight to misgivings about performance in mathematics and science. According to Prais and Wagner (1983), the level of attainment of the lower half of German secondary pupils was higher than the average level of attainment in England; Postlethwaite (1988) showed that 14 year olds scored lower than their peers in 17 countries with whom they were compared; Ball (1990) reported that 'on average, British children are two years behind the Japanese in terms of basic mathematical competence'. The Engineering Council (1993) claimed that only 27% gained GCSE grades A–C in the core subjects of English, mathematics and science, compared with 60% in the equivalent in France and 62% in Germany. Although one needs to be careful in interpreting such figures (for example, more emphasis may be placed on aspects of mathematics such as geometry which do not enter the comparison), there is cause for concern, as Tables 2 and 3 show.

Table 2: *16 year olds' achievements in the equivalent of GCSE A – C in mathematics, national language and science (National Commission for Education 1993, p.3)*

Country	Percentages
Germany	• 62
France	66
Japan	50
England	27

However, there have been improvements since these comparisons were made. More people remain in full-time education than ever before. HMI (1993) have reported improved standards. Better A Level results were reported in 1993 and 1994. GCSE results similarly improved in 1992, 1993 and 1994. Far more take public examinations and proceed to higher education. On the other hand, there is a disappointing fall of

Table 3: *Percentage of young people gaining a comparable upper secondary school qualification at 18 in 1990 (National Commission for Education 1993, p.3)*

Country	Percentages
Germany	68
France	48
Japan	80
England	29

interest in the sciences at A Level – a decline in 1993 of 10% in entry to physics, 5% to chemistry and 3% to biology.

There are particular problems in comparing standards which are rarely addressed but which, given the concerns of this book, need to be noted straightaway.

First, it is true that performance in examinations is a measure of standards. But what constitute the standards are the values, the educational aims that the schools pursue. Different values require different measures of success (see Pring 1992). Behind the concern over standards is a deeper concern over the aims of education, but this is usually obscured by the technical debate about examination results and by the simplistic conclusions drawn from their publication. The significance of this point became apparent with the introduction of the Technical and Vocational Education Initiative (TVEI) (see pages 62–5). The more technically and vocationally oriented curriculum appealed to different standards of achievement – equally demanding, equally rigorous in their application, but related to different educational purposes. Success by those who would not normally have shone in the traditional examinations, and mediocre performance by others who normally would have succeeded, led some wrongly to argue that TVEI represented lower or inappropriate standards. They were wrong. Different, and too long neglected educational aims, assumed different standards of achievement, requiring different measures of performance. Similar mistakes are being made in criticisms of the standards applied to GNVQ.

Second, examinations have traditionally been norm-referenced, that is, measuring each person's performance against the 'norm' for the group as a whole; ideally the examination would differentiate as much as possible between candidates on both sides of the norm so that individuals can be compared with each other. However, there is a problem in deducing from norm-referenced tests what students actually know; their purpose is to differentiate, not to say what people know or can do. This would suggest the need for 'criterion-referenced' assessments – spelling out exactly what young people need to know and then checking whether or not they know it. Differentiation between candidates is not the purpose of the assessment. The GCSE examinations, when they were introduced in 1988, and the national assessments introduced from 1991 onwards and grading performance at ten levels against explicit criteria, aimed to be criterion-referenced rather than norm-referenced. But that has not been fully achieved. How does one arrive at the appropriate criteria except by reference to a set of norms? On the other hand, the National Vocational Qualifications (NVQ) do measure what a person can do and are criterion-referenced.

What, however, is not technically possible is to make with confidence *longitudinal* comparisons, essential if one is to judge whether standards are rising or falling. What 14 year olds in 1995 can be expected to know might be significantly different from what was expected of a 14 year old in 1980 – even in mathematical development, reflecting changed emphases in mathematical teaching (the more practical and applied approaches, for instance, or the relevance to the world of work or the universal use of electronic calculators).

Concern for standards is, therefore, an essential part of the context against which we must view current changes in education. But agreement on the values within which standards are defined, the establishment of clear criteria against which performance might be judged, and the longitudinal comparisons of the 'rise and fall of standards' are highly complex and controversial matters. On the other hand, the notion of 'standard', however elusive, is an essential one in education, and, therefore, must be central to the more philosophical critique of the current changes, in Part III.

Extending education and training

One characteristic of the country's education and training provision has been the comparatively small number of young people availing themselves of it full time, once they have reached the end of their compulsory schooling, although, as Table 4 shows, part-time participation is much higher than elsewhere.

However, these figures do represent a trend to remain in education, as Table 5 shows.

This might be explained partly by the recession – there simply are not the jobs for them. But more young people see the need for further study. On the other hand, the staying-on rate tails off rather quickly. It is 67% at 16, but only 50% at 17 and 35% at 18. It is as though young people are easily tempted from education and full-time training as soon as there are jobs available – seduced by employers who remain wedded to 'the low skill equilibrium'.

Table 4: *An international comparison of full-time and part-time participation in education and vocational training for 16–18 year olds in 1990 (National Commission for Education 1993, p.275)*

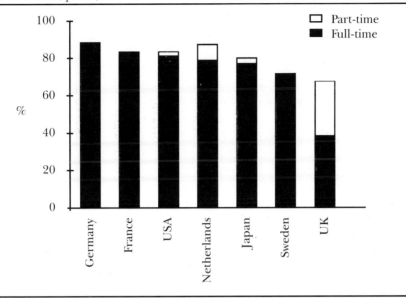

Table 5: *Trends in 16 year olds staying on in education 1980 to 1992 (National Commission for Education 1993, p.241)*

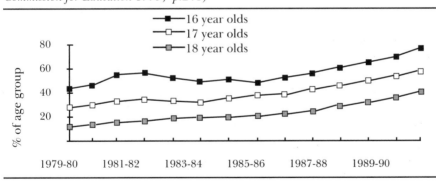

The importance of remaining in education is often assumed to be self-evident for two reasons. First, it is argued that personal development is curtailed if a person no longer continues with further studies after the age of 16. Liberal education is a worthwhile end in itself. Second, much more powerful politically is the view that economic performance is related to the amount of investment in 'human capital' – to the degree to which a society improves and extends the education and training of its future workforce.

Such claims need to be treated with care. Not *any* form of further study, liberally or vocationally conceived, is necessarily a good investment. Indeed, a narrow and rigid training might be an obstacle to the kind of preparation required of a sophisticated and swiftly changing economy. And a form of liberal education which disdains the practical and the economically relevant might be a barrier to economic success and to personal fulfilment. Nonetheless, as the economy has less room for the unskilled and the semi-skilled worker and as economic performance depends upon knowledgeable, adaptable and intelligent people, there is a strong case for the continuation of those studies which extend the powers of the mind and of the imagination – and which provide those more general skills and personal qualities upon which subsequent training can build.

The pressure, therefore, to encourage more to remain in some form of education and training after the age of 16 has been immense. It has been the focus of major reports by the CBI and by the TUC; it is central to the expansion plans of all major political parties; and it has been seen by several independent reports as essential to our future welfare. With this end in view, major revisions are advocated for the pattern and content of post-16 education and indeed of the curriculum pre-16, so that more will be motivated to postpone entry to full-time work.

Conclusion

There is a political and economic context to education that we need to take seriously – although that view is not shared by those who, within a particular tradition of liberal education, believe that what we teach should be untouched by the more immediate concerns of the economy and social need. There is also a public concern about the values and the standards that are promoted in our schools. That concern may be ill-informed, but, even so, it remains a reality affecting what those who run the system can do. The last ten years, therefore, have witnessed a re-assertion of these links between educational aims and values, on the one hand, and, on the other, the economic and social realities in which those aims are to be achieved. This has brought education into the forefront of politics. The purpose and the content of what is taught must serve wider social and economic purposes, and be accountable to a wider public. And political action is taken to make sure that this is the case.

But the appropriateness of that action depends upon several things. It depends on the correctness of the economic and social analysis. What exactly is the relation of our economic performance to the kind of curriculum that children experience at school? Can schools contribute to the formation of social attitudes and values? Can they prepare students in a significant way for the uncertain future they are entering into? Furthermore, it depends upon the underlying philosophy of education. Can what is being proposed be educationally justified – that is, defended in terms of those values which make the whole enterprise morally worthwhile? Are there assumptions about the nature of learning or about the nature of knowledge that might not stand up to too close a scrutiny? And is there a view of society, and of how it relates to the individual, which needs a more critical examination?

This introductory chapter argues that the following are the salient points in any understanding of the changes presently taking place in school and college courses:

- it is now expected that all young people should be in some form of education or training up to the age of 18. It was pointed out in the DES White Paper (1985, p.4) that 'it is only in Britain that the majority of 16 year olds seek to enter the labour market direct from school'. This affects the appropriateness of courses both pre- and post-16, the kind of guidance required, the atmosphere of the institutions in which the young people are expected to learn, and the routes through which they might be enabled to progress;
- standards are being reassessed as education and training are no longer seen to be the prerogative of a privileged few and as the connection between education and economic, social and personal welfare is recognised;
- distinctions between education and training blur as education becomes more vocationalised and as training requires the broader educational base;
- there are greater demands upon schools and colleges to meet the personal needs of young people as they try to make sense of a future which, in personal and in moral terms, is less clearly mapped out than it was for previous generations;
- schools are expected to assume greater responsibility for the social formation of the next generation – promoting values that underpin law and order and that support economic enterprise and regeneration;
- everyone professionally involved in education – teachers, administrators and politicians – are accountable to a wider public, including parents and employers, who will have views on aims and standards;
- what we do in England and Wales can no longer be considered in isolation from the rest of Europe – including Scotland whose own innovations are too often ignored in the search for responses to the pressures outlined above.

Above all, however, these changes reflect at a deeper level conflicts about the relation of education to training, the relevance of education to economic and social aims, the criteria of success that should define educational achievement, the educational significance of practical talents and moral qualities, and, indeed the compatibility of liberal education with vocational preparation.

2

Changing Political Control

The key educational legislation, until recently, was the 1944 Education Act. That Act supported a partnership between central government, local education authorities (LEAs), teachers and the churches – with central government playing a minimal role in the curriculum. But the changing context outlined in the last chapter has caused the government to re-examine the nature and the composition of that partnership. Has central government the power (or has it exercised its existing powers sufficiently) to make the system respond to the changing context? Are the local authorities too local for administering a national system and too distant for supporting local, especially parental, involvement in schools? Have the parents been genuine partners in an enterprise that affects profoundly the personal and social welfare of their children? And what place, if any, in the partnership has been allocated to the employers, who believe they have a contribution to make to the preparation of young people for the future?

Responsibility for the curriculum

The 1944 Education Act required the Secretary of State:

❝ To promote the education of the people of England and Wales and the progressive development of institutions devoted to that purpose and to secure the effective execution by local authorities, under his control and direction, of the national policy for providing a varied and comprehensive educational service in every area.

In the decades following the Act, 'promotion' was perceived in very general terms – ensuring that there were resources adequate for all children to receive an education according to 'age, ability and aptitude'; providing the broad framework and regulations within which the otherwise varied provision of education should operate (for example, the length of the school year or the division of education into primary and secondary phases); and initiating major reports on such important matters as language and mathematics teaching. Ministers may have had opinions about the curriculum, but, if they did, they kept quiet about them.

Within this framework, the LEA organised the schools (and different LEAs developed different patterns of organisation). The LEA raised money through the rates to provide (with the help of the central government rate support grant) education from primary right through to further and indeed higher education, and made sure that the schools and colleges were working efficiently. The LEAs owned the schools (except in the case of those that were voluntary aided and controlled). They employed and paid the teachers. And ultimately they had responsibility for the quality of teaching within those schools. LEAs had, too, considerable discretionary powers over such matters as the provision of nursery education or the provision of grants.

The Churches were key partners because historically they (particularly the Church of England) had provided a large proportion of elementary education and owned many of the schools. The 1944 Act had to establish a new partnership between state, LEAs and the church schools. It created the status of voluntary controlled and voluntary aided schools through which the Churches retained a certain control over the appointment of staff and over the curriculum.

Even then, the responsibility for quality of teaching was handed over in practice to heads and teachers. The curriculum was regarded as a professional matter to be left in the hands of those who had been professionally trained. Indeed, when in 1962 the Ministry of Education, as it then was, established a Curriculum Study Group to identify gaps in, and then to promote, curriculum development, the teaching unions, supported by the representatives of the LEAs, created such a furore over what they saw to be state encroachment upon professional territory that the Group survived only two years before it was replaced by the teacher-controlled Schools Council. But, even in the case of the Schools Council, care was taken not to prescribe what should be taught – simply to support what schools and teachers chose to do in the light of professional judgement.

Two comments are required at this stage in anticipation of what I shall have to say in subsequent chapters. 'Partnership' had, through practice rather than through interpretation of the 1944 Act, been understood in a particularly partisan way. There seemed little room for parents or employers in the partnership. Indeed, it was not until the 1980 Education Act that a place for parents on the governing bodies of schools was made obligatory. And the governing bodies themselves played little part in the running of the school and in oversight of the curriculum. Futhermore, the partnership, as it had developed, assumed a clear division of function, with deliberations over aims and quality of learning seen as a professional matter – something that teachers only, as a result of their training, were able to make decisions about.

The emergence of central direction

Memories are short lived, and those who believe that central government has traditionally remained aloof from the details of what should be taught forget that only in recent years did it relinquish control of the curriculum. Only in 1926 did the Board of Education forgo its right to determine in broad outline the curriculum of elementary schools; and only with the 1944 Act were the regulations controlling the secondary curriculum abandoned.

There have been many indications in the last two decades of the government's determination to change the terms of the partnership as that had developed since 1944 and to reverse the retreat from curriculum responsibility. And, indeed, that is not surprising in the light of the changing context outlined in the last chapter.

First, the government initiated a national debate, soliciting the views of employers in particular, following Callaghan's Ruskin speech in 1976. It was clear, for the first time in 50 years, that deliberation about the content and the quality of education was not the prerogative of the teaching profession.

Second, following the 'great debate', the DES asked the LEAs to furnish details of their respective curriculum policies. Most LEAs were unable to do this. Thereafter, LEAs began to monitor what was taught in each of their schools. Furthermore, in the light of the LEA returns, the DES circulated its version of what the curriculum should look like in *A Framework for the School Curriculum* (1979) and then in *The School Curriculum* (1981). The latter suggested the percentage of time to be allocated to different core subjects. Finally, *Better Schools* (1985) set out the criteria which the curriculum should meet. Meanwhile, HMI began, in 1985, *Curriculum Matters* which set out attainment objectives in different subjects from ages 5 to 16.

Third, in responding to the criticisms of falling standards, the DES established the Assessment of Performance Unit (APU) to monitor performance across the curriculum at different ages, in such a way that longitudinal comparisons could be made. Technical problems prevented precise comparisons. But the mechanism was thereby created for national testing and databases in mathematical, linguistic and scientific development.

Fourth, the Taylor committee produced a report in 1977, *A New Partnership for our Schools*. This report argued for a more active role for governing bodies in reviewing school policy, including the curriculum. And, in thus arguing, it advocated a different composition of those bodies so that they would be more representative of the different members of the partnership – equal representation of parents, teachers, LEAs and the community, including employers.

Fifth, the government began to affect the curriculum through specific grants – making funds available to schools on conditions laid down by central government. Clearly TVEI grants (see pages 62–5) were the most spectacular example of this, but there were many other instances. Through specific grants, the government could, for example, determine the quantity and shape of inservice training of teachers.

The old partnership, therefore, would not be allowed to survive the changing economic, political and social scene. Government, sensitive to the charge that schools were not preparing young people adequately for the future, sought to change the terms of the partnership – to find a place for parents, employers and government in the formulation of educational values and of how they should be transmitted. The losers quite clearly were the teachers, because what was being challenged was their professional right to dictate the terms of the educational debate. But also questioned was the role of the LEAs which could jeopardise central direction.

There are in this changing partnership several, at times conflicting, ideas that need to be identified – and this we shall do in chapter 7 where we examine the underlying social philosophy. For the moment we need to note the apparent paradoxes: the strengthening of central direction and yet emphasis upon parental choice; anxiety over the preservation of standards, and yet appeal to market forces as judge of those standards; recognition of the need for a more 'vocationally relevant' curriculum, and yet the creation of a national curriculum that ignores that relevance; the recognition of the central role of teachers, and yet the undermining of their professional status. My task in this chapter, however, is not to explore these paradoxes, but simply to establish the key changes in the control of education as that responds to the changing context.

The changed partnership

In essence the new partnership, that was to assume control of education, had to reconcile the apparently contradictory pulls between national direction on the one hand and consumer choice on the other. Central direction was seen as necessary if the schools were to meet the needs of the economy and the criticisms of employers; and yet the conditions of a free and open market were essential if parental choice were to be enhanced and if standards, helped by a more competitive spirit, were to be raised. How in practice is this being achieved?

New governing bodies

The Taylor Report (1977) argued that the governing bodies should exercise the power, and perform the functions, as these were outlined in the 1944 Act but largely ignored. Governing bodies were part of the partnership – but, so far, a dormant one. The committee, therefore, recommended: that there should be change in the composition of the bodies so that there would be equal representation of teachers, parents, LEAs and the community (including employers); that the bodies should, within the overall policy of the LEA, determine the general direction of the school, including its curriculum; that they should assume responsibilities for admission, finance, staff appointments and upkeep of premises – within the overall framework set by the LEA. The report stated that there was:

> no area of the school's activities in respect of which the governing body should have no responsibility, nor one which the head and the staff should be accountable only to themselves or to the local education authority.

Subsequent legislation implemented some of these ideas and made schools more accountable to the different interested partners. The 1980 Act changed the Instruments of Government such that teachers and parents had a place on the bodies; and it obliged the governors to publish information about the school that would enable parents to make informed choices. The 1986 Act went further. It increased the number of parent and community representatives and reduced LEA representation. It also extended their powers and responsibilities in anticipation of the 1988 Education Act, which devolved the financial management of schools to their governing bodies. Moreover, each LEA was to have a curriculum policy that would need to be considered and implemented by each body, unless it had grounds to modify that policy. The bodies would also have to establish a policy on sex education and ensure that political indoctrination would not take place. Accountability of the work of each body was to be assured through an annual report to be presented to a public meeting of parents.

Therefore, there was a significant shift in the terms of the partnership, at least on the surface: greater parental and community presence in the governance of the school; the involvement of non-professionals in the defining of educational values and the shaping of curriculum content; and the provision of information so that parents and the community might judge the performance of the school against criteria laid down by government. The role of the LEA was thereby diminished, and the monopoly of curriculum thinking removed from teachers. The curriculum was to serve purposes other than those 'internal' to the educational traditions into which the teachers had been initiated, for parents, employers and other members of the community might have different educational aims. They, in their different ways, were the 'consumers' of education, and 'consumerism' had become a factor in determining the shape of the secondary curriculum in a way that had not been the case before. The deeper philosophical significance of this I shall deal with in chapters 5 and 7.

Central control

When Dr Marjorie Reeves was appointed to the Central Advisory Council for Education set up under the 1944 Education Act, she was told by the Permanent Secretary, John Maud, that the first duty of a member of the committee was 'to be prepared to die at the first ditch as soon as government tried to get its hands on education'. Such was how government was seen in the partnership established. However, we have intimated how, in response to the changing context of education, the government sought to exercise greater influence and to be a more active partner. There are two main aspects of this: the control and distribution of money, and legislation.

With regard to money, the normal way of funding the educational service had been through local rates, supported by grant, from central government. Receipt of that grant was not conditional upon what was taught or how. The LEAs were responsible for content of the curriculum, but they in turn distributed the grant to individual schools and colleges according to formulae that did not specify how they should be managed or what the students should learn. The government, therefore, through its general grant, had no leverage over the curriculum – no means of making the schools respond to the changing context as the government understood that. Because of this lack of leverage, Shirley Williams, Secretary of State for Education in 1977, put money into local authorities through the rate support grant to enhance the inservice training of teachers. The money, however, often did not reach education, let alone inservice training. The government did not have the powers to determine *how* money should be spent, whatever the national priorities for education. There was a need, therefore, if government were to be more directive in the spending of public money, to transfer funds from *block* grant, with no strings attached, to *specific* grants that did have strings. LEAs, colleges and schools might be more responsive to government initiatives if that was the condition for funding.

The most significant examples of specific grant have been TVEI and the subsequent grants for inservice training. The general rule is that central government sets the priorities and offers a large percentage of the cost so long as the rest is paid by the LEA. Increasingly these priorities concern the efficient delivery of the national curriculum.

Therefore, although in the changed partnership emphasis is given to local participation by the consumers of education (the parents and the employers in particular), such participation is to be within a framework set by central government through controls it had gained in its distribution of specific grants.

Legislation in 1988, 1992 and 1993 gave the government powers to exercise detailed control over the organisation and content of education.

The 1988 Education Act legislated a National Curriculum and the detailed assessment of it. But significant changes were enacted to make possible the central financing and thus control of schools through, first, the provision of city technology colleges (CTC), and second, the creation of grant maintained schools (GMS). It also abolished ILEA, a major epicentre of power within the system. The implications for secondary education were the strengthening of a traditional, subject-based curriculum at the expense of one more relevant to the economic and personal needs of so many young people (exemplified in TVEI), and the subjection of schools to 'market forces' incompatible with a coherent response to the changes outlined above.

The 1992 Act gave corporate status to further education and sixth form colleges, no longer to be under the control of the LEA. This created different funding arrangements for students in schools and in these newly incorporated colleges. It created competitive conditions between institutions and destroyed a system of systematic planning of scarce resources.

The 1993 Act promoted the flagging policy of grant maintained schools, establishing a Funding Agency for Schools (FAS), making it quicker and easier for schools to become grant maintained, and providing the framework within which LEAs might share the administration of schools with the FAS after a certain proportion of schools had abandoned their LEA. The implications for secondary education is an even more fragmented, competitive and politicised system under the banner of 'choice and diversity'.

What are the implications of these developments? There is a powerful shift to the centre of the financing and thus control of schools, thereby weakening, if not extinguishing, local responsibility for educational policy. At the same time, within this more centralised system, there has been, at least in theory, the creation of greater parental choice through the establishment of different kinds of schools and through the granting of parental rights to send their children to the school of their choice.

The Acts, therefore, give legislative force to a massive change in the terms of the education partnership. First, the Secretary of State has arrogated to himself powers over the details of the curriculum and testing which would not have been contemplated a short time ago. Second, the mechanism has been created whereby there can be more participation by parents, and to a much smaller degree by employers, in decisions that affect the aims and the content of education. Third, the LEAs have transferred many decisions over finance, staffing, and admissions to the schools and colleges themselves. Fourth, the LEA responsibility for the curriculum (usually delegated in practice to the schools) was transferred to the Secretary of State. Little mention was made of the place of the teacher or, indeed, of the child in the partnership.

What role then is left for the LEAs? In his address to the July 1989 conference of the Council of Local Education Authorities (CLEA), the Secretary of State spelt this out. The national curriculum would need to be monitored; the framework for a competitive local system would need to be maintained; LEA help would be needed in the establishment of financial delegation; the quality of teaching would need to be scrutinised through locally developed systems of appraisal; professional advice and support would need to be provided. Subsequently, however, these words ring hollow. FAS is supported by the government in taking over an increasing amount of LEA responsibility; LEA monitoring and inspection is handed over to independent teams; LEAs, strapped for cash, find it difficult to maintain a high quality advisory service.

Quangocracy

A quango is a 'quasi autonomous non-governmental organisation'. Quangos have been an interesting feature of government in the last decade. Many areas of government have been removed from public accountability, either at local level or nationally through Parliament, to bodies which, although they are responsible for the dispensing of billions of pounds of public money, are not accountable and whose membership is at the discretion of the Secretary of State. Examples are the new Funding Agency for Schools (which, despite the necessary co-operation between it and the LEAs in the provision of educational services, is not open to public scrutiny in the way that LEAs are), the CTC Trust, the Further Education Funding Council (FEFC) and the new Teacher Training Agency. Other quangos, which may not directly dispense money but which have immense power to determine the shape of education and training, are the School Curriculum and Assessment Authority (SCAA) and the Office for Standards in Education (OFSTED).

The power and patronage of unaccountable, politically appointed bodies affects the nature of the partnership profoundly. Indeed, the respective roles of parents, employers and governing bodies depend upon the decisions of those bodies. And these have been influenced by particular pressure groups and political advisers, in particular the Centre for Political Studies and the Institute of Economic Affairs, which have pursued relentlessly a political and ideological campaign for a market-led organisation of education and training, and for an undermining, first, of the professional independence of teachers in shaping the aims and the content of education, second, of the LEAs in the organisation of the system of education and training and, third, of Her Majesty's Inspectorate in the maintenance of standards. To that we must return in chapter 7.

Parental power

The Parent's Charter (DES 1991b) stated:

❝ Good schools work better if they have your active support ... you will want to play your full part at every stage.

This required annual written reports on a child's progress, regular reports by inspectors, published tables on assessment and independent assessors on appeals panels. Parental power, therefore, was seen as a cornerstone of the changed partnership. It was stated clearly in the 1993 White Paper *Choice and Diversity*:

❝ Parents know best the needs of their children – certainly better than educational theorists or administrators, better than our mostly excellent teachers. (DES 1993, p3.)

The justification for the ability to choose is threefold. First, freedom to do what one thinks best is a prima facie good. Second, the customer (in this case, the parent on behalf of the child) knows best. Third, in so choosing, the receiver of the service keeps the providers on their toes –

thereby enhancing the quality of provision. Power has shifted from provider to consumer.

This changed partnership was to be reflected in the governing bodies. The Secretary of State, Mr Baker, said at the 1988 conference of CLEA:

> ❝ the Act ensures much less interference by local government in matters of detail and more voice from the consumer – parents and employers. (*Education* 15.7.88)

The extension of parental choice was to be achieved through: having parents on governing bodies; declaring an 'open admissions policy' which deprived LEAs or governing bodies of the right to restrict entry; making provisions in the 1988 Act for a simple majority of parents to initiate proceedings for a school to opt out of LEA control; and the creation of new categories of choice that are not under LEA control – namely, the grant maintained (the 'opted out') schools and the city technology colleges (partly funded by businesses that sponsor them). As the Secretary of State explained:

> ❝ The voice of the consumers, the parent, the employer will be heard more. Schools and colleges will be more accountable ... LEAs are confidently planning to ensure that the services that they provide are going to be competitively acceptable ... . The respective roles of the local partners will have to be recognised. There will be a much greater desire for less interference in many matters of detail. This will establish a whole new set of details in the partnerships that will develop. (DES Press Release 21.5.88)

Whether things have turned out like that is a different matter. Certainly the greater involvement of parents in school governance and the greater accountability to parents are major improvements. But choice of schools is more often than not a myth. One person's choice can be another's enslavement; the schools themselves can become selective in that, once full, 'less desirable' children who otherwise would have attended the school get turned away. Choice depends on mobility and that might serve the well-heeled but not those who are less able to manipulate the market. And decisions are being made by one generation of parents (for example, in opting out) which bind the next generation.

Employer involvement

'The voice of the consumers will be heard more', and the consumer includes, as we have seen, the employer. But what place is envisaged for the employer in this new partnership? There are two distinct roles – in relation to schools and general education, and in relation to further education and vocational training.

With regard to schools, several initiatives encouraged employer participation. First, and possibly the most important in the long run, has been the placing of business representatives on governing bodies of schools. Remember that the Taylor Report proposed that a quarter of the membership should be drawn from the community, including local employers. And that has proved to be beneficial as schools gain the support of the community and as they obtain access to expert advice. Second, there has been a range of initiatives which have given employers an even greater say in the purposes which schools are expected to serve and in the means of attaining them. There are 'compact schemes' (an idea borrowed from the USA) in which schools and their pupils undertake to attain specified objectives, and in return for which the employer agrees to certain kinds of support – such as providing training places for school leavers or sponsorship or work placements for students and teachers, and sponsoring schools, as in the case of city technology colleges or the Burger King school in Tower Hamlets. The result is a blurring of the distinctive tasks of general education and vocational training, reflected in the language through which educational achievement might be understood and criticised. The seriousness of this I deal with in chapters 5 and 7.

With regard to further education and vocational training, it has been the explicit aim of the government to place this much more in the hands of the consumer (the employer) 'who knows best' and thus to move it from the control of the provider (the college).

On the other hand, this creates a paradox. Britain has a poor record of youth training compared with that of its competitors.

Apprenticeship schemes, which for centuries had provided the main training in craft skills, were criticised for three reasons: they were not adapting to a fast changing and technologically based economy; they did not apply to new areas of industrial development; training goals were not spelled out in terms of the competences to be acquired. Training was on the whole left to industry, with supporting courses provided mainly by FE colleges. But industry failed to provide the training.

Attempts by government to change attitudes and to provide incentives for greater employer responsibility for training had not been successful. Therefore, the DE, in its 1981 White Paper, *The New Training Initiative: a Programme for Action*, aimed to change that, spelling out the need for a national youth training scheme, competency-led qualifications, adult re-training, and the demise of apprenticeships. Therefore, one major task of the DE's Manpower Services Commission in the eighties was to establish a major national training scheme for youth, together with a framework for national vocational qualifications. The

Youth Training Scheme (YTS) was put in the hands of 'managing agents' who had to be approved by the MSC, whose training programmes had to meet criteria established by MSC and whose performance was monitored by the MSC. A managing agent was usually an employer, in either the private or the public sector. YTS eventually guaranteed a training place either in industry or in college for everyone between the ages of 16 and 18. There were financial incentives for the employer to take on the trainee. There were grants for the trainee. And the YTS became a major route into employment.

Here my concern is with the changing control of education and training. Clearly YTS represented a major government intervention in national training. It was the government, through the MSC and later the Training Agency, which funded the scheme, including allowances to the trainees and subsidies to employers. It was the government which laid down the training conditions for grant and established a National Council for Vocational Qualifications (NCVQ) to specify, with the help of industry, the skills to be trained for. It was the government which, following the recommendations of the (1984) White Paper *Training for Jobs*, transferred from the LEAs to its own MSC responsibility for 25% of work-related non-advanced further education. Money had to be bid for which previously would have come 'unbidden' through general grant. And the bids had to comply with the regional training needs as these were perceived by the MSC.

The intention, however, was to shift responsibility eventually back to industry. With the creation of the Training and Enterprise Councils (TEC), following the recommendations of the 1984 White Paper *Training for Jobs*, the new partnership finally became clear. There are nearly 80 TECs in England and Wales with an annual budget, initially from government, of over £3 billion. The executive boards are drawn predominantly from private industry. Each TEC establishes the training needs of its region in response to national guidelines, allocates funds to institutions and courses which it approves of (whether in existing colleges or in private training agencies), and raises the money which temporarily is granted by central government. Indeed, most college courses, other than those for A Level, depend on the patronage and on the money distributed by the TEC. This is a massive shift of control from the education service of the LEA to private industry under conditions determined by government. On the other hand, it also signifies an abdication of direct responsibility by central government for training programmes – except in so far as government maintains a controlling influence over the national qualifications provided by NCVQ and through the grants to the TECs.

The success or otherwise of TECs cannot be ascertained for some time. But it is important to think what would count as 'success', because the implications of this development for institutions and for the relationship between education and training are considerable. First, it is difficult to see how FE colleges, cut adrift from local *systems* of education and training (which is what the LEAs were), can be but one amongst many kinds of institution competing for the approval of the TECs, based on quality of course and on cost. Already we are seeing the employment of instructors to do the same job as FE lecturers, but at a much reduced rate. Indeed, the FE sector is the one which will need to be most adaptable in the wake of market forces. Second, for that very reason, the institutional gap between education and training will be widened, thus making it more difficult to broaden and to 'liberalise' vocational preparation which, for economic as well as for educational reasons, is essential.

This potential (though not essential) conflict between a liberal education of all young people and the preparation of them for the world of work needs to be recognised at the earlier age, too. The 50 or so 'compact schemes' will, after four years, be handed over to the control of the TECs. Certainly in one scheme the compact arrangements will reach down to the eleven year olds and thus we shall have a large part of compulsory educational experience under the control of private employers whose main interest lies in industrial training.

The role of assessment

Two distinct approaches can be taken towards the role of examinations in educational policy. The examinations can be the servant of the curriculum, reflecting what has been taught and remaining in the hands of those who control the curriculum. This was the intention behind the Certificate of Secondary Education (CSE) introduced in 1964. Mode III enabled teachers to set and mark the examinations on syllabuses they had devised, though approved by the examining boards. The Boards moderated the marking to ensure comparability of standards across subjects and across institutions.

Examinations, however, can be the masters of the curriculum, establishing the standards that need to be reached and thus determining what has to be taught. To some extent, the GCE 'O' level was an example of examination-led teaching – but only 'to some extent', because some GCE Boards were responsive to school-based innovations and reflected this in the style and content of the examinations. However, clear examples of examination-led curriculum development are to be found in the vocational area where very specific objectives of what is to be achieved can (so it is thought) be established beforehand by the experts. Certainly, therefore, the examination boards have a dominant place in any partnership.

Given the potential of examinations to determine what is taught, it is to be expected that a government seeking more central direction of what is learnt should want to exercise greater control over the examination system. Furthermore, the public concern over standards, to which the government felt obliged to respond, could possibly be met through a reformed system of examinations which would specify the standards against which performance of schools and of pupils might be measured.

There are four ways in which the government assumed this control.

Initially, it established in 1987 the School Examinations and Assessment Council (SEAC) to scrutinise and to approve all syllabuses and examinations leading to public awards up to the age of 16, with the right to extend such powers to post-16 examinations. Such approvals had to be endorsed by the Secretary of State himself. And Sir Keith Joseph, as Secretary of State, was swift to use such powers. He rejected early drafts of GCSE syllabuses in physics and history because he did not approve of their content.

Then, SEAC's predecessor, the Schools Examination Council, created with the approval of the Secretary a single system of examinations at 16+ to replace the dual system of CSE and GCE. The GCSE limits the range of subject titles and the syllabuses to be approved under those titles – thereby enabling much closer control to be exercised over what is to count as the standards to be applied within each subject.

In 1986 the NCVQ was established to create a unified system of competency-based and occupationally defined certificates at five levels – NVQs which set standards in the preparation for the world of work.

Finally, the 1988 Education Act legislated for assessment of pupils at the ages of 7, 11, 14 and 16, using the attainment targets in the foundation subjects agreed by SEAC (and thus the Secretary of State) as the criteria of measurement.

The government, therefore, created an examination and assessment system which, independently of financial inducement or curriculum directives, determines the content and style of learning.

One can now see how central direction is reconciled with consumer choice. Attainment targets, defining standards and enforced by examinations, are what are controlled, not the means of reaching them. But the 'market', in which institutions compete to ensure their students reach those targets, is 'open' because, first, access to institutions with a good track record is offered and, second, the conditions for consumers to choose between institutions is secured through publication of standardised information.

The privatisation of education and training

One of the several intertwining threads of the account so far has been the role of private institutions and enterprise in the new partnership that shapes education and training and redefines the boundaries between the liberal tradition, on the one hand, and vocational preparation, on the other. How much can be left in the hands of the publicly funded educational establishment? And even if it is so left, how far can that 'establishment' be insulated against other interests – particularly those of parents and of employers? The arguments about the privatisation of education take on a new twist in the light of such considerations.

By 'privatisation' I mean two things. First, there is the growing dependence of the public and maintained sector on private means – on donations from parents for essential goods such as books, equipment and even teachers; on sponsorship by industry such as in the compact schemes, eventually to be run by TECs or CTCs; and on selling services such as renting sporting facilities and premises. Annual reports by HMI on LEA expenditure policies demonstrated that there were not enough resources in the public sector to provide a satisfactory educational service for all. Therefore, parents often feel obliged to opt for the state supported private sector or to top up the inadequate funds received from government. There is much evidence now of schools *dependent* on donations and covenant schemes. And it is clear that, as schools move towards control of their own budgets, they will be expected to improve their resources through external funding. This picture is much clearer still in the post-16 world of further education.

Second, privatisation refers to the encouragement given to the private sector through subsidies – and indeed through the impoverishment of the public sector. The most significant subsidy is through the 'assisted places scheme' which enables those who otherwise would not be able to afford it to send their children to private schools. But we have seen, too, the growth of private training agencies replacing further education colleges in programmes which until recently were the prerogative of the colleges.

However, the position may best be understood not so much between 'public' and 'private', since, with 'the private' being subsidised publicly and 'the public' being subsidised privately, the boundaries between the two in terms of funding become blurred. This is even more so with the creation of CTCs and the changed funding arrangements for schools that opt out of LEA control. And with Further Education, as we have seen, it may soon be difficult to see any boundary at all. Rather may the position best be seen in terms of the degree of independence from government control, or of readiness to compete in the market conditions that once affected only the private sector but now provide the framework for all. Of course, those market conditions are unfair and indeed rigged (think of the massive government subsidies to CTCs and lesser ones to the grant-maintained schools). But those are the conditions in which the values of liberal education have to be taught and reconciled with the demands for vocational preparation.

The issues are complex indeed. The national context would seem to require a *systematic* response, and yet market forces and the weakening of LEAs undermine the only system there is; low standards are deplored and appropriate standards redefined through the National Curriculum and assessment, and yet the promotion of standards is increasingly left to the vagaries of consumer choice; there is a recognised need to integrate as far as possible educational and training provisions, and yet the two are being put into the hands of quite different agencies with different ends in view; and, above all, success or otherwise depends on the professional quality of the teachers, and yet they, representing different traditions of education and training, have less of a voice in determining the goals towards which we should be striving.

In response to the context outlined in the last chapter, I see a hierarchy of institutions emerging which, rather than reconcile the different traditions of liberal education and vocational preparation, simply exacerbate them – and raise questions about the relation of schools to society. At the top of the list are the genuinely independent schools which are able to define liberal education and its relation to vocational preparation in their own distinctive way. Second, there are 'independent schools' that, free of obligation to a National Curriculum, nonetheless are dependent upon government subsidy. Third, there are the CTCs which, contrary to the original intentions, have received government grants undreamt of by other institutions but sponsored by industry and thus dependent on industry for patronage and general direction. Fourth, there are grant-maintained schools, initially with extra grant from government to give them a head start and to encourage others to 'opt out' of LEA control. Finally, there are the remaining LEA maintained schools, increasingly dependent on donations and on successful bids for specific grants which arise from someone else's perceptions of economic and social needs. Such a divided and hierarchical system, with different sponsors, sources of finance and degrees of independence, cannot constitute a coherent system and thus a systematic response to the problems outlined earlier.

Conclusion

Changing context, changing partnership. It is perceived by government that the educational system should be more closely linked to future needs – especially of industry. It is also thought by government that the system should be more responsive to consumer needs, as parents and employers see them – namely, improved social and personal responsiveness, improved academic standards and improved vocational relevance. A changed partnership is thought to make the response to government and to 'consumers' more effective. This is achieved by strengthening parental and employer choice (and thus power over local politicians and bureaucracies), albeit within limits more explicitly circumscribed and regulated by central government. The chief 'losers' in this changed partnership are local government and the teachers: the former through diminished financial control and responsibility for shaping policy, the latter through the encroachment of government on areas that previously were professional territory.

However, deeper and more philosophical questions arise.

Who should determine the aims of education? Does there not remain a distinctive role for teachers trained within a tradition of liberal education?

Given that there should be freedom of choice for those who 'consume' education, who are the consumers – present or future parents, employers or pupils? Who should guard the interests of the ultimate consumers, present and future pupils, other than the teachers who initiate them into forms of knowledge which protect them against the propaganda of politicians and the fashions of the market?

Given the government's interest in ensuring that education paid for out of taxation serves the public interest, how far should the state be allowed to determine the aims and content of education? If education is conceived 'liberally' as a 'conversation between the generations of mankind', should government or employers, each with their partisan interests, be allowed to dominate that conversation?

Key concepts are those of freedom, choice, enterprise, market economy, regulation of standards, competition. And that places the answers to these questions firmly in Part III. Meanwhile, in the light of this new partnership between government, parents, employers, examination boards, LEAs, and teachers, I shall describe in the following chapter the changes taking place in courses, curriculum and assessment.

PART II

COURSES AND CURRICULUM

3

The Changing Framework

Parents, governors, and teachers must feel bewildered by the changes taking place in the organisation of education and training. Choice is fine, but how can one make sensible choices where the different options and routes are unknown, or when one's knowledge is based on systems of education that have been replaced?

The last two chapters have shown how the changing context is seen to require a closer integration of education, training, and employment; nonetheless, a sharper focus on personal development; greater concentration upon standards; a redefinition of the partnership to include employers and parents; and a dominant position given to central government in stipulating outcomes.

In this chapter, I show how the framework of the system is gradually adapting to the new context. What is emerging is a re-appraisal of the purposes that education should serve and, therefore, of the ways it should be organised. But this is by no means straightforward. Different traditions compete to dominate the reshaping of education and training.

Subject-based courses

Pre-16

The secondary school curriculum up to the age of 16 is generally thought of as an aggregate of subjects, covering (normally) English, mathematics, the sciences (three), history, geography, religious education, a foreign language, art, music, crafts and physical education. Of late, economics and technology have been added to the list. Of course, there are variations on this, and there are examples of integrated subjects and cross-curriculum projects. But these examples have not been numerous enough to disturb the traditional picture.

Such a curriculum has a long history. The 1904 regulations for the secondary schools stipulated the subjects of the curriculum, and in broad outline these remained much the same up to the 1944 Act. Moreover, they came to be reflected in an examination system which ensured the maintenance of a subject organisation together with an appropriate style of teaching, even after the regulations enforcing the subjects had ceased – and even though the educational misgivings of this mode of organisation had been picked out by the Spens Report over fifty years ago (Spens 1938). That report, so often regarded as the advocate of the tripartite system of grammar, technical and modern schools that followed the 1944 Education Act, criticised the grammar school curriculum for being too theoretical and not relevant enough to the needs of young people.

The maintenance of this shape of the curriculum was a major function of the GCE O Level examinations, which themselves were a preparation for the post-16 courses leading to A Level. These in turn constituted a preparation for the single or double subject honours degrees at university. The shape of the curriculum for the majority has been determined by the needs of the academic few aspiring to a university place.

The introduction of the Certificate of Secondary Education (CSE) in 1964 loosened a curriculum based on a limited range of subjects. CSE was geared to the 40% ability range below the 20% who were deemed fit to take O Level. Those who first conceived the CSE intended that the primary mode of examining would be mode III, namely, teachers conducting their assessment of students' work based on syllabuses devised by the teachers themselves, though moderated by the regional examining board. Many of the syllabuses were within recognisable subject areas, but many were not, focusing upon integrating themes such as 'people in time and place' or upon broad areas such as the 'Humanities'.

Another major reform was the introduction of the GCSE, which replaced GCE O Level and CSE in 1986. One reason for this change was the difficult and unpopular task imposed upon teachers of directing children into different routes at the age of 13 or 14 which would affect subsequent education, training, and employment. This, however, reflected a deeper worry, namely, the division at an early age into two types of educational experience – a *liberal* education as that had been traditionally defined, and a more *relevant* education in the senses of being closer to the interests of the child and useful as a preparation for the future. What was needed, it was felt, was a form of education that combined the two. However, success would depend on what would be judged acceptable as a liberal education and upon how far it might accommodate the 'relevant' and the 'useful'.

The changes introduced by GCSE lie in the different control, content and assessment provided by the new examination – which together affect approaches to teaching and learning: *control*, in the reduction of 24 GCE and CSE Boards for England and Wales to five groups, with national criteria for syllabuses and examinations in a limited number of subjects dependent on the Secretary of State's approval; *content*, in the much greater focus on the processes of enquiry than on the product of others' enquiries; and *assessment*, in the encouragement given to course work, to criterion-referenced grading, and to 'differentiation', so that almost the entire ability range might be awarded some recognition.

Nonetheless, the national criteria which govern the GCSE examinations reinforce the subject-based approach. And this is further reinforced by the National Curriculum. This prescribes: three core subjects (English, mathematics, and science) and seven other foundation subjects (history, geography, foreign language, art, music, physical education, and technology), in addition to religious education required by the 1944 Act. In Wales, Welsh is added to the core subjects. The subjects are defined in terms of attainment targets made explicit at ten levels (which are related to four key stages of development) and of programmes of study leading to those attainment targets. National tests at the ages of 7, 11, 14 and 16 measure the degree to which children attain these targets. In that way, targets can be openly scrutinised – which in turn will help to improve the standards.

However, criticism of the National Curriculum that it had crowded out other studies which were often seen to be more motivating and relevant to many young people emerged in the Dearing Report (1994). That Report recommended (and these recommendations were accepted by the Secretary of State) that certain subjects were not compulsory until 16 – history, geography and the arts – and that it would be possible for students to opt for more vocational studies – including part 1 of a GNVQ. And so the traditional subject-based National Curriculum was dented, and the way was opened for a more vocational track after the age of 14.

Post-16

After the age of 16, most successful GCSE students move on to the subject-based A Level courses, taken usually in groups of three. The successful completion of these is generally necessary for access to higher education.

The A Level system was criticised by the Higginson Report (1988) which advocated radical changes. It was argued that in the 37 years since A Levels had been introduced, syllabuses had become 'too volumi-nous and candidates over-burdened with having to memorise a large amount of information to the exclusion of other important demands'. Programmes of study had become too narrow and specialised. To meet the problems, the Report argued that there should be more concentration on quality of thinking, analysing, understanding and act-ing intelligently – following, indeed, the enlightened innovations of GCSE at the pre-16 age range – and to do this on a broader subject base. A different sort of examination was required in five rather than in three subjects, the syllabuses for which would be leaner, concentrating upon central concepts, facts, ideas and principles. It is interesting also to note that, in advocating this broadening and liberalising of the examination, the committee appealed to the example of the country's economic competitors. At the same time the report wanted to preserve the flexibility of discrete subjects rather than integrated courses, because that would open up more chances of combinations of A Level with BTEC courses.

The Higginson Report was rejected by the government, thus joining earlier 'N and F' and 'Q and F' in the waste-bin of rejected post-16 proposals. The A Level system was felt to be too sacred to meddle with to that extent ('gold-standard', 'flag-ship', 'jewel in the crown'). The compromise position is that, alongside A Levels, there are AS (Advanced Supplementary) Level examinations. These are worth half an A Level and would enable able students to broaden their educational experience with a 'contrasting' subject (for example, the science special-ist taking a foreign language). Or it would enable a student to select a wider range of subjects, each representing half the equivalent A Level course – in many respects like the Higginson proposals but under a different name. The weakness in this particular solution was quickly revealed in practice. Schools were wary of directing students along the AS path because of uncertainy of the reception they would receive from universities. And the idea of 'half an A Level' is a muddled one – half the syllabus, the core without the frills, different but taking half the time? Therefore, instead of supplementing or replacing A Levels, they often became no more than an extra assessment point on the way to A Level.

But the problems identified by Higginson and others will not go away and the Secretary of State continues to explore ways in which they might be reformed – without being changed.

There are several reasons why the present A Level system needed a thorough reform. First, it limited choice of subjects at a time when a more general education should be encouraged. Second, approximately 30% of subject registrations either drop out or fail – a massive failure rate amongst a group of young people from the top 30% of academic achievement who therefore have no qualification after two years. Third, the content and assessment of most A Level syllabuses (and therefore the sort of teaching encouraged) are incompatible with the approaches to learning fostered by GCSE – a switch from practical modes of learning, assessed through coursework, to an emphasis upon content coverage, less practical enquiry, and written examinations. Fourth, the concentration on academic success thus conceived has little room for the vocationally relevant skills and personal qualities stressed by education's critics and fostered by expensive government initiatives such as TVEI. Fifth, there are no connections between the academic, prevocational and vocational routes such that credit can be transferred from one to the other if the student or trainee wishes to change track. Finally, there were over 600 A Level syllabuses from eight independent examination boards often with overlapping titles and content, often with obscure connection between title and content, such that the 'user' of the results (the admission's tutor or the employer) has little idea of what the successful student actually knows or can do.

These criticisms are widely shared – indeed, it is difficult to find anyone except a few politicians who do not accept them. Therefore, there have been several initiatives by schools and colleges to provide an academically respectable alternative to A Levels, modelled on the Baccalaureate. There are several schools which now offer the International Baccalaureate (IB). Students take six subjects chosen from a range which covers Arts and Science. In many respects it is similar to the Higginson recommendations, ensuring intellectual balance as well as specialisation. General education, including philosophy, plays a central role. On the other hand, it is geared to the more able, and, if adopted, might nonetheless reinforce the academic/vocational divide. The Institute of Public Policy Research (IPPR) recommended a different version of the Baccalaureate, one much closer to the French one, in which there are different kinds of balance depending on the specialist focus – the professional baccalaureate, the technological baccalaureate, etc. That would enable the vocational emphasis to be given within a liberal and common framework. City and Guilds of London Institute (CGLI) offers its own Technological Baccalaureate at three levels – the Advanced Level being equivalent to three A Levels plus core skills, examined through demonstration of practical competence and by portfolios of evidence, together with end of course tests.

The inadequacy of this and of other solutions to the A Level problem lies in the failure to look at the post-16 arrangements as a whole – the failure to question the deep divide between the different routes, or to see how the best of the prevocational innovations can be integrated into the curriculum experience of all, or to ensure that attainments throughout the respective courses are properly credited, or to examine carefully the different ways in which the students' learning experience might be broadened, or to ensure continuity with the educational and training experience before 16 and after 18. But rectifying these failures needs much more than an ad hoc tinkering with part of the post-16 examination system. Indeed, it is difficult to see how any solutions are workable until more important questions are asked about the nature of liberal education and its relation to vocational training.

The first point to note about the changing framework is that, in some areas, it is not being changed too much – a balanced, subject-based route from 14 to 16 is reaffirmed, narrowing to a small cluster of (usually) three subjects which enable students to study to a greater depth in preparation for university. Such little change is defended by the 'standards argument' – namely, that standards are defined within the subject disciplines, and thus, at the end of schooling, are best measured by A Level examinations, which thereby become a necessary bulwark against the threatened decline in standards. Reference to economic relevance has not loomed large in the reform of this part of the system.

The second point is this. The reaffirmation of traditional subjects, now defined in detail by government as never before, is also a reaffirmation of a particular idea of 'liberal education' that has little place for the more student centred practices or for the vocational relevance that were emerging within the changing context. It is this concept of liberal education that will be examined in Part III, in particular the idea of a subject as a logically coherent intellectual discipline and as the basis of liberal education which is concerned with intellectual excellence.

Vocational courses

Education and training targets

'Preparation for adult life' includes training in the skills required for a job. These skills can be pitched at different levels – highly job specific and not requiring much thought in their application, or 'generalisable' and applicable to a range of employments. The more generalised are the skills and the more judgement is required in their application, the more blurred is the distinction between education and vocational training. Nonetheless, a distinction there is and it is recognised in differences between courses and between institutions. And the nature of the differences affects what one means by liberal education, as we shall see.

The blurring of the distinction is to be seen in the National Targets for Education and Training which the CBI specified and which the government endorsed – and handed over to the TECs to achieve.

Table 6 : *National Targets for Education and Training (originally proposed by CBI 1988)*

Foundation Learning	*Lifetime Learning*
1. By 1997, 80% of young people to reach NVQ 2 or equivalent.	1. By 1996, all employees to take part in training or development.
2. Training and education to NVQ 3 available to all young people who can benefit.	2. By 1996, 50% of the workforce aiming at NVQs or units of NVQs.
3. By 2000, 50% of young people to reach NVQ 3.	3. By 2000, 50% of the workforce qualified to at least NVQ 3.
4. Education and training provision to develop self-reliance, flexibility and breadth.	4. By 1996, 50% of medium/large employers as 'Investors in People'.

How then can such educational and training targets be achieved?

Vocational education in schools

Vocational courses are concerned with the teaching of job-related skills, whether specific or generalisable. They can be based in industry, and 'open learning' techniques make this increasingly likely. But in the past, they have normally been taught in colleges of FE, with students given day release from work. Vocational training, therefore, has not been the function of schools. But some, in facing the difficulties out-lined in chapter 1, think that schools should provide it for those not cut out for academic study – thus introducing to schools an academic/voca-tional divide between courses and between students. As the then chief executive of NCVQ, Professor Peter Thompson, said:

> If the Government is serious about these ideas it must make a significant amount of room in the timetable. We need a first-class alternative to acade-mic education, like the Germans, to tackle the great drop in youngsters in full-time education after 16. It makes a great deal of sense to be looking at provision from the age of 14. What is actually being proposed is a crystalli-sation of vocational provision, including the TVEI, into a coherent programme. (*Independent* 31.10.90)

This reflects ideas that had been floating in government circles for some time. In November 1982 the MSC announced that it was prepared to set up its own vocational technical high schools. The reasoning behind this was that the curriculum in schools tended to be too academic for many students.

> What I am trying to show is that there is another line of development that is equally respectable and desirable which leads to vocational qualifications such as BEC and TEC, OND and HND. That is the message that we have to sell to the public and the parent. (David Young, Secretary of State for Employment, quoted in *Education* 19.11.82)

Age 14 was seen to be the critical age at which to start vocational training (although not for the top 15%) because that was the age when children were said to become switched off from the traditional school curriculum. David Young thought that 30% of the curriculum at the age of 14 should be vocational but increasing as time progressed, with courses based in industry for the final two years. In fact, the TVEI scheme which followed was not narrowly vocational as it had been intended, but it did introduce vocational relevance for all students, thereby evoking angry criticism from the guardians of the liberal tradition. More recently, the Dearing Report (1994), in reforming the National Curriculum, provided opportunities for vocational studies to be introduced at 14. Though not intended for the less able, it is possible that this is how this option will be exploited.

Certainly, prior to the introduction of the National Curriculum, there had been attempts to bring vocational studies into the schools. BTEC and CGLI provided a Foundation Programme pre-16. After 16, there had been opportunities to study for the Certificate of Pre-Vocational Education (CPVE). Subsequently that had been replaced by the CGLI Diploma of Vocational Education. Furthermore, there has always been the possibility of studying for various RSA qualifications in commercial, secretarial and word-processing skills. And the CGLI made its Technological Baccalaureate widely available in 1994 following a three-year pilot phase. But the sheer number and changing nature of these courses made it necessary to bring order into the system. After all, for these qualifications to have cash value, the 'customers' (students and employers, parents and higher education) needed to understand them – what they achieved and what they could lead to. Even the most ardent free marketeer must see that. Hence, the scene was set for a national qualification relevant to schools which incorporated the vocational orientation of these different initiatives but which, as in their case, was not too vocationally specific. I refer to what I call the *prevocational* developments of GNVQ, an attempt to integrate the liberal education with vocational preparation. And this provided the opportunity for Dearing to introduce vocational studies pre-16, for his Report proposed to introduce to 14 year olds a GNVQ part 1 which would comprise three vocational units and three core units of Communication, Application of Numeracy and Information Technology.

But the real changes in *vocational* training were to be seen outside the schools – and in some respects outside the educational system.

Vocational qualifications

The curriculum in further education has been closely determined by vocational examination bodies which say what one should be able to do if one is to receive a qualification as, say, a plumber or a hairdresser. These qualifications were pitched at different levels – from relatively low-skilled operative to higher-skilled craft and technician. Obtaining these qualifications often required an apprenticeship, with day release in a college of further education for more theoretical study. Different examination boards specialised at different levels and in different vocational areas, in particular, the CGLI at operative and craft levels, the Royal Society of the Arts (RSA) in the business and commercial area, and the Business and Technology Education Council (BTEC) at technician level.

For instance, CGLI was founded over 100 years ago as an independent examining body incorporated by Royal Charter. It determined standards in over 300 vocational areas, thereby determining the content and shape of the vocational preparation for about half a million people a year. The certificates of competence were obtained mainly at the operative and craft levels, but some were at the technician level, thereby overlapping with the provisions of BTEC. Many young people who entered employment upon leaving school at 16 would study part time for their 'city and guilds'. The courses were conceived as leading to awards which spelt out the precise competences related to specific jobs. The awards thus reflected close co-operation with industry and at the same time an assurance of nationally agreed standards. CGLI also had schemes for career extension and a licentiate, the latter being akin to the status in Europe of Master Craftsman.

Entry to BTEC's First Certificate was normally at 16. With better school results, entry could be straight into the National Certificate. There could be progression to a Higher National within higher education and thence into the professions. At every level the courses were characterised by: a modular breakdown of the whole course; an explicit statement of achievement in each unit; the possibility of credit transfer of relevant experience and qualifications; core units that were common to a range of vocational routes; core skills, including interpersonal skills, necessary for success at work; core themes which were a means of relating core skills to course content; and task-related learning so that general and vocational skills were acquired 'in the doing'.

There was, therefore, a progressive pattern in vocational awards accessible to full-time students after the age of 16 and to those in employment on a part-time basis. Such awards arose from the analysis of the skills and qualities identified in different vocational areas. Moreover, within BTEC certainly there was a great deal of flexibility; the courses were spelt out in terms of general framework and criteria, rather than (as in the case of A Levels) content to be covered. Different tasks or assignments (thus different contents) might develop the same skills or meet the same criteria. Courses were related more closely to objectives to be achieved (skills to be acquired, performances to be successful in) rather than to content to be covered – a distinction to be examined more carefully in Part III.

But criticism there was. The qualifications, and the courses leading to them, were thought not to meet the needs of the changing context which I have outlined. There was a 'jungle' of many overlapping qualifications. They were not responsive enough to the changing economic and technological base of society. The apprenticeship system, leading to these qualifications, was 'time serving' rather than competence based, and needed to be reformed. Even the vocational qualification system excluded so many young people at a time when many more needed to be trained.

Youth training

Britain's relatively poor performance in vocational training has been referred to, together with the government's attempt, through YTS, to redress the balance. But not until the MSC was created in 1973 did the government have the machinery to interfere in what was seen to be a private matter.

The 1981 DE White Paper *The New Training Initiative: a Programme for Action* stated three major objectives in the Government's training policy: a national training programme (though voluntary) for all the nation's youth who did not remain in full-time education; a revision of the apprenticeship system in line with changed categories of employment and industrial need; and an adult retraining programme.

The consequent Youth Training Scheme was intended to be much more than a cure for unemployment. There were different kinds of scheme – some employer-based, some college-based. But all schemes had in common: off-the-job training, prolonged work experience, opportunity to gain a qualification, development of personal and social skills, and a system of profiling which reflected the range of experiences and achievements that the trainee had received.

Responsibility for the most recent schemes has been devolved to the TECs. These estimate the regional training needs and ensure adequate provision of training places. Trainees are qualified on the basis of what they have achieved. Therefore, at least in theory, there is a national scheme of training for all those who, at the age of 16, choose not to take the academic route into further education and employment. The scheme leads to a range of awards at progressively different levels, still in the main bestowed by the examining bodies referred to (CGLI, BTEC, RSA) but accredited and pulled together in a more coherent national scheme by the NCVQ.

It is not easy to pass judgment on YTS. The intentions behind the scheme were admirable – trying to create a national system of training suitable for a rapidly changing industrial scene in a much tougher, more competitive and more technological economic world. But such intentions have to be carried out against a cultural background in which education and training are related to each other in a particular way. No amount of money will make a dent on that. YTS continued to be seen as a low status option, a basic training route leading to relatively low level skills, often forced on young people by the removal of social security benefits if they did not volunteer. And it was seen by many employers as a way of screening potential employees for relatively low-skilled jobs. There were, of course, exceptions, as in the case of the Engineering Employers' scheme which integrated YTS with a reformed apprenticeship.

Vocational training always has had a relatively low status in Britain. The 'practical' and the 'vocational' have seldom given access to university or to the prestigious and professional jobs as they do, say, in West Germany. Those for whom a more vocationally relevant course had been thought more appropriate had not been encouraged to continue in full-time courses. Indeed, Britain was, until recently, unique amongst the major industrial nations in having a majority of its students leave full-time education or training at the age of 16. It was essential, therefore, to do more than to provide resources for youth training, often at the reluctant expense of the employers. There was a need to start from the qualification end – to define more precisely and more systematically the *competences* required at different levels and in different areas of employment, and to do this in co-operation with the employers, thereby ensuring progression and status for these qualifications. What should matter is not the course one has been on or the institution one has been a student at, but the competence to do a job. At first sight, this seems a great equaliser. The creation of NVQs aimed to do precisely that.

Nonetheless, this major divide between academic and vocational, between education and training, between 'thinking' and 'making', is deeply rooted in our culture. Until recently technology had no place in the general education offered at school, certainly not in the grammar school or in the top ability range of the comprehensive school. The technical schools of the post-war tripartite system, intended to provide a more vocational preparation for skilled jobs for the middle range of ability, never succeeded. The present attempt, therefore, to create a system of training adequate to the nation's economic requirements needs to relate to a school curriculum suitably reformed to play its part in overcoming the academic/vocational divide and to provide, however minimally, a vocational preparation for subsequent vocational training.

How can that be done whilst a defensible tradition of liberal education is maintained?

National Vocational Qualifications

National Vocational Qualifications (NVQ) were established in 1986 to reduce the 'jungle' of vocational qualifications to an intelligible *system*. They assess competence at work. Those competences are identified in precise terms as a result of detailed analyses of the 'can dos' necessary for a job to be done competently. These 'can do' statements are pitched at five different levels:

1. competence in the performance of routine work activities;
2. competence in activities, some not routine, requiring individual responsibility;
3. competence in a wide range of activities – complex, not routine, and in different contexts, requiring responsibility for self and others;
4. competence in a broad range of complex, technical or professional work activities in a variety of contexts, with a substantial degree of responsibility – for self, others and allocation of resources;
5. competence in pursuit of a senior occupation or profession, including ability to apply a significant range of fundamental principles and techniques in a wide range of unpredictable contexts, with considerable responsibility for others, resources, analysis, diagnosis, design, planning and evaluation.

These levels of competence are then applied to eleven occupational areas, which are thought to include all possible occupations, namely: Tending animals, plants and land; Extracting and providing natural resources; Constructing; Engineering; Manufacturing; Transporting; Providing goods and services; Health and social care; Business services; Communicating; Knowledge industries.

To identify and to express all the 'can dos' for every conceivable occupation at every level of difficulty is a mammoth task. A lot of progress has been made at the first three levels, but there are considerable difficulties in reducing higher level cognitive abilities to a finite and measurable list of competences. This task is shared by the NCVQ with about 160 Lead Industry Bodies, but, as I shall argue in chapter 6, these difficulties are, at base, of a conceptual and philosophical kind and need to be recognised as such if the whole enterprise is not to be brought into disrepute.

To get an NVQ, the trainee would perform competently against performance criteria specified for that level. There would be several tasks in which the person would be assessed for different competences. These tasks, and their competences, are grouped into 'units'. Each unit comprises a set of 'elements' in which that competence is measured in a 'range' of situations. Hence, the building blocks of the framework for NVQ certificated competence are: *elements, performance criteria, range statements,* and *units.*

For example, within the occupational area of 'Construction', there is a range of crafts which receive NVQ awards at Level 2: these include bricklaying, carpentry and joinery, painting and decorating, and shop-fitting. In the case of 'Bricklaying (Construction)', a 'functional analysis' breaks job roles down into 'elements of competence'. These are grouped into 'units', and a group constitutes an NVQ. Table 7 shows an example of an 'element of competence'.

Table 7 *(from FEU 1992)*
Element: for opening and positioning lintel, steel and concrete beams

Range:	concrete and metal lintels steel and concrete beams
Performance criteria:	lintel/beam +/- 2mm uniform bearing +/- 10mm horizontal position uniform +/- 3mm opening formed to specified position and size plumb to within a tolerance +/- 6mm in 1m
Evidence required:	purpose of a lintel reason for position of reinforcement distributing load from steel beam identification of types of lintel, length and 　　size for safe load bearing

There is pressure upon NCVQ to issue separate certificates for units which together add up to an NVQ. Thus, in Hairdressing, one would receive a certificate in cutting men's hair, a necessary but not sufficient condition for the full certificate: one needs to be successful in other units, too. Hence, standards are expressed in precise outcomes, which meet prespecified behavioural criteria and which refer to the range of situations in which these criteria apply.

The interesting points to be noted for my purpose are: NVQs assess competence in the work place, not in the academic environment of school or college; those assessed need to *demonstrate* their competence, not talk or write about it – theoretical understanding is shown in intelligent practice, not in separate assessment of the talking or writing about that practice; undertaking an apprenticeship or a college course is of no consequence, only the demonstrated capacity 'to do'; accreditation of prior experience and competence becomes part of the accumulation of evidence in the assessment.

There are three major criticisms.

First, the validity of the claims of NCVQ depends on the extent to which relevant vocational capacities can be reduced to finite lists of prespecified and measurable competences. There are logical differences between descriptions of 'skill', 'mental quality', 'knowledge', 'understanding', 'judgment' and 'appreciation' which are too crudely passed over by the NVQ definitions – a philosophical question which we shall return to in chapter 6.

Second, Smithers (1994) argues that, in concentrating upon the 'can dos' – the practical manifestation of competence – NCVQ has neglected the theoretical knowledge which is essential for a sophisticated and flexible workforce. Thus, the plumber, under CGLI courses which NVQ has replaced, would have had to learn underlying knowledge of physics, electronics, mathematics and technical drawing, whereas none of the units in the NVQ contains the relevant scientific knowledge as such. NCVQ (1994) in reply deny this, pointing to the theoretical knowledge which is explicitly mentioned in the assessment schedule. But that is only partly an answer. There is a distrust of theoretical understanding divorced from practical outcomes, and yet mastery of that theoretical framework requires an understanding which, although practically relevant, cannot be cashed out in terms of practical outcomes.

Third, the measurable statements of competence can easily become the language of control where the funding is 'output related'. Might not such funding arrangements encourage training agencies to submit candidates for lower level awards, where success is guaranteed – or even cook the books, since failure of a candidate entails clawback of income?

Modern apprenticeships

Possibly the greatest contrast between the developments just referred to and the vocational arrangements of ten years ago lies in the replacement of the centuries old apprenticeship system by one based on measured competence – of a system based on processes over a fixed time by one based on proved capacity to do a job competently without reference to the processes by which that competence has been achieved or to the time required for achieving it.

Indeed, that is part of a more general view about the process of learning which is affecting our understanding of higher education. Why, for example, do universities insist that a course leading to a first degree should be three years? Why do they insist that the student should attend lectures and seminars? Why are not degrees awarded on the basis only of successfully completed examinations? Courses and attendance might be considered necessary only in so far as they help students pass those examinations – not as a necessary condition. Indeed, already we are seeing the accreditation of prior learning as a major component of some university degrees. Perhaps the time-serving degree course is the last attempt to preserve the apprenticeship system.

That indeed is the thinking which underpins recent developments (see, for example, Jessup 1991). It is something which is eating away at the liberal/vocational divide, as the vocational language of 'competence', 'output' and 'measurable behaviour' replaces the liberal emphasis upon process and judgment and the non-measurable benefits of exposure to the intellectual life of a university.

However, anxieties about this way of thinking affect not just the defenders of liberal education. There is renewed interest in an apprenticeship system due to perceived failures in recent arrangements for vocational preparation. 'Modern apprenticeships', announced in the Autumn budget of 1993, are aimed at 16/17 year olds in certain occupational areas (such as engineering, chemical industry, child care); they are selective; they aim at NVQ level 3 in a range of skills and knowledge; they are tied to careers advice from the age of 14 so that right choices will be made; and they, like the old apprenticeships, are part of an employment package in which the apprentice has the status of an employee. The DE White Paper (1994) announced an accelerated extension of the scheme for 18/19 year olds.

Prevocational courses

It is important to distinguish between vocational in the *job-related* sense and vocational *preparation*, stressing 'relevance', especially for those who have limited educational ambitions. The Spens Report of 1938 wished to see vocational in this broader sense extended to the grammar school – thereby challenging a central tenet of the prevailing idea of liberal education. Rural grammar schools might, for example, build science around such relevant rural pursuits as bee-keeping.

This '*pre*vocational curriculum', incorporating vocational relevance without providing vocational training, has become a feature of secondary schools and colleges of FE, and is essential to our understanding of the changing framework – first, because of the extra dimension it gives to the already complex course structure, and, second, because of the reshaping it gives to educational aims.

In the mid-seventies, many young people remained in full-time education, not because they wanted to, but because there was nowhere else for them to go. They were not able, or willing, to pursue A Level courses. They had no clear picture of a vocational route into training and employment. Normally, such students would have proceeded straight from school to work, often with no further education or training. But the country was then beginning to suffer a level of unemployment that hit hard the young school leaver without qualifications or useful skills.

The arrival in colleges of FE of a type of student which they had not previously catered for required new courses 'relevant', and thus motivating, to students who were disgruntled at having to continue full-time education instead of earning a living. After all, many were failures of the education system – those who had left school with no qualifications and would normally have moved into unskilled jobs.

But 'relevance' depended on the analysis of the changing context in which this situation had arisen. Were they unemployed because they lacked qualities and skills that industry needed? If so, 'relevance' would mean the acquisition of those qualities and skills. In a rapidly changing industrial scene, these would be personal qualities, capacities and 'transferable skills'. Such a person would thus be better prepared, when employed, for specific on-the-job training.

On the other hand, the fault of unemployment might lie, not in the student or in the schools, but in the demographic and economic circumstances in which a 'bulge' in the output of school leavers coincided with a contraction of traditional manufacturing industries. 'Relevance' would mean the development of those qualities of character that sustained them personally as they faced an unpredictable future.

It was clear to many within the colleges that continuation of the same kind of subject-based curriculum as at school would not provide 'relevance'. There needed to be a continuation of general education, but in a different form. The students were not ready for vocational training, but general education had to be vocationally relevant – not vocational, but *pre*vocational.

'A Basis for Choice' – the prelude to prevocational courses

A broadly based general education, with a vocational orientation and with the opportunity to experience different kinds of employment, was required – courses which prepared young people psychologically and economically for a rapidly changing and uncertain future. Such courses should be based on the needs of the young people themselves and of the society into which they were entering. There should be a closer connection between their extended education, albeit with a vocational bias, and the adult world, than had been experienced in the subject-based courses of school.

A key document was *A Basis for Choice* (*ABC*) published in 1979 by the Further Education Unit (FEU) at the DES. The FEU had been established in 1976 to provide support to those involved in post-16 education and training. *ABC* proposed a framework of general education within which there would be sufficient vocational orientation to enable students to choose more intelligently their routes into the adult world, particularly that of employment. Such courses would thus provide 'a basis for choice'.

ABC provided a threefold framework: a common core, a vocational orientation within broad occupational groups, and work experience. The common core arose out of an analysis of what young people needed if they were to be effective within the adult world. The analysis attended both to what the young persons themselves required in order to live fulfilling lives and to what society required of them if the economic and social base of their lives were to be sustained. The common core therefore was expressed in a list of aims that reflected these individual and social needs, and these were translated into more detailed objectives. The aims included such abilities as 'working co-operatively', 'developing a defensible set of moral values', 'communication skills', 'practical numeracy', 'literacy', 'social and economical awareness', 'responsibility for decision-making', 'approaching problems creatively', and 'having a practical grasp of relevant technology' (especially information technology). Moreover, such aims, bearing little obvious relation to school subjects, could be pursued through the more vocational activities. Education could be undertaken *through* training, if the right qualities of mind were thereby developed; aims need not be compartmentalised into separate subjects. Emphasis was laid upon personal qualities of confidence and responsibility, and this was reflected in the importance attached to the negotiation of individual learning objectives, to experiential and activity-based learning, and to a more generous conception of assessment. In providing a 'basis for choice', guidance and counselling were brought from the fringes of the curriculum, where they normally belong, to the very centre.

A Basis for Choice became the basis of the CGLI course 365 and of the RSA Vocational Preparation course, first in colleges of FE, then, in 1983, in schools for students from the age of 14. In 1984, following the DES consultation paper *Examinations at 17+*, the Certificate of Prevocational Education (CPVE) was available in schools and colleges post-16. In 1987, CGLI and BTEC jointly offered Foundation Courses at 14 leading to the CPVE. Thus, the prevocational principles were translated into recognisable qualifications within mainstream education from 14 to 18. Courses, thus defined in terms of criteria that allowed for local development, practical learning, links with the community, and personal needs, seemed to solve a curriculum problem that many teachers had been feeling their way towards.

This brief history is important because one needs to be aware of the fact that GNVQ, although started by NCVQ, is in fact rooted in attempts by teachers to provide a relevant general education for young people from 14 to 18 based on educational principles different from those of the liberal tradition we inherited. Furthermore, these attempts were *educationally* argued for. Indeed, it is because NCVQ seems unaware of this history that the prevocational tradition is in danger of being impoverished by the narrower tradition of vocational training.

Five features of prevocational courses should be noted.

First, emphasis is upon *processes* (not outputs) that embrace: a more experience-based and practical mode of learning; the utilisation of the community, including the world of work; reflection upon personal and social relevance, requiring guidance and counselling; personal learning agendas, requiring negotiation of learning objectives; and the capacity to work and communicate with others.

Second, connected with that process is a system of profiling by which a person's competences, qualifications, experiences, interests and achievements might be recorded.

Third, vocational studies, as the vehicle through which general qualities might be acquired, could be taken at different levels – in the case of CPVE at introductory, exploratory, and preparation levels – so that there might be progression finally into vocationally specific courses of training.

Fourth, these broadly conceived vocational studies required the identification of occupational groupings, each of which would cover a range of similar kinds of employment. And this encouraged the formulation of 'generic' or 'transferable' skills which, at a time of rapid industrial change, provided greater flexibility in the workforce.

Finally, course design in these prevocational developments was different from what teachers were accustomed to and which was implicit in the *dirigiste* 1988 legislation for the National Curriculum. The prevocational (but not the national) curriculum framework provides broad criteria within which a local and individualised curriculum might be developed. And those criteria combine an occupational focus with emphasis upon the processes of learning and upon skills and qualities not limited to subjects.

We must, however, be wary. Appraisal of such courses needs to be critical of key concepts such as 'process of learning' (rather than 'product'), 'skills' (of decision-making or problem-solving), 'personal effectiveness', 'negotiation', 'communication skills' or 'social relevance'. The connection between this way of understanding the curriculum and that embodied within the subjects needs to be explored in Part III, lest, in the pursuit of 'relevance', liberal education is neglected.

TVEI – a prevocational programme

The Technical and Vocational Education Initiative (TVEI) was not a course. It was a large sum of money (altogether over £1 billion) made available to schools and colleges to create courses that met broad criteria. Therefore, as with the prevocational courses referred to, it was an arrangement that stimulated local curriculum development, but at a price. For it was one aspect of that shifting control of education, referred to in chapter 2, whereby the source of funding is transferred from LEA to government and made available only if spent as government approves. In fact, that control through TVEI was benign and the conditions educationally defensible – and flexible enough to enhance rather than diminish the professionalism of teachers.

But that might not have been. TVEI was announced in November 1982 by the Prime Minister. She saw it as a response to the inadequate provision in schools and colleges for technical and vocational education. And the chairman of the MSC, David Young, to whom the responsibility of establishing TVEI was given, saw the initiative in narrower vocational terms than many teachers and LEAs found acceptable. In defending the haste with which the scheme was introduced, Young spoke of TVEI as a major part of the answer to the growing unemployment of young people, giving them the skills with which they would become more employable; and an answer, too, to the inefficiency of industry in the face of competition – providing the trained manpower that employers needed. Hence, the school curriculum was to be brought closer to the economic and industrial needs of society as the government saw these, and was thereby to challenge the prevailing view of a liberal education. Clearly there would be opposition from those who represented that liberal position but, in the face of a changing system of funding and thus of control, such opposition could be ignored. Thus, if schools did not respond to the initiative and provide a more effective preparation for work, then Young would create technical schools outside the educational system, run by the MSC itself (see Gleeson 1987).

In September 1983, 14 pilot schemes started. By September 1987, the scheme was extended to every secondary school in the country – although phased in over a number of years.

Proposals for TVEI funding had to meet these criteria: the promotion of equal opportunities; the provision of a four-year curriculum designed as a preparation for adult life; the encouragement of initiative, problem-solving and personal development; the containment of a vocational component throughout; the relation of vocational and technical elements to employment opportunities; the provision of work experience; the establishment of links with subsequent training and educational opportunities; the inclusion of regular career and educational advice; the preparation of students for one or more nationally recognised qualifications; the design of courses that could be replicated elsewhere.

As with the other prevocational innovations, a *framework* was determined centrally within which there could be variation in course structure and content. And schemes showed considerable variety. Put practically, there were some schools that benefited from the legitimation TVEI gave to radical curriculum thinking (organising the curriculum through active assignments and cross-curriculum themes; taking the school into the community and industry; promoting team approaches to technical and social problem-solving), whereas others saw TVEI as a 'subject' within self-contained option periods. What emerged, despite Young's announcement, was not vocational preparation in a job-specific sense but an emphasis upon the quality of the learning experience. In that way TVEI provided a fundamental challenge to the content and to the teaching methods employed in the curriculum as it had been traditionally experienced. This is expressed well in the summary of a major evaluation study (see Harrison 1987).

This report distinguished between the 'reality dimension' of learning and the 'participation dimension'. Within the reality dimension, there can be varying degrees to which the learning activities in school reflect the activities of the world outside the school, arise from the students' own interests and problems, and have the same sort of 'messiness' that real-life problems have. It was the aim of TVEI to open up the learning process to this more realistic dimension, and its success lay, therefore, in the extent to which that happened. Connected with that is the 'participation dimension', namely, the degree to which the pace, style and content of learning shifts from the control of the teacher to that of the pupil. The success of TVEI came to be assessed on the degree to which the learners assumed greater control of their own learning – hence, the importance of study skills, of counselling and guidance, and of 'formative profiling' (see chapter 4). The Interim Report proposed that

> TVEI aims are best served by teachers who seek to develop their teaching away from routine exercises (a) towards realistic tasks and (b) towards enabling their students to use the concepts and skills for themselves upon problems that they perceive to be important in the real world. (Harrison 1987)

TVEI, therefore, referred to a set of criteria, which themselves indicated a particular style of learning and curriculum content, and to a lump of money that would enable courses to be developed within those criteria. But courses get off the ground only if they are certificated and linked with recognised qualifications. Hence, the award system provided by the Foundation Courses, before 16, and the CPVE, after 16, came to be incorporated into many of the TVEI schemes. However, if TVEI was to gain acceptance and respectability across the ability and social spectrum, then it needed to get certification also within GCE and subsequently GCSE. Much of the energy of TVEI co-ordinators was spent in trying to achieve this.

TVEI, therefore, was the stage upon which different traditions competed with each other for control of the curriculum. On the one hand, it was first announced, in narrowly vocational terms, as an implicit criticism of a liberal education which had failed so many and which had not produced the kinds of skill, knowledge and attitude required by a successful economy. On the other hand, such a narrow vocational focus became, in the hands of teachers, something educationally defensible, although still a challenge to a liberal tradition which was disdainful of commercial or practical relevance. The important question for my purpose is whether within the curriculum thinking exemplified by TVEI and other prevocational developments, there are the seeds of a defensible educational philosophy which bridges the academic/vocational divide – by liberalising the vocational track and by vocationalising the liberal one without betraying the best that is within each.

RSA, Education for Capability and the prevocational virtues

The educational principles embodied in the prevocational courses have a respectable history, although that is unrecognised in much of the background debate. That is a pity because, had there been recognition of that history and of the courses associated with it, the relevance of prevocational courses to mainstream education would have been more obvious.

The Royal Society of the Arts (RSA) was founded in 1754 for 'the Encouragement of Arts, Manufactures and Commerce', and for 200 years sought, in its membership, lectures, awards and courses, that integration of theory with practice, of art with design, and of industry with the academic world which is incorporated, though implicitly, in the prevocational innovations. Therefore, the RSA has made a significant contribution towards the development of prevocational courses through its own Vocational Preparation Course, based once again on the principles of CPVE; through its 'Certificate for Vocational Preparation Tutors'; and through its 'Education for Capability Award Scheme'.

'Education for Capability' started as a campaign in answer to some of the criticisms referred to in chapter 1 and promoting the kinds of courses that the RSA had traditionally stood for. It resulted in the Education for Capability Award Scheme which

> was set up to identify, encourage and publicise educational programmes designed to help people, whether pupils, students or adults, to learn to live and work more effectively'. (RSA 1984)

Its manifesto first appeared in the national press in 1980, supported by nearly 250 leading figures in industry, politics, education, the arts, the trade unions, and the media. What united them all was the belief that courses of instruction at every level were 'imbalanced' towards an academic tradition and needed to give more recognition to 'competence, to coping, to creativity, and to co-operation with others'.

Schools/industry links – the prevocational context

Integral to prevocational courses has been the close link between education and the world of work. Schools have established collaboration with industry in the development of the curriculum, even though such collaboration had no place in the examination system upon which public prestige depended. Work experience has not been confined to TVEI. Indeed, it owes more to the perception of teachers who have seen the importance of industrial and economic awareness in a liberal education.

Why have teachers seen this to be important? First, they appreciated the connections that students and their parents make between school and subsequent employment prospects (a matter often treated with disdain by exponents of liberal education); second, they see that to be intelligent about how to live is one of the most important benefits of an education – and central to 'how to live' is the choice of a job which opens up further worthwhile experiences.

Schools and industry have linked in many ways. The first is that of work experience, and prevocational courses have integrated this into the total curriculum rather than leave it as a vicarious experience squashed between examination courses. Second, there have been the extra-curriculum activities such as the Young Enterprise Schemes which encourage economic awareness through practical business ventures. Third, industry links have been built into science, geography and other courses with a view to demonstrating the economic relevance of what is learnt. Fourth, understanding the economic base of society, and one's own practical place within it, is seen as an important aim of education too often ignored by those who, in the name of liberal education, are contemptuous of the practical and the useful.

The government has demonstrated its keenness in these developments. The industrial connection is built into projects such as TVEI; moreover, the DTI, in its 1988 White Paper, set three objectives: 10% of all teachers to be placed annually in industry; all students to have at least two weeks' work experience before leaving school; and teacher training to incorporate these objectives in the preparation of teachers. On the other hand, the National Curriculum, spelt out in terms of Foundation Subjects, found little place for the schools/industry links – as though TVEI and all the rest had never happened. In addition, other organisations such as the CBI and a satellite of the CBI, Understanding British Industry (UBI), stimulate joint activities and provide placements for students and for teachers. Hence, the whole scene is complex and a bit muddled, with three government departments promoting in their different ways 'enterprise' and 'entre-preneurship' and links with industry.

One significant development has been the 'compact'. This was introduced into Britain by ILEA in 1987, based upon the pioneering work of the Boston compact scheme in the USA. There are now about 50 compact schemes in the UK. They are a special arrangement made between industries and their local schools, especially in the inner cities, whereby guarantees of training and employment are made to young people if they reach certain targets in behaviour, attendance, qualifica-tions or continued education. These schemes were then funded by the TECs which, together with local education/business partnerships, had an increasing influence on the school curriculum – a further example of the changed partnership affecting the understanding of educational aims and their relation to vocational training.

The importance of close and reciprocal links with industry is widely accepted. But it is not *universally* so, for such links threaten a tradition of liberal education which separates the world of learning from the world of business and industry. And even where the principle is accepted, the practice may not be. Work experience may not be of educational value; that depends on the nature of the experience, on the preparation for it and on the debriefing afterwards.

GNVQ – the prevocational qualification

General National Vocational Qualifications (GNVQ) were first announced in the DES (1991) White Paper *Education and Training for the 21st Century.* The Secretary of State explained their significance as follows:

> We are aiming to establish three broad qualification pathways for our young people – the A Level system, NVQs and the new GNVQs .... which will stand alongside academic qualifications on their own merits. GNVQs will play a central role in our strategy for 16–19 year olds. I want GNVQs in at least two subjects to be available in at least 1,500 schools and colleges by 1996.

GNVQs, then, are within the prevocational tradition already described. They are concerned with the continuation of general education whilst having a definite vocational orientation. They are intended as an alter-native to A Levels for those who want a more relevant and practical extension of their learning. And yet, like A Levels, they are intended to lead on to higher education for those who want that.

GNVQs are pitched at three levels: Foundation, Intermediate and Advanced (called vocational A Levels) since a GNVQ level 3 is said to be equivalent to two A Levels at grade E or better, enough in theory for university entrance. GNVQs, therefore, have replaced the other prevocational qualifications of BTEC, CGLI and RSA – although GNVQ is administered by these three examining bodies. (For an excellent account of GNVQs see Hayward 1995.)

GNVQs are modular in design. Level 3 requires eight mandatory units, covering the principles, processes and skills common to a range of occupations within a broad occupational area, and four optional units. There are in addition three core skill units, in numeracy, communication and information technology, which are taught through the mandatory and optional units. A very able student might take six extra units (thus equivalent to three A Levels) or take one A Level along with the GNVQ. Level 2 (known as Intermediate GNVQ) requires four mandatory units and two optional units (plus core skills), and Level 1 (known as Foundation) requires four mandatory and 3 optional (plus core skills).

The occupational areas are Health and Social Care; Leisure and Tourism; Business; Art and Design; Manufacturing; Science, Construction; Hospitality and Catering; Engineering; Information Technology; Distribution; Media; Management; and Landbased and Environmental Studies. All will be phased in by 1996.

In the short time they have been available, GNVQs have proved to be very popular. In September 1993, 70,000 registered for GNVQ, long before the full range had been phased in. And there are plans to extend GNVQ to Levels 4 and 5 for higher level occupations – a broader focus than the equivalent NVQs but sharing the same structural features of competence-based outcomes, with emphasis upon core skills and, as a result of the modular structure, upon credit accumulation and transfer. GNVQ attempts to provide a common currency at different levels of both vocational training and higher education. There is an emphasis upon 'rationalisation' and 'common framework'.

There are, however, criticisms of the GNVQ from quite different quarters.

First, with regard to status, equivalence (for example, to A Level) cannot be achieved by government edict. Indeed, there is something odd about saying one is equivalent to the other when they are so different in conception and in standards appealed to.

Second, Smithers (1994) argues for a two-track system. The more vocational would emphasise the virtues of precision, perseverance and patience, and practical engagement which nonetheless incorporates a theoretical perspective, leading to subsequent occupational flexibility. Such a vocational track, far from being the route for academic failures, should be a rigorous and respectable alternative. His criticism of

GNVQ is that it falls between the academic and the vocational – failing to be either. Practical and vocationally oriented GNVQ certainly is, but it lacks the focus upon precise and detailed skills and, in concentrating upon measurable competences in practical situations, it is deficient in theoretical understanding. In other words, in listing the 'can dos', the NCVQ has failed to provide syllabuses and the subject-matter which need to be learnt – the concepts, principles, facts and theories which ought to be studied and understood. It is assumed that those who carry out a task successfully will have grasped the implicit theory. But that is not going to convince universities who want to know the level of theoretical understanding of those seeking entry to degree courses.

Third, there is the criticism that the prevocational tradition has been hijacked by the vocational one, heavily dependent upon measurable outcomes. In other words, the NCVQ imposed upon the prevocational courses of RSA, BTEC and CGLI the inadequate language and behavioural psychology of NVQ. Quality of learning, as that is experienced by the learner, or the complex processes of learning leading to different sorts of understanding, or the subtleties and unpredictabilities of judgment as those are respected within a more liberal tradition, have no place in the GNVQ language.

Fourth, the government, in its concern for externally moderated standards, has insisted that there should be external written tests for all mandatory modules. It has also said that the pass rate should be 70% (formerly 80%). The items for such tests, to fulfil their function, are banked in their thousands, ready to be drawn upon whenever a candidate chooses to be tested in that specific module. They are not based on any explicit syllabus. The cost of developing and refining such test items for all mandatory modules at three levels in each occupational area is enormous.

Youth Award Scheme – a prevocational initiative

The 1960s saw many local initiatives as teachers thought through the problems of educating all young people, irrespective of motivation and ability, and of enriching a curriculum which was too narrowly academic. But recent initiatives, such as these, have little chance of surviving government requirements for the National Curriculum or the all-embracing demands of NVQ and GNVQ. Many teachers, especially following the criticism of Smithers, are concerned that the principles of the prevocational tradition might be squeezed between the academic tradition, on the one hand, and the narrowly vocational one, on the other.

The Youth Award Scheme is a remarkable witness to personal initiative and teacher response to young people's educational needs in an increasingly bureaucratic framework. This scheme was started in the early 1980s by Roger White and David Brockington based on their work with young people (see White 1980, White and Brockington 1978 and Crombie-White, Pring and Brockington 1995). Presently, over 1,000 schools and colleges have registered 80,000 students for various levels of the scheme – more, at the moment, than are registered for GNVQ. The scheme offers a progressive series of awards at Bronze, Silver, Gold and Platinum levels as a curriculum enrichment activity. To get an award, the student must complete a range of assignments within such areas of activity as International Relations, World of Work, The Community and Economic and Industrial Affairs. It provides evidence of achievement in those skills and personal qualities sought after by employers and admissions tutors in universities and colleges. In other words, it is not a substitute for the content of the academic curriculum, but rather a complementary experience which expands and enriches the learning which too often is narrowly academic in content and approach. It has CBI endorsement and specific mention in the UCAS guidelines for University admission.

This has been a long section for two reasons. First, it introduces the reader to a range of courses, developed in response to the context described in Part I, which, despite their importance, are not well known. To get a comprehensive picture of the changing educational and training scene, one must understand these prevocational developments. Second, the prevocational courses are also a response to the academic/vocational gap which is the main focus of the book. They are an attempt to close that gap – to offer an alternative vision of education in which education and training are not in opposition and in which personal needs of the learner illuminate the often impersonal nature of traditional learning. Sadly, it has not always been recognised as such, and thus Kenneth Baker, when Secretary of State, spoke of the 'three broad qualification pathways', GNVQ producing a third alternative to the academic, on the one hand, and to the vocational, on the other. But that is missing the point. The prevocational tradition at its best liberalises the vocational and vocationalises the liberal, seeing no opposition between academic respectability and vocational relevance. It should not be seen as a third and different track.

Problems of coherence and progression

Lack of coherence

The relationship between NVQ, GNVQ and academic qualifications is illustrated in Table 8, showing the three separate tracks.

Table 8: *The national qualifications framework*

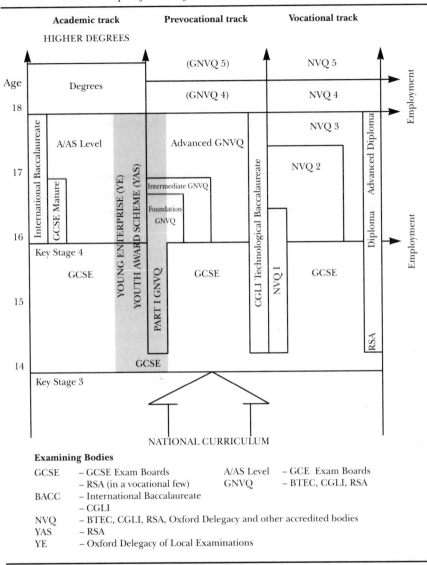

Examining Bodies

GCSE	– GCSE Exam Boards	A/AS Level	– GCE Exam Boards
	– RSA (in a vocational few)	GNVQ	– BTEC, CGLI, RSA
BACC	– International Baccalaureate		
	– CGLI		
NVQ	– BTEC, CGLI, RSA, Oxford Delegacy and other accredited bodies		
YAS	– RSA		
YE	– Oxford Delegacy of Local Examinations		

To illustrate the consequent lack of coherence and progression, let us take five examples. First, there is the student who registers for a youth training scheme but who subsequently wishes to transfer to full-time education; there is no chance that his NVQ units will be credited to his A Level assessments and little chance that they will be credited to his GNVQ. Second, the student enthused by her GCSE double science (as advocated within the National Curriculum) is prevented from pursuing A Level physics at her local Tertiary College because she had not covered the relevant content. Third, the student, highly successful in technology (boosted in its importance by TVEI), finds that no university acknowledges it as a matriculation subject for engineering.

Fourth, the A Level student who drops out after one year has no record of achievement that she can transfer to other courses – she simply has to start from scratch on a new course. Fifth, the student who is persuaded to remain in full-time education to take a prevocational course finds no route into local engineering employment because places have been taken by 16 year olds who have moved straight into employer-based training leading to NVQ.

Lack of coherence is reflected in other ways. The National Curriculum is defined in terms of Foundation Subjects, and these in turn are spelt out in attainment targets peculiar to those subjects. But the prevocational courses are not. They are organised within occupational areas rather than within subject disciplines; they are spelt out in terms of outcomes to be assessed rather than in terms of content to be covered.

Again, GCSE has encouraged more practical modes of learning and forms of assessment based on course work. But the national assessments at 16 created by the 1988 Act, apart from making the system creak from assessment, runs counter to that trend. And A Level courses need to alter radically if they are to be continuous with the levels of attainment of the National Curriculum or the styles of learning of GCSE which, in seeking to improve the quality of learning, have cut back the content to be covered.

This lack of coherence and progression can be understood at different levels. On the one hand, there are so many independently operating providers that it is difficult to see how there could be a coherent system – not only three departments of state, but a range of well-established examination bodies responding to perceived needs independently of each other. Moreover, the encouragement of competition amongst the immediate providers – LEA and grant maintained schools, independent schools, city technology colleges, colleges of FE, all operating under different legal and financial arrangements – prevents the co-operative use of resources and the appropriate careers guidance that a coherent system requires. For example, schools under local management, conscious of the financial benefit of extra sixth-formers but unable to provide vocational courses, are persuading students to remain on A Level courses even though it is clear that such students are more suited to the prevocational routes at the college of FE. And schools, anxious to retain as many students as possible, create prevocational courses in rivalry with the local FE colleges, when they may not be equipped with resources or expertise required for effective teaching. The problem is that there are now more qualifications pursuing more students in a competitive and fragmented market of institutions, each of which is differently funded.

However, at the base of this lack of coherence between tracks are the different traditions of learning as they are reflected in A Level, on the one hand, and the NCVQ's qualifications on the other. A Levels refer to courses (normally of two years) with syllabuses, in which understanding will be developed and in which judgment will mature. Vocational courses, on the other hand, do not specify time or syllabuses – only competences to be measured in the outcomes of specific tasks. Judgment and understanding are implicit in the successful performance. Moreover, what is needed to be understood within the A Levels will be determined by the tradition of public knowledge within respective subjects, and those subjects (and thus those traditions of knowledge, understanding and enquiry) are very different from the 'functional analyses' of the NCVQ – thus making judgments of equivalence between the two qualifications a nonsense.

This distinction between academic traditions, on the one hand, stressing knowledge and understanding, and not specifying precisely what the successful student should be able to *do* as a result of the course, and, on the other, the vocational tradition which emphasises skills and competences and which does insist upon very precise objectives, is more significant than the proponents of NVQ realise in their attempts to reconcile liberal education with vocational training.

Profiling and Records of Achievement

Prevocational courses, following the research and practice already initiated in Scotland, promoted the practice of student profiling. Profiles are in effect an attempt to give a more generous account of the experiences and achievements of students than is normally captured in reports or certificates, on the understanding that there is more to education than academic results. Moreover, this further information needs to be recorded in such a way as to be useful to teacher and learner alike, particularly as the school attaches greater importance to the guidance and counselling of students as they decide what to do with their futures.

There are many kinds of profile but they nearly all have the following features in common: an account of non-academic as well as academic achievements; the incorporation of skills and personal qualities which, because they transcend subject boundaries, often go unassessed and unreported; a progressive up-dating of the account in the light of further experience and achievement; the 'formative' use of the profile in the determination of learning objectives; the involvement of the learners themselves in the self-appraisal and in the negotiation of the judgments which enter the profile; the presentation of a summative account that can assist the transition to the next stage of education or training or employment. It is claimed that the final product or report is of less educational importance than the process of producing it, because the process requires agreement, and thus conversation, between teacher and student over what it should contain, what has been achieved and where they need to concentrate effort.

Profiling was strongly supported by *A Basis for Choice*, and subsequently became an essential ingredient of TVEI, the YTS, and full-time courses, such as CPVE, which were trying to bridge the academic/vocational divide. A national *system* of profiling would help overcome the problems of coherence and progression. But how far would the academic tradition be able to absorb such a practice?

There were hopeful signs. The DES produced in 1984 a statement of policy *Records of Achievement*, suggesting the possible extension of profiles to all secondary schools. Grants were given to 20 pilot schools in eight English schemes. An evaluation of the pilots by HMI (1988) came to the following conclusions. The benefits were greater variety and effectiveness in methods of assessment; improvement in teaching methods; better personal and social education; improved relationships between student and teacher; self-awareness in the students; and the effective use of the final report in the transition to subsequent training, employment or education. However, profiling was very time consuming. Teachers needed time with the students on a one-to-one basis as part of the timetabled curriculum. And that could signal the demise of this attempt to meet the problems of coherence and progression which had the support of teachers, employers, and the Secretary of State. As HMI explained, 'in all but the most generously staffed schools some extra provision of staff time will be needed' – hardly probable under the local management of schools.

Despite these difficulties, the National Record of Achievement (NRA) has received support from NCVQ which now administers it. The NRA is a national scheme for recording vocational and academic and other relevant achievements at school, in further education and throughout working life. It is intended to encourage people to identify their own agendas and to have greater control over their own progress and development.

Core skills

In 1990, the Secretary of State indicated that he wanted all 16–19 students to develop 'core skills', and to enable much easier transfer between A Level and vocational courses. The National Curriculum Council (NCC), therefore, produced its booklet *Core Skills 16–19*. This drew upon the prevocational tradition that had stressed vocationally related 'process skills' and identified the core skills of communicating, problem solving, personal effectiveness, numeracy, information technology, modern language competence. One way of vocationalising the academic curriculum and liberalising vocational training would be to ensure that these vocationally relevant 'core skills' were common to both and received due credit in assessment. Thus the revised general principles governing A Level syllabuses would specify how these common core skills were included and what weight was being given to them in the scheme of assessment. They would also have a place in the record of achievement that ideally would be the same for academic and for training courses.

The NCC booklet received a fairly uncritical welcome. But possibly the acceptance of the NCC recommendations arose from the rather elastic use of 'skills'. What are 'problem-solving skills', disconnected from particular sorts of problem and from particular theoretical frameworks? Can the complex capacity to communicate to different audiences and about different subjects be reduced to a finite list of skills?

Such philosophical points are ignored at one's peril. If something simply does not make sense then it is difficult to know what to do about it in practice. Thus, a range of attainment targets for 'communication', as for all the core skills, have to be put into measurable statements and these will have to be differentiated into levels – so that, as a result of assessment, there can be seen to be progression. But 'communication' (similarly 'problem solving') is not that kind of thing. It involves skills certainly – a massive number of them which cannot be reduced to a small number of statements – but it involves much more than that, namely, the sensitivity to different contexts (a good communicator at Old Trafford may be pretty poor at the Athenaeum), empathy with different sorts of people, an extensive vocabulary representing conceptual complexity, a grasp of the different uses of language, and so on.

Access to higher education

Britain has fewer students continuing into higher education than its main competitors, and it is the declared policy of the government to increase the number of HE students – although not at the same unit cost – and the results of that policy are well known. Indeed, the changing shape and quality of higher education is reflecting the theme of this book, namely, the relation of a system of education designed for an elite few to one that will prepare a large number for the more sophisticated technological and competitive world – a shift from selective to mass higher education. These changes are not unaffected by what is happening in schools.

What then are the main issues?

First, the changing school curriculum means that many will reach higher education without the qualifications that once were required by universities. For example, students who have studied double science, instead of the three single sciences, will not have covered the content that will enable them to progress to some science courses.

Second, the emphasis at school upon the *process* of learning, encouraged by the prevocational courses leading to GNVQ, will make demands for different modes of teaching in higher education – more activity-led assignments and greater emphasis upon practical ways of learning.

Finally, the post-16 framework is characterised by independent initiatives, each showing the hallmarks of the distinct traditions referred to above, and then by the frantic and futile efforts to connect them – asking the A Level boards to incorporate core skills in otherwise content-heavy syllabuses or trying to attribute NVQ equivalences to the very different vocational and academic qualifications. But this surely is the wrong way to set about it.

The appropriate framework for 14 to 18 education and training should arise from the answers to three questions: What sort of curriculum is needed to meet the personal needs of all up to the age of 18 and to meet the needs also of society (*not* what curriculum is needed in schools in order to prepare a few for university)? What system of institutions is needed to ensure that all have access to that curriculum according to 'age, ability and aptitude'? What sort of teaching is required so that all students will benefit from that curriculum?

Institutional framework

I recently had to explain the system of education and training to a group of Americans. It was impossible to make a general statement without pointing out so many exceptions that the generalisation was almost worthless. Let us start with the simple picture. Compulsory education is from 5 to 16. This period is split between primary and secondary at 11 on the Hadow Report (1926) principle that 'a tide begins to rise in the veins of youth at the age of 11; they call it adolescence'. At 16 most go to work, where some will receive further training and day release for more theoretical work at the local college of FE, but some will continue in full-time study in the sixth form of the school or at the college of FE mainly for A Levels. At 18 a minority will proceed to university or to a college of HE.

Furthermore, there is a fairly simple picture of how this is arranged financially. Most students (about 93%) go to schools which are entirely paid for from the public purse, the rest attending private schools. Similarly, those who are released to study at colleges of FE, as part of their training whilst in employment, will not have to pay fees. And the minority who go to the university will have fees paid and will also receive a maintenance grant if their parents earn below a certain amount.

Immediately, however, the exceptions have to be given. In some parts of the country, entry to secondary schools is at 12; in others, 13. Again, secondary schools may be comprehensive, dealing with the full ability range, or they may be divided into grammar (selective for those judged to be academically most able) and secondary modern.

The funding arrangement is not so simple either, and this makes the above scenario even more complicated. Thus, the division between public and private – between state maintained and privately funded – becomes blurred as public money supports private education through the Assisted Places Scheme and as public education becomes increasingly dependent on private sponsorship. Furthermore, the creation of city technology colleges – officially independent but 90% maintained by public funds – further fragments the system. And, finally, the parallel development of Local Management of Schools (in which almost the total budget is devolved to the school) and of grant maintained schools (in which the schools are directly funded by the newly created FAS) brings with it different bases for funding the maintained system, together with a growing but unplanned tendency to select on a variety of bases (academic, musical talent, etc.).

And that refers to schools. Post-16 there are school sixth forms, sixth form colleges (which until recently specialised in A Level), colleges of FE (which specialised in vocational studies, full time and part time, but which increasingly attracted A Level students) and tertiary colleges (which provided *all* the post-16 education and training for a particular locality).

However, that is becoming more complicated mainly because of changed funding arrangements. Thus, colleges of FE, tertiary colleges and sixth form colleges are no longer funded through the LEA, but receive money directly from the Further Education Funding Council (FEFC) – on a different basis from sixth forms in schools and with different strings attached. For example, those funded by the FEFC have been told that, in order to maintain the same level of funding, they must increase their student intake by 7% per year for three or four years – a public saving of money by cutting the 'unit of resource' called 'efficiency gains'.

Furthermore, money which previously LEAs paid to support vocational courses in their colleges of FE, is now paid via the TECs, and those TECs may choose instead to divert the money into private training agencies. In that way a public tradition of education and training is being transformed into a private profit-making one.

Therefore, a coherent system of education is transformed into a fragmented one, with different institutions funded according to different formulae, private sponsorship encouraged, and competition replacing the co-operation between institutions within a balanced system. Sixth form colleges now poach vocational students from colleges of FE where previously there was an agreed division of labour.

There is growing, therefore, a hierarchy of schools and institutions, each recreating its identity in competition with its neighbours as it seeks a particular niche in the changing 'market' of educational and training provision and a range of resources to replace the once sufficient provision from the public purse.

Conclusion: the way forward

This chapter has set out the complex framework of courses and examinations through which students progress from 14 to 18 – from school into employment or vocational training or further and higher education. I have shown the different institutional arrangements through which this progression is to be made. What this chapter has revealed is the existence of three quite different traditions with different cultural roots and with strong forces within each ensuring their continued separation. Let us call them the 'academic', the 'vocational training' and the prevocational or 'life-preparation' traditions.

The **academic** tradition is encapsulated within a curriculum that is the aggregate of subjects. These subjects incorporate a particular understanding of 'liberal education', namely, that education aims at the acquisition of worthwhile knowledge; knowledge is divided into forms structured by their own distinctive concepts, facts, theories and methods of enquiry; and a selection is made from this vast amount of knowledge of what is worth learning. Such knowledge goes beyond common sense and therefore can be acquired only from study and systematic teaching – it is not picked up from experience. And it is taught by those who, due to their own prolonged initiation into that tradition, are now its custodians, and are authorities in particular parts of it. This initiation is long and arduous. It requires separation from the practical affairs of life. The initiates are therefore placed in special institutions called schools. (It is significant that many of our major public schools are in isolated rural areas and that the new universities were built mainly on old country estates.) Relatively few students have the ability or resources to undertake this arduous journey and so liberal education is a rather elite accomplishment, picked out by special kinds of knowledge (theoretical rather than practical or useful) and by distinctive sensibilities, cultivated through the arts and through a selective literature.

The **vocational** tradition is reflected, of course, in the youth training schemes, but also in the many developments that are affecting full-time education both before and after the age of 18. In particular we have pointed out the development of NVQ. This vocational tradition, by contrast with the academic, celebrates the practical and the useful. It sees knowledge not as something worthwhile in itself but as something useful for purposes that are externally determined – by employers, say, or by parents who see the value of qualifications for getting jobs. Indeed, the primary purpose of the knowledge and the skills acquired at school is the promotion of the economic base of society and of the student. Furthermore, the superiority of theoretical over practical knowledge is denied – indeed, theory is only valuable in so far as it is useful. Hence, the starting point of curriculum analysis is not the time-honoured traditions of literary criticism, historical scholarship, scientific enquiry or aesthetic appreciation, but the particular skills, useful knowledge and personal qualities judged necessary for success in industry and commerce. And such knowledge, skills and qualities can be trained in and precisely measured.

However, possibly the most interesting course developments of the last decade have been those associated with the FEU and TVEI, the **prevocational** courses, which fall within what might be referred to as the 'life-preparation' tradition. This is implicitly critical of the other two. First, it accepts a continuity between what is taught and the experiences that the students bring with them to school. Learning is a matter of building on that experience, reflecting on it and refining it. Second, the purpose of education includes vocational training, but it is much more than that. It has a moral purpose, enabling students to develop a set of defensible values that will sustain them when life gets tough, encouraging the interests that will enable them to enjoy their leisure time profitably, providing the guidance and counselling which will enable them to find the appropriate routes into further education, training and employment. It is difficult within such a tradition to specify in advance precisely what has to be learnt – so much depends on the aspirations and on the prior experience of the student. The emphasis therefore is not upon the content to be covered, as in the academic tradition, nor upon specific competences as in the vocational tradition, but upon general capacities for living effectively and upon the processes of learning, of problem-solving, of co-operating and of enquiring.

This is a sketchy set of distinctions, and no doubt it has its defects. Does anything fit neatly into any one category? But I shall expand on this analysis in Part III, showing how they do in practice embody different philosophical beliefs about the nature and the value of knowledge – and indeed about the nature of liberal education and its relation to vocational training. The point is that the different pathways outlined in this chapter embody separate traditions, thus preventing a coherent development of a 14 to 18 curriculum.

4

Curriculum and Assessment

The idea of a curriculum

A distinction needs to be drawn between *courses*, referred to in the last chapter, and *curriculum*. Take, for example, a BTEC course I observed. The *course* in media studies refers to a set of arrangements: contact hours, assessment procedures and college syllabus which meet the BTEC criteria. The *curriculum*, on the other hand, refers to the learning experiences (planned, for the most part, by the teacher) through which that course is put into practice. Thus, the teachers set practical assignments leading to learning outcomes – specific skills such as questionnaire construction, knowledge such as the quality of different Dorset cheeses which they were planning to market, concepts such as the idea of market research, and qualities such as entrepreneurship. Furthermore, in promoting those outcomes, the teachers related to the students in a way appropriate to the learning which they wanted to encourage. Teaching and learning styles are part of the curriculum.

The point is that 'curriculum' is a richer concept than that of 'syllabus' or 'course'. The curriculum incorporates the aims, philosophy, resources and (in the light of all these things) the planning of the teacher. It refers to the carefully nurtured 'social process in which learning takes place, discoveries are made and pupils come to terms with culture, and, we hope, learn to think independently within culture' (Stenhouse 1967). And that in turn will be profoundly affected by the atmosphere (the 'hidden curriculum') of the school. The same syllabus can be taught in different courses, the same course taught by different teachers – in each case producing different curricula. And this is either worrying or consoling, depending on one's standpoint, for the contribution of the teacher is an integral part of the curriculum, and no amount of government directives or legislation can produce a national *curriculum*.

This point is not insignificant, for, in neglecting it, bureaucrats talk about the 'delivery' of the curriculum, as though it were a 'thing' like a course or a syllabus and as if the teacher were no more than a delivery boy. And that (with the other language changes foisted on schools) has a profound effect upon how we come to see the relationship between teacher and learner within the tradition of liberal education.

It is often argued that planning the curriculum requires initially a clear understanding of what the teacher wants the student to learn. It is necessary to distinguish between the *aims* (the overall orientation of the teaching) and the more precise *objectives* (the shorter-term, more specific learning outcomes). Only then, so it is argued, can one plan *rationally* the means for achieving those aims – namely, the texts, the activities, the learning experiences to which the learner should be exposed. Finally, there should be an evaluation of the whole process – checking whether the means really do achieve the ends and re-assessing, in the light of experience, the worthwhileness of the ends themselves. Part of that evaluation will be an assessment of the students' performance. All this is what has been referred to by Tyler (1949), and those following in Tyler's footsteps, as 'the rational curriculum model' (aims, objectives, content, method and evaluation), and the validity of this view seems, at first sight, to be self-evident. Indeed, that (with adaptations) would seem to be the model adopted by NCVQ (see Jessup 1991) and of the National Curriculum, with its emphasis upon precise and assessable outcomes.

There are, however, qualifications which need to be made to this account, lest, seduced by a particular understanding of 'being rational', we concede the liberal case to the vocational trainers.

First, the model ignores the social process of the curriculum – the transaction between teacher and learner where the learners themselves make a significant contribution to what is learnt. What the teacher plans the student to learn has to be filtered through the thoughts, beliefs, understandings of the learner.

Second, to work towards an objective is itself ambiguous. To some, it requires a clear exposition of the outcomes of teaching. How else, one might ask, can one tell whether or not one has been successful? To decide what to teach and how to teach it would surely require clear understanding of the ends. And it would help if these goals were to be described as precisely as possible – in terms of behaviours and compe-tences. As we shall see (pages 94–7), this view of rational curriculum planning is a dominant feature of vocational courses. However, it is not obvious that it applies to a more liberally conceived education. Certainly, the teacher has to plan and to decide what texts and activities the student should get to grips with. But the teacher may be reluctant to state with precision what the student should be doing or thinking as a result. An educational experience is an encounter with other minds, whether those of the teacher or those of the authors to whom the learner has been introduced. Indeed, the success of one's teaching may lie precisely in the ability of the learner to sift the evidence, to challenge conclusions, to criticise an argument, to imagine alternative viewpoints. The teacher, well versed in the arguments within the tradition of that subject, but without a clear view of the conclusions to be reached, could still exercise judgment over the quality of the student's argument or deliberation. One should distinguish between teaching to objectives and teaching to those processes of thinking which are compatible with a range of possible and unpredictable outcomes. This distinction is essential to an understanding of the division which has been established between liberal education, on the one hand, and vocational preparation, on the other.

Third, there are difficulties in seeing how the overall aims are to be established – or who should have responsibility for establishing them. This problem is linked to that of the changed partnership referred to in chapter 2. Not long ago aims were implicit within a tradition of educational practice almost entirely under the control of the professional educators – teachers, examiners and admission tutors of higher education. But the discovery of the 'consumer' of education (the employer and the parent particularly), and the government's involvement in defining 'standards', have altered the control over educational aims and have thereby redefined them. There is a greater vocational orientation. There is a more explicit articulation of the kind of learning which is regarded as acceptable. There is an attempt to say what qualities (such as enterprise and entrepreneurship) are desirable. But puzzles remain about the authority of those who now pronounce on aims of teaching. Have the Secretary of State or the director of the CBI any particular expertise here? And these puzzles give rise to deeper questions in ethics about the values that education should serve and in social philosophy about the control of those values. These questions will be the focus of chapters 5 and 7.

Fourth, this lack of the more philosophical reflection required for establishing curriculum aims has resulted in surprising gaps and inconsistencies in the proposals put forward by government, examination boards, employers and others who tell teachers what they ought to be teaching. Thus, what is taught should, we are told, relate to the needs of society, of the economy, and of the learner's own personal growth.

But there is no evidence of the cultural analysis essential for knowing what these social needs are and to which Lawton (1989) draws attention; nor, with regard to the economy, is there clarification of the skills, qualities and knowledge which a successful economy requires of the educational system; nor, finally, are we given a clear picture of the kind of personal growth which education aims to enhance. Above all, there is no attempt to see how these different aims can be reconciled with each other – what, in the light of present day social, economic and personal circumstances, is a desirable model of an educated person which the educational system should foster.

Given these problems over the aims and objectives of the curriculum, it is not possible to decide rationally between the different ways in which the curriculum might be organised without raising the ethical questions which are considered in chapter 5.

'Subjects' as the framework for learning

What a subject is

There is an enormous amount to be learnt and, for teaching purposes, it is necessary to break it up somehow. A subject is a way of breaking it up and of organising a manageable and relatively coherent area of learning.

There are two characteristics of a subject which make it both manageable and relatively coherent.

The first is that a subject has its own history and social characteristics. Books (e.g. in geography) are written in its name and are classified accordingly in libraries; departments are created in schools and chairs are established in universities; professional bodies are formed and teachers give allegiance to them (for example, the Association of Science Teachers); there develops a spirit and tradition of criticism associated with the subject. Of course, as in the history of anything, divisions arise and new allegiances are formed. Subjects split and new ones vie for recognition. This usually takes place in the universities but partly is reflected in the schools. Economics, sociology, politics and socio-biology are relatively new subjects on the school curriculum. But the list of school subjects remains relatively stable, and those in the National Curriculum are much the same as those in the 1904 Regulations for secondary schools.

The second characteristic of subjects, which no doubt partly explains their relative stability, is that they each have a distinctive 'logical structure'. This I shall explain at greater length in chapter 6, but it means, for example, that there are features of the learning that take place within 'history' which make it quite different from the learning that occurs within 'science'. Such features include the distinctive ideas or concepts, the distinctive modes of enquiry, the distinctive ways of testing the truth or validity or relevance of what is said. Therefore, a subject is understood to be, not an arbitrary division of knowledge, nor one that is based on historical contingencies alone, but one that makes logical sense. To master a subject, so it is claimed, is to acquire distinctive mental capacities which enable one to think more effectively. It is to be initiated into a tradition of scientific enquiry, of aesthetic appreciation, of historical understanding, of literary criticism. And these mental capacities and these traditions are not picked up vicariously. They need to be focused upon systematically. Hence, the central place for subjects in the curriculum.

Prior to the National Curriculum, there was a gradual acceptance within the DES and amongst HMI of the subject-based framework for the curriculum. The DES established the Assessment of Performance Unit (APU) in 1974 to monitor the performance of pupils at different ages across the curriculum. Its main aim was to provide the data on which judgments could be made about standards in schools and therefore about the allocation of resources. To do this the APU needed a curriculum model. That model suggested that all school work contributed to learning in one or more of the following areas of development: language, mathematics, scientific, aesthetic, personal and social, physical, and foreign language. There was disagreement within the DES over whether to admit 'economic' and 'technological' as distinct areas of development. And such subjects as history and geography were seen to contribute to the personal and social – the key focus of the humanities. The HMI produced in 1977 *Curriculum 11–16*. This suggested eight 'areas of experience' as a basis for the curriculum: aesthetic/creative, ethical, linguistic, mathematical, physical, scientific, socio-political and spiritual. Remember that these were 'areas of experience', identified by their distinctive logical structures, not subjects which were the means through which the students might enter into these areas of experience. In subsequent publications, this list and this approach became reinforced, and referred to as the 'entitlement curriculum'. However, the 1977 Green Paper *Education in Schools* affirmed the Secretary of State's responsibilities for the curriculum. Subsequent documents, *A Framework for the Curriculum* (1979) and *The School Curriculum* (1981), proposed the subjects, not areas of experience. The former document even suggested the percentage of time to be allocated to each subject.

Implicit within both the DES and the HMI thinking was a criticism of the range of options often available to students after the age of 14, in that these options might not give entree to the different forms of knowledge and understanding to which they were 'entitled'. There was an implicit criticism, too, of the organisation of the curriculum around themes and interests without due attention being paid to these distinctive forms of particular subjects. The DES was becoming much more prescriptive in the actual organisation of the curriculum.

The National Curriculum

The National Curriculum was a major part of the Education Act of 1988. It was the culmination of a process of government intervention in an area of public life which previously had been left to the professionals. In that respect it reflected a distrust of professional power, which extended to other areas of public service such as medicine, social work and the law. It was argued that many of these services would be better in private hands, responding to customer demand and discrimination, subject to market forces, free of the power of the self-perpetuating middlemen – the professionals. Indeed, teachers were no longer considered to be authorities on what should be taught; rather did their expertise lie in the skills of delivery. Nonetheless, there were limits to the operation of market forces in education, and therefore it was seen to be necessary to ensure that those educated in the public sector would be taught according to objectives defined by those who are elected to represent the public interest and to manage the system, namely, the government.

What, then, were the reasons for the government wanting to take on this role?

As I explained in chapter 1, there was a concern that standards were not as high as they might have been – to the disadvantage both of the students and of the economic welfare of the country. And to overcome this problem, there was a need to identify much more clearly the objectives which the teaching should be aimed at.

Furthermore, the exercise of professional autonomy had resulted in different curricula, and that was inappropriate in a mobile society; the parents, the customers, had a right to a service which was truly national to ensure continuity from school to school and ultimately from school to college.

Finally, in pursuit of consumer rights, the government required a proper description, not only of what the school did, but also of how the pupils had performed, compared with other children in other schools. The National Curriculum, defined partly in terms of objectives pitched at different levels, would become the yardstick against which the performance of schools and of pupils might be measured – necessary if 'customers' were to be able to make rational choices or have objective grounds for evaluating the services they were to 'buy'.

The National Curriculum, therefore, defined the curriculum primarily in terms of attainment targets and programmes of study within a range of core and foundation subjects. Attainment targets were not, in theory, age related, but for each subject programmes of study specified what content needed to be covered for each key stage. Key stages were age related: key stage 1, age 5–7; key stage 2, 7–11; key stage 3, 11–14; key stage 4, 14–16 (linking up with GCSE syllabuses). The attainment targets in each subject were at ten levels, so that progression in each subject could be established and teacher, child and parent would know how the pupil performed relative to the objectives to be reached and to other pupils. The appropriate level of performance in each attainment target was that which the average student in that age group would perform at. Such a student would be expected to improve by one level every two years. But of course, as one goes up the age range, there would be greater variation in performance, some performing well above the norm, others well below.

The 1988 Act established the NCC to advise the Secretary of State on the National Curriculum, but the operative word is 'advise' because the Secretary was empowered under the Act to decide what should be the attainment targets and the programmes of study within each subject, a power which he was ready to use when his view of history or geography, say, was at odds with that of his professional advisers.

Working groups similarly had to think hard about the essence of their respective subjects – the logical features by which they maintained their distinctive identities, but also the social and cultural context within which the subject might be redefined or at least made relevant. And this was rarely uncontroversial either because the experts disagreed amongst themselves or because the Secretary of State, for political reasons, disagreed with the experts.

Indeed, debates within the working group were often acrimonious about many aspects of the new 'curriculum' (for example, the place, if any, for teaching 'standard English' and the examples given of the 'best that has been thought and said'). And that is a significant point. In inducting the young into a form of thought – for example, in the appreciation and mastery of English – the teacher introduces them to a conversation which is not over, to a set of arguments yet to be resolved, to a conflict of values which lends vigour to the conversation. And yet the detailed prescriptions by government on such matters assumes that there are experts, known to the Secretary of State if not the Secretary of State himself, who *do* know what the outcomes of the conversation should be. But where in the tradition of liberal education is there room for such authority in academic and moral matters? And how can one reconcile that definition of a curriculum in terms of prespecified learning outcomes with the curriculum as described earlier, namely, as a social process planned by the teacher in which a particular kind of transaction takes place?

The main lessons to be drawn from this section on the National Curriculum, and of the controversies that it has given rise to, are these.

First, the government thought it important to define a National Curriculum in terms of specific objectives or attainment targets and programmes of study leading to them within traditional discrete subjects – rather than in terms of vocational competences or of general mental and personal qualities or of transactions between teacher and learner. And that very decision embodied an understanding of liberal education and of its relation to vocational preparation.

Second, the achievement of these targets was to be measurable at ten levels, each level representing the progress an average pupil could be expected to make in two years. And yet little attempt was given to show how the criteria, against which the attainment of the targets at each level would be judged, represented either a logical sequence in the subject knowledge or a typical two-year progression in learning.

Third, in defining these attainment targets and the criteria by which their attainment would be measured, the working groups examined and debated the educational aims of each subject. In so doing, they took account of the relevance of the subject to employment and life after school.

Fourth, even though the definition of these targets was initially put in the hands of subject working groups on which there was representation from appropriate professional and academic experts, the final version depended, not on the agreement of the working group, nor on the consensus reached after wider consultation, but upon the political decision of the Secretary of State. The result is that the legally binding National Curriculum assumes certain characteristics of each subject (for example, the integrative nature of general as opposed to single-subject science) which are controversial in the sense of being disputed by serious people within the relevant professional and academic bodies.

Themes, dimensions and processes as the framework for learning

The desirability of organising the curriculum into subjects may seem self-evident. But there are criticisms – at least if subjects are the sole elements of organisation. Shortly after the publication of the National Curriculum Consultation Document in 1987, questions were raised about the place of health education, personal and social education, environmental studies, careers and guidance, indeed many of the curriculum activities pursued by schools which were educationally justified and yet which would be omitted from a curriculum defined solely in terms of traditional subjects. There were further, more radical criticisms from those who thought that curriculum planning should start, not from an analysis of subjects, but from an analysis of personal and social and economic needs, the satisfaction of which may or may not be met by traditional subjects.

There are two kinds of response to these concerns which we should consider if we are to understand the variety of courses and their under-lying philosophies: the introduction of cross-curriculum themes, dimen-sions and skills; and a focus upon the processes through which young people come to make sense of their experiences. This double response makes it more even more difficult to provide a coherent system 14 to 18.

Dimensions, skills and themes

The NCC quickly came to see the importance of cross-curriculum planning, thereby overcoming the potential danger of a curriculum conceived in terms of disconnected and logically distinct subjects. For this purpose it distinguished between 'dimensions', 'skills' and 'themes'.

Dimensions are the particular emphases that might be given to the teaching of a subject so that students acquire ways of thinking, feeling and behaving which transcend particular subject boundaries. The two main dimensions are those of 'equal opportunities' and 'multicultural perspective'. This means at one level addressing those elements in the organisation and curriculum of the school which militate unfairly against the success of particular groups – particularly girls and those from ethnic minorities. There is a need, for example, to pay special attention to the reason *why* girls do less well than boys in public exami-nations in chemistry and physics. At another level, however, it means addressing deep-rooted gender or ethnic stereotyping – for example, about intelligence or social habits. Such dimensions to teaching do not constitute subjects in themselves, although there are new subjects in higher education called 'women's studies' and 'black studies', and these have been reflected in curriculum developments in some schools. But the problems to be tackled are more to do with the 'hidden' or implicit message conveyed by textbooks, teachers' attitudes and student preju-dices. They can nonetheless be approached directly through existing subjects, as, for instance, when racial or gender themes are dealt with in the study of literature or in the discussion topics in the humanities.

A multicultural dimension to the curriculum is specified for several reasons. First, students from different ethnic minority groups constitute a significant minority in many schools (and a majority in some) and their self-respect requires the recognition of the culture which is distinctively theirs and upon which their own self-identity to some extent depends. Second, the presence of different ethnic cultures is a richness to be exploited rather than a problem to be overcome. Third, however, is the need to counter the racism which is endemic in society, reflected as much in schools as elsewhere. That surely is the main reason for a multicultural perspective even in areas where there are few if any ethnic minority groups.

The second aspect of cross-curriculum planning is the teaching of **skills** in communication, numeracy, studying, problem-solving, personal and social relationships and information technology. Moreover, these cross-curriculum skills have been extended to post-16 education, where it is argued that there should be core skills integrated into the otherwise disconnected A Level courses.

There are three reasons given for introducing cross-curriculum or core skills. The first concerns the importance of vocationally relevant elements in otherwise academic courses. The second lies in the bridge-building that such skills provide between the academic and vocational courses. The third lies in the belief that such core skills are more important than the content of particular subjects; core skills extend the mental capacities which transcend specific subject matters and which affect most profoundly how we think and feel and operate in the world. However, despite the almost universal acclaim for core skills (the FEU, the NCC and the NCVQ have all produced their own but similar lists), there are problems, developed in the previous chapter, in the very concept which have not been addressed by these different bodies. Possibly it is because of these conceptual difficulties that it has not been possible to find ways to assess them – or indeed of incorporating them into the curriculum both pre- and post-16.

However, that should not detract from the very real importance of addressing within particular subject areas the personal qualities and self-confidence that communication in different contexts requires, the numeracy that is needed for everyday living, the habits and techniques of study which enable students to become increasingly independent of the spoon-feeding approaches, or familiarity with basic techniques of word-processing. Behind the confused talk of core and cross-curriculum skills lie important truths.

Finally, cross-curriculum planning within the context of the National Curriculum includes **themes**. These are: economic and industrial understanding, careers education and guidance, health, citizenship and the environment. Some of these could be thought of as 'dimensions' – the distinction remains unclear. Thus, history can be taught from an economic point of view, the erstwhile pirates, Drake and Raleigh, being redescribed as 16th century entrepreneurs; literary texts can be selected to reflect aspects of industrial culture (Mrs Gaskell's *North and South* rather than Hardy's *Woodlanders*). But the pro-theme argument is that such topics require thematic treatment if justice is to be done to them; there is a need to focus upon a particular content and to make sure that this is incorporated somewhere in the curriculum either as a 'mini-subject' or as content to be covered within the foundation subjects. Thus, sex education is often regarded as part of health education, and cross-curriculum planning would ensure that it is covered in relevant subjects – biology, literature, physical education, religious education and so on. There would no doubt be a need for special classes in particular aspects (for example, AIDS), but this would not add up to there being a subject in sex education – although I understand that there are universities where one can get degrees in it.

Of particular significance has been the cross-curriculum theme of 'citizenship'; and indeed here most of all we see the distinction between a subject and a theme. *Education for Citizenship* is introduced in the following way:

> Education for citizenship is essential for every pupil. It helps each of them to understand the duties, responsibilities and rights of every citizen and promotes concern for the values by which a civilised society is identified – justice, democracy, respect for the law. (NCC 1990)

Unlike the normal subject, it starts not from a tradition of enquiry but from a vague political analysis of what students should know and experience so that they might fulfil their civic duties. The concept is spelled out in terms of four kinds of objectives – relevant knowledge, skills, attitudes, and moral codes and values. These are pitched at different levels linked to the key stages. But it is essentially concerned with producing a certain sort of citizen and thus represents a more direct intervention in personal and social formation than has been generally found within the liberal tradition. And that raises questions about educational aims which we shall come back to in chapter 5.

Processes of learning

A more radical response to the perceived problems of a curriculum organised in traditional subjects was, as I explained in the last chapter, provided by the prevocational courses, reflected in the TVEI initiative particularly. These developed a set of curriculum principles which were neither narrowly vocational nor subject specific. Too many young people were completing the compulsory stage of their schooling disillusioned, failures in the sense that the schools defined failure, ill-equipped for the world into which they were about to enter, often socially inept, without the 'tools' that would give them some prospect of economic independence. At the same time, employers argued that the young people lacked the qualities necessary for employment. In unpacking these problems, teachers argued that the curriculum was too disconnected from the personal experience of the students. It tended to be too abstracted from the concrete and practical world that the students felt at home in and could understand. It too frequently did not meet the aspirations (particularly those concerning employment) which the young people had for the future. More often than not, assessment emphasised what they could not do rather than what they had achieved. Continuity from one stage of education to the next or to vocational training or to employment was only dimly perceived. And too often the traditional curriculum put them off learning rather than whet the appetite and create the capacity for more.

The courses developed in response have been described in the previous chapter. They provided a more student-centred approach to learning. Therefore, the *curriculum* thinking began, not from a distillation of the knowledge and understandings represented by the major subjects, but from an analysis of the personal needs of the student and of the economic needs of society. Of course, such an analysis might well point to the importance of traditional learning, but it might not – at least for some of the time. Such a curriculum emphasised reflection upon, and making sense of, the students' experiences in or out of school. It contained more practical and co-operative modes of learning, gradually leading the learner on to the deeper significance and the more theoretical understanding of that which was practically engaged in. A central place was given to helping students to identify and to negotiate learning objectives significant to them; to that end the teacher would provide guidance and counselling. Assessment was transformed into a more generous profile of achievements and personal qualities, partly with a view to helping with the guidance and counselling. The distinction between the vocational and the academic was intentionally blurred as vocational interests and aspirations became the vehicle for more general understandings of the economic and social context. Opportunities were provided for an exploration of the personal and social values which ultimately would guide them in life and sustain them when things got tough. Links were made with the wider community (employers, voluntary agencies, political groups, etc.) as sources of information and of help. In sum, therefore, the emphasis was more upon the process of learning (the development of study skills, the readiness to work co-operatively, the capacity to explore and to test out ideas, the ability to engage in discussions about work or values, the acquisition of basic skills of communication and numeracy and information technology) than upon the product of other people's learning; more upon personal and social qualities (those of self-confidence, enterprise and co-operation) than upon the disinterested pursuit of knowledge; and more upon general capability than upon specific work-related skills.

Such a curriculum would be organised around practical assignments, so structured as to require the development of these capabilities and skills and the more reflective and co-operative modes of learning. Linked with the assignments would be the timetabled periods for guidance and counselling and for the recording of achievement. There would also be the opportunities to acquire those skills (in, for example, word processing or information technology) which would be required for the carefully selected and structured assignments. A key element would be 'the group' through which ideas are developed and to whom assignments are presented for critical appraisal. Vocational interests would be explicit and often the more general qualities and capabilities would be developed through those interests.

Such a way of thinking about the curriculum is not a pipe dream. It was intrinsic to many of the TVEI developments and it characterised the course developments in CPVE and BTEC. Thus, BTEC specifies the criteria which a college-based course must meet rather than specifying the precise content to be covered. And those criteria will be concerned primarily with the processes of learning rather than with specific content or outcomes.

The irony is that curriculum initiatives, launched and conducted under the aegis of vocational preparation, were reminiscent more of the child-centred philosophy of the Plowden Report than of the assessment-dominated initiatives of the National Curriculum or of the NVQ. What so often was condemned as a narrowly vocational subversion of liberal education came to be defended as a bulwark against the illiberal curriculum of both the subject-based National Curriculum and the objectives-led vocational training.

But problems there were, because there is a limit to how far one can go along this student-centred route before essential questions about standards are raised, against which success is to be measured, and before consideration is given to the relationship between these personal and social achievements, on the one hand, and a wider cognitive perspective, on the other, which traditionally has been a hallmark of the educated person.

Competences as the framework for learning

Harking back to my account above of rational curriculum planning, one can see the attraction in dismissing so much education as ill planned and amateurish. Teachers and those who plan the curriculum rarely clarify where they want to go – what exactly the students need to learn – and then what are the best means for the learner to get there. They should stress outcomes rather than inputs or content to be covered, for these are but the means to an end, not the end itself. Furthermore, the outcomes should be so specified that one knows what performances will indicate that the goals have been reached. Assessment consists of whatever evidence demonstrates that the learner has so performed and has acquired the particular competence aimed at.

Such a model has frequently been advocated in curriculum textbooks, but it has recently acquired fresh importance through the attempts to make the curriculum more relevant to the perceived economic needs of the country. It is argued that, despite the massive investment in education, too many people are incompetent at various levels of their working life. Preparation for life requires the identification of those competences which will enable people to be more effective, especially at work. Therefore, it is considered necessary to 'particularise' the specific activities that working life consists of and to turn the competences, necessary for these activities, into the curriculum objectives. This turns educational planning upside down. Normally education is 'provider-led' – the system providing syllabuses irrespective of the potential learners' interests or needs. Here it is suggested that it should be learner-led, or, more precisely, led by the specific competences that the learner wants to acquire.

Although the claims for such a model of planning are extensive indeed, blurring the distinction between liberal education and voctional training, they arise particularly in the vocational area and are built into the ambitious programme of the NCVQ. The central concept is that of 'competence'. This refers to the ability to perform an activity to a specified standard. The list of different competences, therefore, will be accompanied by a list of performances, the execution of which demonstrates that the person has that competence. The wider or more 'generic' the competence, the more tentative must be the relationship between it and the specific performance by which it is assessed, because actual performances can never exhaust the total number of possible performances which the competent person is expected to be able to do.

A functional analysis of working occupations will reveal the many different activities that are performed and thus the list of competences needed in order to perform them. The most detailed and specific description of a competence is called by the NCVQ an *'element'*. Jessup (1991) gives two examples of an element within the broad occupational areas of catering and health care: 'maintain standards of hygiene in food preparation areas' and 'assess physical conditions of patients by inspection'. In each case, there is a list of particular performances that a person with those competences would be able to do and that therefore could be the criteria for judging whether the person has the competence. Furthermore, there would be a statement about the range of situations to which this competence would apply. Thus a person judged competent to drive a motor vehicle (he performed a three-point turn and reversed accurately into a side road) would be excluded from driving heavy lorries – they were outside the range of competence.

A number of 'elements' (that is, the basic statements of competence) can be grouped together into a unit of competence. Thus, the ability to drive would be a unit of competence made up of elements such as the ability to reverse, to stop in an emergency and to park. And a specified number of units would be credited to a NVQ. This specification of competence in terms of units and their constitutive elements, together with the performance criteria related to each element, provides the objectives which define the vocational curriculum and which are reflected in a wide range of qualifications. These objectives (and thus the qualifications) arise from an analysis of what is needed to work in different occupations, although in many cases the elements and in some cases the units together with their respective qualifications are common to several occupations. Furthermore, these competences can be pitched at several levels, the levels depending on the degree of complexity, the amount of knowledge and the assumption of personal responsibility in being competent. Thus a driving instructor would be competent at a higher level than an ordinary driver because he or she would have more explicit understanding of the principles behind the various driving activities.

Some competences are very broad – indeed, so broad that they enter into almost every activity that we do. They are the core skills such as communication or problem-solving. Once acquired, they are transferable to many different situations. To that extent they are the most important outcomes to aim at – although, also to that extent, they seem distanced from the elements and their performance criteria which are the essential building blocks of the whole system of vocational outcomes.

It is the intention of the NCVQ to provide a framework of nearly 1,000 vocational qualifications affecting over 80% of the workforce, and to specify, at level 5, a further set of competences which are needed in the work of professional people such as teachers and doctors. To this end, there are about 150 Industry Lead Bodies engaged in the occupational analysis which will produce the full list of competences that the work place could possibly want from its workforce. All these qualifications, and the massive range of elements of competence that go into them, will be on a database so that people can check what competences they already have, and what further ones they need, in order to obtain a particular qualification. They will be able to see which elements, in the qualifications they already have, might be transferred or credited to another qualification. In this way there will be a system of qualifications through which clear routes of progression can be charted.

The competence-based curriculum, therefore, is focused upon prespecified and precisely stated outcomes. Indeed, the concept of 'curriculum' is almost an irrelevance because, the outcomes having been logically severed from the means of getting them, there need not be any curriculum at all. The crucial institution is not the school or college but the assessment centre where it is judged whether or not people are competent, and what needs to be done if they are not. To become competent might require a course or it might simply mean more practice or individualised study or more intensive supervision in the work place. Eroded is the requirement of a distinctive place of learning with courses of a prespecified length. Instead there would be a system of assessment centres with accompanying facilities for guidance through the different qualification routes, and resources that enable the learner to devise an individualised 'action plan'.

The model is not, however, confined to the specific competences and skills related to the work place. As we have seen, 'core skills' such as 'communication' are embraced within the same programme, despite the problem of making logical links between such all-embracing notions and the highly specific elements of competence to which they would have to be related. Moreover, it is argued by Jessup (1991), one of the chief architects of the NVQ programme, that the same model could and should apply to general education, including the National Curriculum. Indeed, links are being attempted between the attainment targets in the National Curriculum and the statements of competence within NVQ. Difficulties are recognised because the National Curriculum attainment targets are not (yet) broken down into elements with performance criteria attached. It is as though the National Curriculum is still hung up on an outdated liberal ideal, and that School Curriculum and Assessment Authority (SCAA) has not yet had courage to embrace the 'outcomes model'. A focus on the learning competences to be achieved, instead of upon the experiences and syllabuses of the provider, would 'eradicate the distinction between education and training' (Jessup 1991, p.4). And it would solve the problem of coherence and progression outlined in the last chapter.

Assessment

Assessment is an integral part of teaching because the teacher is constantly assessing what the students know, why they are having difficulties and what has been achieved as a result of the teaching. Usually this is done informally, but that should not detract from the importance of it.

More recently, however, the aims, techniques and social purpose of assessment have come to the forefront of the public debate on education. And this affects our concern about the relation of liberal education to vocational preparation – and our understanding of the problems of coherence and progression outlined in the last chapter.

Assessment has several functions and these distinctions need to be kept clear. First, it says what students know or understand or can do with a view to finding out whether there are any problems – a kind of screening device which can be applied in the school or across schools locally and nationally. Second, assessment says which students perform better than other students, with a view to selecting some for a different kind of teaching or education. Third, it diagnoses what, if any, the learning difficulties are. Fourth, conducted at different times, it can give a longitudinal comparison of performance to see if standards are being maintained. Fifth, assessment can gather data for comparing the performance of different schools. Assessment, therefore, either surveys attainment or puts people in rank order of achievement or diagnoses learning difficulties or provides comparative data or provides evidence of school performance.

It is important to remember that the same assessment cannot fulfil each of these separate functions. Thus, the kind of assessment which tells what students can do may not be good at separating out the students with a view to selection (to use the more technical language, criterion-referenced testing is required for the former, norm-referenced for the latter). Neither will be any good for the third, diagnostic function, namely, identifying what the problems are. Finally, there are well-known technical problems in using either criterion-referenced or norm-referenced assessments for comparing performance either longitudinally or across schools where there are so many variables affecting performance.

All this is important if we are to understand the courses and curriculum described in this and the preceding chapters. Take, for example, the competence-based curriculum described in the last section which is seen by many of its proponents as a model for education generally. The curriculum is assessment-led: the outcomes aimed at are competences and these are spelt out in terms of the performances through which competence is assessed. The curriculum comes later, for it is the means selected for achieving those outcomes. The competence-based system, therefore, is a system of interrelated assessments, pitched at different levels of complexity, which say precisely what the competent person can do. For that reason a range of assessment techniques is used, but a special effort is made to assess 'on the job' – that is, in circumstances in which that competence is realistically displayed. Therefore, importance is attached, first, to continuous assessment (once a person can turn a piece of wood or create a spreadsheet, there is no point in his waiting a year or two to demonstrate this) and, second, to practical tasks and the observation of these (competence in welding or in leading group discussion is not best assessed through essays about these activities).

Typical, therefore, of the vocational courses, and also of some of the prevocational developments, has been the growth of relatively short modules leading to explicit outcomes which are assessed in a realistic and practical manner; the assessments are 'accumulated' and eventually 'credited' to a qualification. A continuous record or profile is maintained of these credits and indeed of any other experience which, properly moderated, might be regarded as credit-worthy. There is, therefore, a 'vision', being brought to earth by the NCVQ, of the whole of working life (and much else besides) captured within a large, but finite, number of assessable competences, which are embraced within an explicit and hierarchically related system. Those working within schools and universities, no doubt subscribing to liberal education as that has traditionally been conceived, will be unaware of this, the most ambitious utopian planning that the education and training system has ever seen.

Contrast this with how formal assessment has been generally understood and practised in schools and universities. It comes at the very end of the entire course with little opportunity for the accumulation of credits; it has sampled in a fairly arbitrary way what the course has covered (for example, in asking for three answers only, in a paper with ten optional questions); it has depended on a limited number of techniques, such as the written response rather than the practical task; it has aimed not so much at finding out what people can do or think, as at separating out the good from the not so good (the traditional form of assessment cannot tolerate a 100% pass rate, however good and hardworking the students, because that would not enable the users of the assessment to make distinctions for purposes of classification or selection).

In defence of such practices, or at least some of them, many teachers in schools and higher education would argue that academic achievement cannot be broken up into these discrete assessable units; that intellectual growth is reflected not in a collection of credits picked up on the way but in the maturity of judgment displayed at the end; that the quality of the transaction between teacher and learner, which, unlike specific competences and skills, is at the heart of the educational process, can only loosely be captured in a system of assessments; that no amount of prespecified 'performance criteria' can be a substitute for the *judgment* of the experienced teacher confronted with the student's work.

It could be argued that what we are talking about is two systems (the vocational and the academic) and about two quite different 'objects' of assessment (skills and quality of understanding). If that were the case it would be an implicit justification for the liberal/utilitarian divide, which is precisely what this book has set out to question.

Therefore, we see three reactions to the problem. The first is to leave things as they are, to let these different 'philosophies' of and approaches to assessment live side by side but in different institutions and for different purposes – one academic, the other vocational. The second response is for those within the vocational camp, who are seduced by the 'rational curriculum model' with its emphasis upon explicit outcomes, to take over prevailing educational practice – to infiltrate the liberal tradition. The third is an uneasy and ill-considered compromise, borrowing from the vocational model where that seems politically useful, but not prepared to go the whole way – and that is what we see in the national assessments.

There is a most important political dimension to the kind of assessment chosen and to the uses it is put to. As I explained above, there are different functions of assessment. One function is the comparison of performance between schools so that the users of the schools (the consumers) can see which school is performing best and, therefore, which educational programme they might wish to choose or buy. In any well regulated market for choosing a commodity, genuine freedom requires properly labelled goods. To choose a school sensibly would, on this view, require precise information about each school's achievements, and this information would need to be in a language that was standard across schools with which it was being compared. Moreover, such precise statements would be about the performance of the students, and would be expressed in terms of outcomes common to all other schools. Such comparison would be made more easily if the facts were expressed numerically. In this way there would be common standards of comparison and easily accessible information to see where the schools stood in relation to these standards.

The National Curriculum does precisely this. It offers a common language with which to talk about student performance. The desirable performance is expressed in terms of outcomes or attainment targets. Assessment lies in gathering evidence, as far as possible, on tasks which should be more or less standard for everybody, and the performance on these tasks is rated on a 1 to 10 scale which represents levels of performance. The meaning of these levels is spelled out in terms of criteria. Indeed, the National Curriculum could be seen, not (as is often the case by teachers) as a well-formulated statement of the subject-based understanding of liberal education, but as a peg on which to hang an assessment system influenced more by the vocational than by the liberal tradition.

The significance of this is not yet generally recognised and yet it does strike at some of the most cherished beliefs of the liberal tradition. That tradition respects the complex and often unpredictable relationship between the teacher, who provides the cultural resources for thought and reflection, and the learner, who strives and struggles to find meaning in the world he is to inhabit. Indeed, the closer the objectives come to more easily assessable outcomes, the less do they arise from the central concerns of liberal education – namely, the search for meaning that each and every reflective person is engaged in.

The clash between liberal and vocational traditions within the context of assessment is well illustrated in the difficulties encountered in the development of the national assessments. Basic principles of the Task Group on Assessment and Testing (TGAT), set up by the Secretary of State in July 1987, included: a 'formative' purpose for assessment (that is, the gathering of information to help the teacher to teach more effectively); a choice of a limited but comprehensive range of activities to be assessed (so that there would be a balanced picture of what had been taught without too much distraction from the job of teaching); a wide range of assessment techniques (so that justice would be done to the variety of achievements to be assessed); the employment of both nationally standardised tests and teacher assessments (so that national comparisons might be made without the subtleties of individual achievement being lost); the development, in each subject, of 'profile components' that might refer to several attainment targets and that would be pitched at ten progressive levels; a formal link, at key stage 4 (the age of 14–16), between national assessment and GCSE; and a Record of Achievement.

However, from the start there was conflict over the relative importance to be attached to teacher and to standardised assessments. The

School Examinations and Assessment Council (SEAC) set up consortia to develop Standard Assessment Tasks (SATS) for use at key stages 1 and 3. But early attempts to produce SATS revealed the immensity and difficulty of the job. Consequently the Secretary of State ordered the job to be simplified – that is, fewer attainment targets to be assessed and a greater emphasis on more easily delivered examinations. Thus, the principles of TGAT were considerably modified.

We must not see the problems of national assessment to be purely technical. More fundamentally they arise from the unresolved conflict between traditions competing for control of education. On the one hand, there are those who, distrustful of teacher judgment and keen to make teachers more publicly accountable and bent on central control, wish to define the outcomes and to prescribe the measurements of those outcomes quite independently of the teachers. On the other hand, there are those who, though agreeing with the importance of external reference points, believe that assessment should relate to the transactions between teacher and learner, and these will vary significantly from context to context. (Can the stage which a student is at as she grapples with a sonnet of Shakespeare be properly represented on a standardised scale 1 to 10?) Such differences do not coincide exactly with the distinction between academic and vocational. But they interconnect and there is a danger of confusing the different functions of assessment, thereby subverting from outside a tradition of liberal learning.

Conclusion

Chapter 3 described the confusing range of courses through which students might move from age 14 into employment, further education, higher education or vocational training. Their present state of incoherence is not suited to meet the problems outlined in chapter 1. At the heart of that incoherence are different ideas about the aims of education and about the relevance of a liberal tradition to our present needs. And this is reflected in the different approaches to the curriculum and its assessment, as they have been outlined in this chapter.

First, the curriculum has been created out of discrete and independent subjects. And there is good reason for this. Subjects at their best represent the different traditions of enquiry essential to the educated person – to the one who is to be liberated from the shackles of ignorance and who is to enjoy the best that has been thought and said and created. The National Curriculum seemed to endorse this, the hallmark of the liberal tradition. But this liberal tradition is, as we have seen, challenged in several ways. The focus upon knowledge and understanding, as they are embodied within the subjects, misses important areas of learning – skills and understandings which transcend curriculum boundaries, feelings and emotions and moral qualities which too often get neglected in the concentration on intellectual development, and practical know-how which can be engaged in intelligently and rigorously.

Second, therefore, the more radical criticism is that the traditional curriculum was misconceived because it started from the organisation of knowledge as it happened to be rather than from its organisation as it might be. If one sees education to be a preparation for life, then one should start with the competences that life requires, not with the content left over from other forms of life long since gone. Hence, curriculum planning should begin with desirable and specific outcomes, not with traditional inputs.

How one makes sense of these competing curriculum ideas affects profoundly one's understanding of liberal education and of its relation to vocational preparation. An emphasis upon the subjects as they are traditionally conceived ensures the continued separation of liberal education from vocational preparation. Indeed, in so far as there are aspects of that liberal tradition which militate against vocational usefulness, then there develops a tension between the two – the vocational, though necessary for the economic prosperity on which the provision of liberal education depends, being treated with disdain.

On the other hand, the prevocational curriculum, though aiming to include within the idea of general education capacities and personal qualities which too often get neglected, tended to overlook the distinctive contribution to personal development of public traditions of criticism and enquiry. To learn to think effectively or to feel sensitively or to reason correctly requires immersion into how others have done so and into how they have tackled the scientific and moral and aesthetic questions that concern us. Too often the advocates of TVEI stressed the *process* of learning as though that were possible without the *products* of previous learning.

Finally, the vocational alternative, taking seriously the injunction to prepare young people for life, argues for a thorough revision of curriculum planning, starting with work-related competences which may or may not lie within the liberal tradition.

The effects of these changes in aim and value are massive. The teacher, once the mediator of a liberal tradition into which the learner is to be initiated and 'an authority' in the ends to be pursued as well as in the means for pursuing them, becomes instead the deliverer of someone else's curriculum – the government's, the NCVQ's, the employer's, the customer's. Schools and universities, once places set aside for learning which would be uninterrupted by external distractions and concerns for usefulness, are linked more closely to Training and Enterprise Council (TECs). They are even threatened with redundancy, for 'preparation for life' may be more effective where life is – within the work place or in agencies specially skilled in training the appropriate competences, not in the university or school. It is not insignificant that work experience for 14 year olds might be extended to work-based vocational training and that major firms are now seeking to prepare their employees for degrees without sending them to places devoted to learning.

We need therefore to return to first principles. In chapter 5 we ask what, given the particular economic and social context in which we live, are the aims of education, and how far does our idea of liberal education have to take into account changed values and the greater emphasis upon usefulness. Given the central concern of education with understanding and knowledge, we ask in chapter 6 what can be said about the nature and organisation of knowledge which should enter into the liberal ideal. And, finally, in chapter 7, we ask what kind of connection can be justified between the educational provision and the community, especially the political community, as it regulates the partnership through which educational aims are determined and curriculum content selected.

PART III

PHILOSOPHY

5

Educational Aims and Values

Introduction

Every society has an educational system – a set of institutions for the upbringing of children and for preparing them for adult life. The more undeveloped the society, then the less developed will such a system be – perhaps little more than an extension of the family. Modern societies, however, require a more sophisticated system because, if one is to earn a living and be personally effective within that society, there is so much to learn.

Such a system of education will necessarily be committed to certain values; out of all the skills, knowledge, attitudes and qualities that could be learnt, only some are selected. What is selected depends on what is valued. Within any culture and system of schooling, there lies an implicit idea of 'the educated person' – the kinds of skill, knowledge, qualities and attitudes that are valued, and thus regarded as important enough to be learnt in the preparation for adult life.

However, the accounts given in the previous chapters reflect the problems that society has in defining 'educated persons'. For example, are they the ones who have succeeded in the academic studies of the traditional (and now national) curriculum? Or are they those who are well adjusted to the demands of the entrepreneurial society in which success goes to the enterprising? Or are there specific moral qualities that an educated person should have?

Some think that the confusing picture painted in the previous chapters can be straightened out by mere change of policy or by purely practical measures – for example, better buildings and resources, or greater emphasis on enterprise, or higher investment in post-16

training, or modification of the National Curriculum, or the more
efficient training of teachers. The Secretary of State would need only to
re-arrange things, to simplify course provision, or to shift resources.

However, such a pragmatic view would be a mistake. Differences run
more deeply. They concern competing views about the quality of life
both for the individual and for society. They concern the knowledge,
skills, values and attitudes which should characterise 'the educated
person' in the economic and technological society we now inhabit. In
effect, we need to address again Herbert Spencer's question *'What
knowledge is of most worth?'* (Spencer 1861)

It is important, therefore, to begin to tackle these ethical questions. I
shall first make some general comments about the concept of education. That at least will show the way to the more substantive questions
about the aims of education. Second, I shall examine critically the
kinds of justification which underpin the distinctive aims behind the
proposals for reform. Third, I shall focus upon one particular answer,
namely, the development and formation of people as *persons*. Only in
the light of what we mean by being and maturing as *persons* within this
society might we come to sensible conclusions about quality of life both
for the individual and for society. It is a matter of some surprise that in
all the proposals for the future of education and training so little
attention is given to the quality of personal and social life which
ultimately must provide the justification for those proposals.

The concept of education

There are three kinds of answer to questions about the aim of
education.

One might point to the benefits which educational activities bring
about – for example, for the individual, a better job and, for society, a
more effective workforce. Here 'education' refers to those activities
which are a means to some desirable end. One is educated *for* something – a certificate which will ensure employment or a skill which will
lead to promotion. Often people will judge the success of 'education'
by the extent to which these activities deliver these particular goods.
Put in modern day parlance, 'education' is a commodity which is 'delivered' so that students might use it for purposes.

However, this answer, by itself, is inadequate because it says nothing
about the specifically *educational* aspect of these activities. To ask for the
aims of education is to ask for the purposes which are *intrinsic* to
activities described as educational. Just as football may be a means to

some extrinsic end such as earning a living, but is defined in terms of aims which are intrinsic to the game (to score goals, but not to earn a living), so the aim of education, in this sense, is *to learn* – to acquire knowledge, skills and understanding – not to get a certificate.

A third answer to questions about the aim of education is to point to the value which one finds in the activity and which provides a justification for engaging in it. Not any kind of learning counts as education. Indeed, we contrast education with indoctrination or conditioning or mere training. *Educational* activities lead to learning outcomes which are regarded as valuable – qualities of thinking and feeling associated with being an 'educated person'. Thus the aim of education as such is not to earn a living (although that might be an extrinsic aim), nor simply to learn, whatever the value of that which is learnt, but to learn those things which are valued and which constitute a valued form of life. In that sense, education is an evaluative term.

Therefore, disagreements about the success or otherwise of our schools, deliberations about the need to invest in our educational system, rejection of education by so many parents and their children, are in effect disagreements about the values which underpin the whole enterprise. On the one hand, people have different implicit ideas of the educated person: some, like the CBI, think that such a person should be enterprising and economically aware; others that he or she should be immersed in theoretical and aesthetic activities far removed from the practical world of commerce and industry. On the other hand, some reject altogether the values associated with learning. For them, the valued life is not the educated one; better a life of beer and skittles.

Ethical questions, therefore, need to be asked at different levels.

Given that there should be schools and universities, then what kinds of learning should go on in them? Why should we force children to learn history rather than chess, or read Shakespeare rather than Harold Robbins, or listen to Beethoven rather than Tracy Chapman? Why should we, in the late 20th century, teach ancient history rather than practical ways of earning money? The key question, therefore, is: what are the knowledge, skills, understandings and attitudes – the mental powers – which a person needs in order to act and to behave as an educated person in our society?

At a different level, what sort of argument enables us to see what knowledge is of most worth? What arguments are there for persuading the reluctant learners of the importance of treading the educational path rather than the one of pure hedonism or of self-interest? Employers, recruiting cheap labour straight from school, parents, unwilling to support financially a prolongation of education, and children, seduced by more immediately satisfying pleasures, remain unconvinced. There is often an antipathy to the values that education stands for. How might such sceptics be convinced that the quality of life associated with education is worth pursuing?

Educational aims

There are different kinds of ethical argument, each having its own distinctive consequences for the practice of education and training.

Intellectual excellence

In 'The Importance of Traditional Learning', O'Hear (1987) argues that education lies in the acquisition of those judgments, sensitivities and appreciations which are transmitted through the traditional subjects of the curriculum. Teachers are the mediators of different intellectual and aesthetic traditions. By 'tradition' is meant a way of thinking and feeling which is socially shared and which has survived the critical scrutiny of previous generations. It possesses an authority which the next generation should respect. Education is an attempt to get the students on the inside of those traditions and, in some small way, to enable them to participate in them. Such traditions are captured in various disciplines of knowledge, understanding and feeling, and are guarded and developed by authorities within a critical community. These disciplines are highly selective both in the key traditions to be passed on and in what, within those traditions, should be learnt. Universities, therefore, are crucial to the educational mission of schools, because the distinctive job of the university is to maintain, to develop and to transmit these intellectual and aesthetic traditions which schools draw upon.

For example, there is a tradition of worthwhile literature (the 'great tradition' according to Leavis, 1948). This has arisen from critical argument between literary 'experts'. That argument is not, and never will be, finished; tradition changes over time. Leavis, having left his mark, no longer 'authorises' what counts as good literature upon which the literary tastes of the next generation are to be nurtured. Nonetheless, so the argument goes, at any one time there is some provisional agreement over what are key works of literature and why these should form the 'canon' upon which the curriculum should draw. Thus, pupils are introduced to Shakespeare, to George Eliot and Jane Austin, to Wordsworth and Keats. Indeed, one would not be considered educated unless one were participating, howsoever marginally, in that literary tradition. The same can be said of music. And, indeed, the Secretary of State has tried to ensure that the National Curriculum in English and music would draw upon an explicitly listed canon of literary and musical work which represents an 'authorised' Western classical tradition. Or, again, within science, there is some consensus on the key scientific theories and concepts that any educated person should know.

This must not be confused with 'knowing about'. The aim, in getting students on the inside of a tradition, is to enable them to think scientifically, to appreciate the arts intelligently, to be critical of literature albeit in an informed way. In the absence of a tradition, in the absence of an agreed literature and critical commentary upon it, in the absence of agreed scientific truths and method of tackling scientific problems, there would be nothing with which the learner might interact in acquiring knowledge and understanding. As O'Hear argues,

> ... the proper and effective exercise of reason must take place against the background of inherited forms of thought and experience. (p.102)

The idea of education as initiation into intellectual and aesthetic traditions which carry their own reward and justification is deeply rooted in our culture. Furthermore, it is seen as the hall-mark of liberal learning. Newman, in his *Idea of the University*, says:

> liberal education, viewed in itself, is simply the cultivation of the intellect, as such, and its object is nothing more or less than intellectual excellence. (1852, p.121)

Newman describes the different forms of knowledge which perfect the intellect because, without them, one would not have the powers of the mind necessary for intelligent thought and reflection.

The same kind of argument is implicit within the work of Oakeshott (1972), for whom education is an initiation into the ideas through which we come to understand the world and operate intelligently within it. There is something inevitable in the wish to improve the intellect because it is through the intellect that one enters the world of ideas and thus experiences the personal, social and physical worlds that one inhabits. These ideas are inherited; they are transmitted through the 'conversations' which take place between the 'generations of mankind'. And it is the job of education to get the next generation onto the inside of that conversation. Otherwise experience and the capacity to act intelligently within the world (the personal world of feelings, the social world of relationships and the physical world of material objects) are curtailed and impoverished. Moreover, there are different voices in this conversation between the generations – the voices of poetry, history, science, philosophy – and the educated person can participate to some extent in all of them.

The identification of education with the development of intellect and aesthetic sensitivity provides the basis for justifying education to the sceptic, because the alternative – the denial of the value of education – would be to deny the value of thinking, behaving and feeling intelligently. And who would admit to that? It *seems* self-evident that the business person would want the mental powers necessary to run a business successfully, the parent the understanding to bring up children effectively, the friend or lover the awareness and sensitivities for enjoying a fruitful relationship, the politician the nous and moral perspective to create a better world. And the subject matter of traditional learning is precisely that – the refinement of, and the selection from, the accumulated wisdom of previous generations which explains and sheds light upon the worlds of politics, of relationships, of economic affairs, or of human development. The development of the mind, in accordance with developed forms of thinking and of feeling, is a value in its own right. That value in no way depends on usefulness; and education is quite distinct from being trained for a job.

This is a powerful argument, but there are problems with it.

The argument might be acceptable in general terms but not lead to the conclusions its proponents wish. One may agree that the development of the mind is essential because it is a prerequisite of all else – ignorance causes powerlessness and illiteracy is a handicap – but only minimum conditions of intellectual achievement need be met. A business person may be successful precisely because he or she is narrow in intellectual development or insensitive to personal needs or unaffected by aesthetic doubts or undistracted by an historical perspective. The perfection of the intellect is one amongst several competing goods and, although the mind needs to be developed to a minimal level for other goods to be enjoyed, that level falls far short of what we normally associate with the educated person.

Furthermore, the initiation into different intellectual traditions is such that only a few people are judged to be successful. Indeed, 'initiation' has been a popular metaphor in describing education (see Peters 1966). That is significant. It presupposes outsiders – those who fail the initiation test. Hence, only a minority is judged to be capable of participating in the conversation between the generations of mankind that Oakeshott speaks about. Those will be 'liberally educated', whilst the remainder are prepared through various training programmes for the world of work, remaining for the most part outside those intellectual and aesthetic traditions which mark out the educated person. Thus the difference between liberal education for the few and vocational preparation for the many becomes institutionalised within society.

Again, the intellectual traditions that constitute liberal education are very selective. Certain voices are not allowed into the authorised conversation – for example, particular musical and literary traditions, moral questions about science and society, and many of the cultural interests which pertain to minority groups or to disenchanted youth. How might one justify certain kinds of knowledge rather than others as the essential core of studies for the educated person?

Finally, education as the 'perfection of the intellect' is very individual-centred. Certainly such a person participates in a *public* conversation; he or she has gained access to a tradition of shared criticism and debate. But the product is a 'personal good' which might be of little benefit to the wider society. Indeed, an educated but immoral person might do more harm than one who had remained in ignorance.

To summarise: one powerful justification for education in general and for a specific content of education in particular is that the development of the mind, through initiation into different intellectual and aesthetic traditions, is a good in itself. It requires no further justification in terms of human happiness or economic utility or social benefit. Because we live in a world of ideas, then it is self-evidently important to master and to be able to use those ideas. Education is about entering into that world of ideas more effectively and to participate in 'the conversations' of which they are a part. However, such an argument does not take us far in determining the content of education. The knowledge required for fruitful participation in everyday life is less than the proponents of 'traditional learning' would wish. Moreover, the defenders of traditional learning unfairly restrict what is valid within that world of ideas and only a relatively few people are thereby permitted to succeed within it. Finally, it leaves out whole dimensions of experience, particularly the practical and the useful.

Social utility

Claims to the intrinsic value of intellectual activities carry little weight in arguments promoting greater investment in education. Indeed, the rapid expansion of post-compulsory and higher education is seen rather as an 'investment' in the future. Arguments point to the danger of being left behind in an ever more competitive world. The curriculum, even for the more able, becomes more vocational through core skills and work-related themes. Universities (through Enterprise in Higher Education) are offered more money if they introduce 'enterprise' into all their undergraduate courses including Latin and Ancient Greek. And Research Councils give priority to research which has industrial and commercial benefit.

Perhaps, in the attempt to reconcile liberal education with vocational preparation, the conflict between those who see the aim of education to be intellectual excellence (accessible to the few) and those who see its aim to be social utility (and thus accessible to the many) is the most important and the most difficult to resolve.

There are two ways in which social utility is understood.

Economic relevance

Social utility often refers to 'economic relevance'. Education should provide the knowledge and skills which society needs if it is to thrive: the trained scientist as well as the trained plumber, a literate and numerate population in a changing and sophisticated economy, and the personal and social skills necessary for the growing service industries. Statistics are produced to show the correlation between educational investment and economic performance. Indeed, economic relevance becomes the main aim of education where political arguments have to be won and resources obtained.

The 'economic relevance' argument works at different levels.

It is argued that to be educated in a broad and liberal sense enables one to work more intelligently and to take on new and challenging employment. The liberally educated person will have the intellectual qualities to get beyond the immediate and the particular and to recognise new challenges. Put in the language of vocational relevance, educated persons will have the generic mental skills which prepare them for the world of work. 'Liberal education' is not an end in itself, but a means to economic well-being.

By contrast, 'economic relevance' is said to require something more specifically vocational in the content and the process of education. It is argued that there is a culture – an elitist culture – which so separates education, as the disinterested pursuit of knowledge, from vocational preparation, that there is a need for radical changes within the liberal tradition if the country is to prosper economically. Such changes would challenge the value of pursuing knowledge for its own sake, and thus of studying particular kinds of knowledge which have little obvious economic use. Already we have witnessed the rapid decline in schools and universities of Latin and Greek, a familiarity with which, until recently, was regarded as an essential characteristic of the educated person. Instead, one of the fastest growing subjects at A Level is Business Studies, and in higher education Management Studies.

Consequently, as we have seen in the last chapter, more vocational studies have been introduced to secondary schools through the prevocational courses, the work experience now required of every pupil in maintained schools, TVEI experiments, the introduction of core skills to A Level courses, schemes such as Young Enterprise in schools and 'enterprise' in universities, and the allocation of grants to *useful* research. And yet, despite these initiatives and pressures, the divide between liberal education and vocational preparation remains, indeed becomes, even more entrenched. Status remains attached to those subjects which are justified in the main by academic rather than by vocational standards.

Hence, the powerful opposition to education being concerned with intellectual excellence for its own sake is met by just as powerful resistance. Of course, educated persons might be more useful than uneducated ones; they have, it is claimed, well-trained minds. But they might not be. Liberal education might produce the wrong attitudes to the practical and the commercial; it might leave huge gaps in the repertoire of skills and knowledge required for survival in today's world. Economic relevance, therefore, becomes antithetical to a tradition of liberal education which remains indifferent to the practical and the useful.

Social relevance

Social utility refers also to *social* relevance – producing the right kind of citizen, training for parenting, preparing pupils to participate in a democracy, helping with the battle against drugs, warning of the dangers of AIDS. Indeed, if there is a social message to be got across, then schools will be asked to teach it.

Such aims are not part of that liberal tradition which is aimed solely at the perfection of the intellect. Indeed, liberal education seeks to *understand* 'citizenship', not to produce good citizens. That understanding includes how the idea has been interpreted in history, not how the pupils might be taught to practise. Therefore, as inheritors of that liberal tradition, teachers often feel uncomfortable in introducing such specific purposes to the curriculum – except for those students, unable to be liberally educated, who need vocational training. Many schools have for a long time had courses in child care for the less able girls. More recently there have been initiatives to help produce the good citizen; certain pupils will work in the community, often with old people. But these have not affected to any significant extent the curriculum experience of the majority, certainly of the more able.

Again important distinctions need to be made. Just as it is claimed that liberally educated people have the generic skills that prepare them for the world of work so it is claimed that a well-balanced education will form the personal and social qualities required for intelligent participation in social and political life. The liberally educated person is thereby equipped to be socially useful. But that is demonstrably untrue, social utility being seen as something much more deliberately planned. There are too many examples of educational 'successes', people academically accomplished and highly respected for their intellectual prowess, whose talents, far from contributing to social well-being, undermine it. There are criminals (confidence tricksters, for example) who are successful precisely because they have been 'well educated'. Therefore, it is argued, social utility cannot be seen as a bi-product of liberal education alone; it must be explicitly taught. There should be courses on parenting, on democratic behaviour, on sexual responsibility, on keeping the streets clean, on road safety, and on caring for animals.

Furthermore, there are those who wish to identify social utility neither with liberal education as such, nor with a specific teaching content, but with the inculcation of certain qualities or virtues. Social utility cannot get away from deeper moral education and training. This comes across clearly in the widespread promotion of 'enterprise' in schools and colleges – a modern day 'virtue' that disposes the learner to behave more positively in relation to work and to business. But it is also reflected in the programmes of personal and social education in which caring relationships and social responsibility are fostered.

This dualism between disinterested pursuit of knowledge for its own sake and learning for some useful purpose, between liberal education with one set of aims and vocational training with another, needs to be examined critically. The beginning of that criticism must lie in the inadequacy of the liberal ideal as it has been outlined: the restricted choice of knowledge which is judged to be worthwhile, the indifference to the cries of many learners simply because they are not speaking the language of the 'educated person', the disconnection between liberal education and its economic base, and the elimination of the practical and the useful from the province of liberal education.

On the other hand, it is mistaken to reduce what is valuable to what is useful. Those who, within a liberal tradition, argue for the importance of developing the capacity to think and to understand, irrespective of the usefulness of that capacity, are surely right. 'Usefulness' itself can be understood only within a framework of ideas which provides the capacity to think usefully – or indeed to choose at certain times not to do so. Engineers are useful but the language of engineering and the theoretical perspectives it embodies are partly the product of disinterested enquiry and intellectual arguments directed by a concern for the truth, not just by the desire to be useful. Moreover, that world of ideas has a life of its own. Mathematicians continue to make discoveries in mathematics. Scientists challenge and put to the test the ideas of other scientists. Historians question the interpretations of fellow historians. None of this intellectual activity, inescapable where the capacity to understand and to think is valued, can be explained or justified simply within the framework of 'usefulness'.

Furthermore, liberal education is concerned with ends, not just with means. Useful for what? Students of literature, history, religion and science are getting to grips with the different ways in which the useful purposes that education might serve are defined. And they question those purposes. The 'useful' is contingent upon what one values, and at the centre of education is the exploration and the discovery of what is worth valuing. Perhaps 'education' is essential for economic or social progress. But why is it called progress? One way of distinguishing between training programmes that are liberally educating and those that are not is the degree to which the ends for which one is being trained are themselves open to questioning and exploration. They themselves become an object of study – by the pupils as well as by the teachers and educational planners.

The pursuit of pleasure

It is commonplace for people, in justifying what they do, to appeal to the pleasure that the activity will bring. Even those who insist upon the usefulness of education will often argue that education is useful in bringing about a state of affairs in which the learner or society is happier. And many pupils are put off school because education brings misery when they fail and requires painful effort when they succeed, and because the pleasure it may bring is counterbalanced by the pleasures missed. Discos seem more worthwhile than homework.

The obvious attraction of the 'utilitarian ethic', namely, that the greatest good lies in the greatest happiness of the greatest number, makes alternative justifications for education less convincing. Why spend so much time getting to know the truth when the truth can be so painful? Why spend so much money on higher education when that same money could bring pleasure to many more people through economic aid or entertainment or medical services? If the educational system had to withstand the test of the greatest happiness of the greatest number, both the practice of education and its distribution would be very different.

There *is* a utilitarian case to be made for education. People get immense pleasure from reading literature or from engaging in historical enquiry. These pleasures would be denied them unless at some time they had been led, often reluctantly, to understand what literary appreciation or historical study was about and thus what intellectual satisfaction each could bring. Or again too much ignorance will lead to unhappiness. A basic education is usually necessary to get a job, and by and large a job is necessary to earn the money to lead a happy life. Moreover, even if, for the creation of a happy environment, not everyone needs to be educated beyond a basic minimum, some have to be educated – there has to be a minority of doctors, engineers and administrators educated to serve the majority.

Such arguments, however, do not justify the importance that is attached to education or the particular selection from the culture which, at school and university, learners are exposed to and judged on. And there are well-rehearsed difficulties in the utilitarian position.

There are valuable aspects of human living which cannot be identified with the amount of happiness experienced. We value loyalty, telling the truth, caring for others, respect for the environment, irrespective of the happiness which these bring. People so value things that they would rather suffer than take the less painful (or more pleasurable) way out. Children wish to be given a sense of dignity as well as a pleasurable time. Indeed, many teachers believe that self-confidence, arising from a deserved feeling of dignity, is a central educational aim.

Of course, virtue has its own reward. It could be argued that loyalty, love, caring, respect, being truthful and discovering the truth bring their own sense of well-being and happy state of mind – thereby subscribing to the utilitarian ethic. But that requires stretching the meaning of pleasure so that any activity, by definition, is undertaken for the sake of pleasure. And it would not solve the problem that we are tackling, namely, how to justify certain activities to be more worthwhile than others – so much so that we make some compulsory for all children up to the age of 16. It is not clear that, for everyone, the mastery of Euclidean geometry or the study of local history or the understanding of the glacial formation of the Lake District brings more pleasure, and is thereby justified, than drinking lager or supporting Sheffield United or attending raves.

Furthermore, the utilitarians are left with the problem that Mill (1861) tried to tackle in *Utilitarianism*. Given that the ultimate good is the pursuit of the greatest amount of pleasure for the greatest number, how can we measure and compare different quantities of pleasure. Bentham, in *The Principles of Utility*, had a rather simple solution in theory, although the subsequent calculus was complex. There are two dimensions to pleasure: length and intensity. Some like their pleasures short but intense, others prefer them less exciting but drawn out. It was thought possible to measure, and thus to compare, along these two dimensions the quantity of pleasure that different pursuits will bring. However, Mill could not reconcile such a simple quantitative measurement with what can only be described as qualitatively different sorts of pleasure. How compare pleasures of the mind with pleasures of the flesh? How compare poetry with pushpin (or, as Wilson 1967, argued, Beethoven with bingo)? For Mill certain pleasures were qualitatively superior to others, and that qualitative superiority, a fortiori, cannot be cashed in terms of quantity. Better Socrates dissatisfied than a pig satisfied.

Finally, even if each is motivated by the pursuit of personal pleasure, there are no grounds for saying that the aggregate of personal pleasures will add up to the greatest amount of pleasure of the greatest number. John's pleasure might depend on Michael's misery. Indeed, the pursuit of personal goods might well lead to a less pleasurable world. The principle of utility needs to be curbed by a principle of fairness concerning the distribution of the chances whereby each and everyone might have the opportunity of enjoying the good things of life. Furthermore, the totality of good things might increase if some people sacrifice their pursuit of pleasure for the general good. Co-operation rather than individual advantage might lead to the greatest happiness of the greatest number, but that requires appeal to the principle of justice as well as to the principle of utility. And how might that principle be acquired except through teaching, if not at home then at school and within a school system that exemplifies it in the fair distribution of resources?

The principle of utility or of maximising pleasure is too flawed to provide an adequate answer to the questions we are asking. The justification for education cannot rely on the individual pursuit of pleasure. Furthermore, human motivation is much more varied than that. People may get pleasure from finding out the truth, but that is not necessarily the reason for pursuing the enquiry. They simply want the truth, and pleasure, if it follows, is a bonus. The importance of learning, and of learning certain things rather than others, requires more justification than that.

Interests

The utilitarians, however, were by no means irrelevant to the problems we are addressing. Pleasure is a protean term. It is often associated with sensual pleasures, but that would be both narrow and misleading, as Mill argued against those who railed against the supposed hedonism of the utilitarians. There is a family of terms for which 'pleasure' is frequently a shorthand though inadequate substitute – mental satisfaction, a sense of achievement, contentment, a sense of well-being, being absorbed or interested. But there is a distinctive pleasure of the intellect, a value which education picks out for our consideration. Indeed, the evil which education fights against is boredom, that deadness of the mind when one cannot find interest in what one is doing.

The importance of the developing interest of the child is long recognised in primary schools but largely ignored by the present day advocates of liberal education. For the latter, certain subjects are educationally valuable irrespective of whether the learner finds them

interesting or whether they help the learner to find greater interest in
what they enjoy doing. Indeed, the student-centred tradition, attributed to John Dewey (see particularly Dewey 1916), is seen by some as
one cause of the decline in educational standards. But, as far as Dewey
was concerned, only certain interests had educational value in so far as
they could lead to yet further enquiries, yet further significant learning.
The development of such interests required expert and careful direction
from the teacher. Not any interest would lead to the development of a
lively mind.

Let us explore this further. There is no doubt that at every level of
activity further learning, leading to understanding and skill, enhances
the satisfaction one gets, and prevents that activity from becoming a
bore. One finds more interest in the landscape if one understands the
historical basis of the field system; an ancient church becomes more
than just another building through the recognition of architectural
features which explain its distinctive appearance; a painting is more
pleasurably appreciated against an understanding of the tradition from
which it comes; the piano continues to satisfy in proportion to the
increased skill in playing. Continuous learning would seem to be essential to that liveliness of mind through which one finds interest rather
than boredom in the world and in the people around one. Such
learning, rightly acquired, develops too the confidence and the capacity
to go on learning and to seek further interest in what on the surface
may seem drab and ordinary.

There are many different kinds of value, certainly, and educational
values are but a subset of them. But they do seem to be central in that,
in the absence of that constant development of the mind, other values
are put at risk and the various interests which absorb one's waking
hours become dull or dead, and boredom sets in.

This argument, however, will not satisfy the advocates of liberal
education. They argue that only certain sorts of interests are worthwhile. Rock climbing may give great pleasure; and that pleasure may
depend on a great deal of skill and technical knowledge. Indeed, anyone who has spent some time in the company of climbers will realise
how sophisticated is that knowledge and how it leads on to yet further
learning and understanding. But rock climbing would not feature in
the liberal curriculum alongside history, geography and science. The
liberal educationists would argue that certain kinds of knowledge and
understanding are more worthwhile than others, irrespective of the
interest that young people find in them. Education presupposes a theory of value which cannot be reduced to the pursuit of what is interesting. In so saying, they conclude *either* that to be educated does
not require interest in that which makes one educated – a knowledge of

history or of the French language is what is required, not a love or a caring for it – *or* that only a few are capable of being educated, namely, those who find interest in the studies that define a liberal education.

Personal autonomy and social responsibility

The conflict between liberal education and social utility – and the possibility of reconciling the two – reflects a deeper divide between the pursuit of individual good and the pursuit of social welfare. But is this not a false division? Liberal education aims at the development of each person through the introduction to those cultural traditions which reflect 'the best that has been thought and said' in literature, the foundational skills and concepts in mathematics, the distillation of the most up-to-date understandings of science and an introduction to aesthetic traditions in music and art. Educated persons are those who, through the acquired capacity to reason and to think critically, have become autonomous – dependent neither in capacity nor in disposition upon authority in making wise and reasonable decisions. Reason replaces authority, and 'reason' participates in that public world of science, history and literary criticism.

There are two distinct, though connected, aspects to autonomy. The first concerns the intellect – the capacity to think things through, to argue effectively, to think critically, rather than to be dependent on authority or on fashion or on the rhetoric of the speaker. One participates in the socially developed world of reasons and evidence, and, in so doing, one is enabled to think for oneself. The second aspect of autonomy concerns the moral character of the person – the capacity to internalise the principles which will guide one's actions and to behave as one's conscience thereby dictates, rather than to give way to every passing temptation and impulse. One could be autonomous intellectually, but, through weakness, lack autonomy in running one's life. Strength of intellect does not guarantee strength of will. But obviously the ideal product of education would be the person who not only has an independent frame of mind built on firm intellectual principles but also the strength and determination to live accordingly.

This stress within the liberal tradition upon the enlightened and well-formed mind, and upon the capacity to act accordingly, is surely correct, and is the basis upon which criticism is levelled against those who impose a narrow or indoctrinatory programme of instruction. Liberal education emphasises the liberation that comes from the acquisition of knowledge in its various forms. But there are two ways in which such an emphasis can both distort the educational values and become inimical to vocational preparation.

There is stress upon the liberated individual without reference to the social context in which that individual operates freely. The emphasis is upon individual perfection, not upon social well-being. And so the expansion of Higher Education following the Robbins Report (1963) was based on the principles that the system should expand to meet, not social need, but individual demand from the expanding number of young people with minimum matriculation requirements; and that those individuals should seek their personal development through studying subjects which were personally satisfying if not socially useful. There is the assumption that the aggregate of people each seeking personal satisfaction will add up to the good of all. But that is very doubtful.

Furthermore, schools and universities are established at considerable expense, in the main paid for by the community. The annual budget for public education in England and Wales is about £16 billion. That tax burden falls unequally on the less well off who pay more in support of education than they receive in educational benefits, since the better off on the whole continue into the more costly higher education. These facts cast a *prima facie* doubt upon the obligation of the community to pay for an expensive service, which is justified in terms of the personal good of the relatively few, unless benefits to the community as a whole can be perceived. Even where the benefit of liberal education is agreed in general terms as a personal good – enlightenment through the acquisition of knowledge and understanding – the precise nature of that education and the length to which it should be pursued are matters of debate. It is currently believed that higher education should be expanded further, giving many more people the opportunity to remain in education until their twenties, without any argument about the content of that education or the values that it should serve. It is simply assumed that the longer the education the better, and that value lies in the liberating effect of prolonged study. Meanwhile, of course, other public services must proportionately be deprived of money – the health service, public transport, the arts, housing.

It is unavoidable, therefore, that questions concerning the social or the communal benefits of liberal education should be raised. And indeed such questions have always been at the forefront of the minds of public educators. The liberal education of the guardians in Plato's *Republic* was for the benefit of all – education gave them the insight into how the world really is, so that they could govern wisely. The great public schools, as they were reformed in the last century, aimed to provide a liberating education so that an empire and its people might be ruled with wisdom and justice. The disciples of T.H. Green and the idealist philosophers of Oxford in the late 19th century were introduced to a moral idealism which set its stamp on public service until this very day.

This connection between the liberal education of the individual and the wider social good has received an added twist in the recent emphasis upon economic and the technological usefulness. But here lies an interesting shift. Previously no such direct usefulness had to be proved – it was assumed that the better educated elite would provide wiser and fairer government. Society did not in the past require the army of professionals and technocrats of today. Education now has to serve more explicitly the specific requirements of a highly technical and sophisticated economy.

There is a further argument which connects the liberal education of the individual with the general good. However selfish and self-centred an educated person might be, such education, liberally conceived, is inseparable from the free flow of ideas and the spirit of criticism which is the most effective bulwark against oppression and injustice. Poets and philosophers are the first to suffer in the totalitarian state.

There is, then, a connection between social well-being and the pursuit of personal good through liberal education. That connection lies in the importance of well-educated rulers if the community is to be ruled intelligently; in the spirit of public service which a certain kind of liberal education provides; in the relevance to a complex technological society of certain kinds of understandings which a liberal education will provide; and in the need for that free flow of ideas and of criticism which is created and guaranteed by a community of liberally educated people.

However, for that very reason, changed social and economic circumstances require a revision of the content of that liberal education. There is a danger of education becoming disconnected from the social and economic world which it should enlighten. The capacity to reflect, to understand and to criticise requires the concepts and the understandings which shed light upon the world which one inhabits. If that is a technological world, and a world where social and personal relationships are determined by economic forces of a different order from those of a previous era, then not to have those concepts and understandings is to be in a state of ignorance. Therefore, we can see that the disconnection between liberal education as a personal good and education for the benefit of the wider community need not be as sharp as all that.

Personal development

Many teachers are suspicious of intellectual excellence as the sole or main aim of education, just as they are of economic usefulness. Those suspicions emerge from the frequently voiced view that all children are important even though many could not aspire to excellence in academic matters or to economic usefulness. Children are *persons*, and to be a person is more than to have an intellect; it is to have emotions and feelings, to enter into relationships, to have desires and aspirations, to have responsibilities and obligations. Moreover, to be recognised as a person requires being treated not simply as someone with great academic potential nor as a means to an end such as the economic success of society. Too many children have been dismissed as unimportant because they are unable to succeed academically – to enter into that intellectual conversation as that has been defined by people in positions of academic control. Therefore, a prominently stated aim of British schools has been the development of persons in a much broader sense than intellectual excellence. And, although this has on the surface appeared to run counter to the growing emphasis upon usefulness, it has in fact received a boost from the vocational education. The future worker needs to have personal qualities which are too often neglected in the pursuit of academic excellence.

There are dangers in so arguing. An uncritical concern for personal well-being might lead to the neglect of those particular values picked out by education. Making children happy, giving them confidence, making them physically healthy, enabling them to enjoy their increased leisure, even instilling in them socially approved behaviours are all worthy objectives but they are compatible with leaving children in a state of ignorance and with the acceptance of low academic standards. These are not in themselves educational aims. That is the criticism many make of child-centred education. Education is concerned with something more than well-adjusted and contented children.

Nonetheless, beneath the concern for personal development espoused by so many schools is the belief in an ethical base for education which is more than academic excellence and which challenges the narrow focus of the vocational trainers, which distinguishes between those interests which are worth pursuing and those which are trivial, and which treats certain pleasurable pastimes, if pursued to excess, as beneath the dignity of human beings. It is impossible, in identifying that ethical base and in asking what is educationally worthwhile, to avoid questions about what it is to be human and what needs to be learnt in order to be so. Academic excellence may tell only part of the story.

This was so well summed up in the letter sent to her new teachers by the principal of a large American high school (Strom 1981):

❝ I am the victim of a concentration camp.
My eyes saw what no man should witness.
Gas chambers built by learned engineers.
Children poisoned by educated physicians.
Infants killed by trained nurses.
Women and babies shot and burned by high school and college graduates.
So, I am suspicious of education.
My request is: help your students become human. Your efforts must never produce learned monsters, skilled psychopaths, educated Eichmanns.
Reading, writing, arithmetic are important only if they serve to make our children more human.

That suspicion of education was of something conceived as only academic excellence, unrefined by other qualities which define one's humanity and which need to be learnt. This same suspicion is implicit in the government documents referred to previously in this book. The White Paper, *Choice and Diversity*, repeats these sentiments in saying

❝ Education cannot and must not be value-free. Recognising this, the Education Reform Act 1988 requires the school curriculum to promote the spiritual, moral and cultural, as well as the mental and physical, development of pupils and society. (DES 1993, p.37)

Unfortunately, in failing to provide any analysis of what this means, it in no way counterbalances the heavy emphasis within the National Curriculum upon the acquisition of knowledge to the exclusion of those wider social and personal qualities which teachers are concerned to develop. But knowing what those qualities are requires further consideration of what it means to be a person – and to be so more abundantly. What then does it mean to develop children as persons, or, in the words of the American principal, 'to make our children more human'?

Being a person

'Persons' refer to men and women and children, but not to dogs and horses however much we love them. Or, if we do refer to animals, we are attributing to them certain qualities which we normally associate only with human beings. What are those qualities?

First, the concept of person picks out more than physical characteristics. It presupposes a form of consciousness, a capacity to experience the world, not merely to interact physically with it.

Second, that consciousness, and the experiences which are constitutive of it, are shaped by forms of understanding – *ways* of experiencing made up of ideas, beliefs, expectations. Such ways of experiencing are learnt. They can remain at a very embryonic stage, or they can be ever more refined through learning. Indeed, education aims to do just that – to introduce the growing mind to forms of understanding and thus to ways of experiencing which transform one's view of the world and make it more intelligible.

Third, part of that understanding is to see certain objects not simply as physical things, to which one is causally related, but as persons – that is, as centres of consciousness in their own right with the capacity to think, and to experience in the light of those thoughts. It is to have the capacity, too, to see oneself as a person – to see oneself as able to have one's own thoughts and point of view. A person is self-conscious – has the capacity to reflect.

Fourth, a person with such understandings has the capacity to relate to other persons in a distinctive way – not only as one physical object to another but as one centre of consciousness with another. Together, persons share a world of meanings, not just a physical world of space and time. However, the exercise of that capacity through various modes of communication and through the sharing of experiences requires much effort and patience.

Fifth, part of the understandings that persons have, and that they share with each other, are practical ones, concerning what one should do and the ends that one should serve. In so deliberating there is the assumption that one can exercise control over one's own life, that one can act autonomously, not being totally under the power of others or of natural forces. One can take some responsibility for one's own actions.

Sixth, a person is highly dependent on others with whom he or she interrelates both on the personal and on the institutional level, i.e. on the level of those formal relationships established to protect and to promote the public good. For example, the period of physical growth is prolonged and there is a need for a wide range of social arrangements to ensure secure upbringing and systematic learning. The quality of life depends on social relationships and the institutional arrangement which support them (for example, in the arts or various voluntary organisations). But these social networks and institutional arrangements, so important in the shaping of oneself as a person, are not *given* – they are the product of human endeavour. Responsibility for one's own life extends to responsibility for the social context of that life, and that requires both the dispositions, the skills and the knowledge to take an active part. In that sense, persons are political animals – capable of shaping the social environment that affects profoundly the quality of life.

Seventh, therefore, 'person' is a moral concept in two senses. On the one hand, it implies the capacity to take responsibility for one's own actions and one's own life. On the other hand, it indicates the desirability of being so treated – of being given the opportunity for taking on that responsibility and of respecting it in others. To be fully a person is to be held responsible for what one does and to be treated as though one is responsible. This is reflected in the moral principles concerned with 'respect for persons' and in the moral claim to be treated with a sense of dignity – not necessarily being loved or even liked. The teacher can respect someone whilst not liking them, and the pupil can be given a sense of dignity (a feeling of having worth) whilst knowing that he or she is not liked. Liking and respecting are different dispositions, with different associated feelings.

Such a characterisation of what it is to be a person stresses the various, though interrelated, *capacities* which may or may not be actualised – the capacity to think and to feel, to see others as persons and to relate to them as such, to be aware of oneself as a person, to engage in the moral deliberations essential to the discharge of that responsibility, to have the ideals which uplift and motivate. But there are barriers to that exercise – ignorance, false beliefs, lack of self-respect, envy and hatred of others, absence of the skills of social relationships, blindness to the goods which will arise from the exercise of that capacity, lack of vision to guide those deliberations. Above all there is boredom, the failure to take interest in things around, which renders inoperative the distinctively human capacities.

The exercise of those capacities is essentially dependent upon learning. One will remain ignorant and unempowered unless, through learning, one acquires the concepts and knowledge which dispel that ignorance and enable one to understand oneself and others, and the obligations and responsibilities that one has. Learning is essential to becoming fully a person. Through learning one acquires the ideals which ennoble and motivate, the standards by which one might evaluate one's own performances and those of others. Adolescence is a period in which young people seek to find their distinctive identities – the sort of persons they are or might become, the ideals that are worth striving for, the qualities that they wish to be respected for, the talents that need to be developed, the kind of relationship in which they will find enrichment, the style of life that is worth pursuing.

There are, however, two things about this process of learning. First, it is shot through with values concerning the ideals worth pursuing, the direction in which the various capacities should be developed, the sort of person that one should strive to become, the standards against which one's performance should be judged. Second, those values have to be learnt, as do the skills and the dispositions required to pursue them. The understandings that dispel ignorance, and the skills and perseverance necessary to acquire those understandings, are achievements requiring guidance and promptings and examples. Liberal education at its best is the attempt to provide the basis of those understandings as they have been developed in different forms of thought. It exposes the young learner to those values and ideals through which they can contemplate the life worth living as it has been differently practised. Liberal education, therefore, is an introduction to those understandings and values – and to the subject matter, the skills and the discipline essential for acquiring them.

There is a danger of failing to see that everyone, even with limited intellectual capacity, can in some measure participate in the enterprise – can, within their own capacity, be liberally educated. It is not a matter of people being educated or not educated – there are no absolute standards for being tagged an educated person. People are *either more or less* educated. There is a danger, too, in being so concerned with the acquisition of a particular knowledge content that dispositions, social skills, capacities for reflection and self-knowledge, moral deliberation, possession of inspiring ideals – all the other aspects of being a person – get neglected. Intellectual excellence narrowly interpreted does not do justice to the formation of the whole person.

That 'whole person' therefore requires the following, all of which depend on learning.

- *knowledge and understanding:* the concepts, forms of thought, beliefs through which one can make sense of the world and operate intelligently within it. To say what those are would be like rewriting the National Curriculum. That I shall not try to do, but in the next chapter I shall argue for the principles, rooted partly in the theory of knowledge, on the basis of which a selection from our intellectual culture might be based.
- *intellectual virtues:* it is one thing to possess knowledge, another thing to care for and to value it. The pursuit of knowledge and the elimination of ignorance require certain dispositions – those of honesty, of not cooking the books, of testing out and sharing beliefs, of openness to new ideas but also scepticism towards untested claims. One might add, too, elegance of and sensitivity to style, welcoming clarity and analytic sharpness and disdaining the bland and obfuscating.
- *imagination:* this refers to many things – conjuring up images often fanciful, lateral thinking, problem solving, and so on. But it signifies, too, the ability to think beyond the given, to make links between the present and the past often in a most unlikely way, to re-interpret experience in the light of previous and different

experience or through metaphor drawn from other fields of discourse. The imagination enables one to see significance in the ordinary, excitement in the otherwise humdrum. Without imagination Greece is a pretty place with sunburnt fields; with imagination it is a land of gods and heroes. But imagination has to be fed with stories and history, with poetry and with art. Again it is acquired through learning – or killed through the wrong sort of learning.

- *intellectual skills:* there is frequently a failure to distinguish between having knowledge and being able to acquire it, between knowledge handed on and knowing how to pursue knowledge through disciplined enquiry, between knowledge as dogma and knowledge as reasoned and tested and corroborated. The distinction can be exaggerated and some teachers wrongly eschew the handing on of any knowledge, believing that it should arise out of the learner's own discovery and enquiry. That quite clearly is wrong, but no more so than the kind of learning that does not also impart the skills of inquiry whether scientific in the laboratories, moral in the cut and thrust of discussion and social in the conduct of surveys. Furthermore, there are skills of reasoning, of marshalling the arguments, of collecting the evidence, of communicating the results.

- *self-reflection:* 'know thyself', enjoined Socrates, and this requires more than having the right kinds of concepts through which one might think about oneself (as gentle or ambitious, as quick tempered or contemplative). It requires too the habit of self-reflection and the readiness to face one's interior thoughts. Such an ability does not come easily to young people surrounded by distractions that are intrusive, and by commercial pressures concerning *appearances*. But self-knowledge needs to be worked at and requires the skills and moral strength which have to be learnt.

- *moral virtues and habits:* intellectual virtues dispose one to act rightly in relation to matters of the truth; moral virtues dispose one to act rightly in relation to one's feelings towards other people, oneself and the world about one. One has in mind such dispositions as kindness, generosity, caring for the environment, sensitivity to others' needs, humility in the face of success, courage in the face of danger or suffering, loyalty to friends. Different cultures do embody different virtues – meekness and humility are distinctively Christian, honour pertains to military societies – and these virtues reflect an underlying understanding of the life worth living. To develop as a person is to acquire dispositions to act in particular ways and these embody ideals of how life should be lived. Although there is and must be considerable variation in the virtues cherished and in the respective importance attached to each, the sort of person that people become cannot be a matter of indifference to society at large. For example, the more we learn about the destruction of the environment, the more important it becomes to dispose the next generation to a respect for that environment.

- *social and political involvement:* social, political and economic knowledge are part of the intellectual achievements referred to above. However, there is a danger within a liberal tradition of stressing the 'knowing about' at the expense of the 'knowing how'. To be a person is to be able to participate in and to influence social activities that affect the quality of one's life.
- *integrity and authenticity:* education is a constant battle between the perceptions of the learner and the public meanings which are mediated by the teacher. A major problem which besets education is the lack of consensus over so many of the values which are the foundation of the curriculum – the literary canon, the style of music or art, the moral virtues, the sort of society to be promoted, the lifestyle to be adopted. People think and live in different moral frameworks. Therein lies the dilemma. Education is based on the values which are connected with personal formation in its widest sense but that formation is to be understood within different and competing moral traditions. There cannot be the confidence, which once there was, in the specific values and qualities that identify the educated person. That does not invalidate the liberal programme in opening to the young what Arnold referred to as the best that has been thought and said. It does, however, make one a little more tentative about it and open to a wider range of possibilities. In respecting learners as persons one must give them credit for the personal search for a meaningful and significant life within the range of possibilities. Recognition of oneself as a person is a recognition of one's own ultimate responsibility for the values that one espouses and for the relationships that one enters into. An important part of education lies in this aspect of personal formation – becoming a person of a particular sort with particular beliefs, values and loyalties. There is a need to reconcile within oneself the different and often contradictory messages about the good life, and to relate these to one's own ability. To engage in this integrating process – to be authentic as opposed to taking on board whatever passing passions and pressures are about – is a daunting and often painful task. It means often the breaking with loyalties and cherished views. But it is part of that seriousness of living – not the games playing, not the dilettantism – that one would wish to associate with the educated person. And that seriousness is by no means confined to the

academically able. Nor does it depend on intellectual excellence. It lies behind the voice of many who want to be taken seriously but who are not, because what they say is discounted by those whose concept of the educated person is confined to academic achievement.

In examining the weakness of the different justifications for education in general and educational programmes in particular, I have suggested that the way forward is to look more closely at the basis of moral life, namely, the values attached to being a person and to becoming one in a fuller and more enriched sense. That requires an analysis of what it means to be a person and of the capacities which need to be exercised to live a distinctively human life. Central to those capacities is intellectual development in its different forms. In that, the liberal tradition is right and needs to be defended against those who, on the one hand, would reduce personal development to training in specific vocational skills, with little importance attached to the serious exploration of the life worth living, or against those, on the other hand, who denigrate the importance of knowledge and understanding as ingredients of the worthwhile life.

However, the liberal tradition has too often ignored the wider aspects of development as a person that I have referred to above, even though knowledge and understanding permeate these – the quality of life to be pursued, the virtues and dispositions to be adopted, the social skills to be acquired, the capacity for serious reflection to be exercised, the fulfilment to be found in relationships, the sense of one's own worth to be discovered through the employment of one's own distinctive talents, the responsibilities met in the participation in social and political life, the satisfactions to be found in the articulation through art and music and dance of one's personal response to the world as experienced. This broader conception of education, which draws upon the liberal tradition but which goes beyond it, has as its central assumption that all young people, whatever their academic ability, can, if given the opportunity, be serious in coming to understand and to articulate their experience of living – that all young people similarly wish for that seriousness to be recognised by others. The alternatives lie in an academic education 'stuck on' as though with chewing gum – the pretence of an educated person, but only skin deep – or in a total rejection of liberal education as something not to be taken seriously.

Social context

This analysis of personal development as the basis of educational aims seems precious like that tradition of liberal education which severs the personal from the useful, which divides education (personal improvement) from vocational training (social utility). But that would be a mistake. Implicit in the analysis of being a person is the necessary link to the wider social group of which the person is a member and which is essential to personal formation. To say that a person is a social animal is a cliché but true for all that.

The acquisition of knowledge and understanding lies in the participation in social traditions of inquiry and argument, of criticism and corroboration. There is little learnt except from other people – writers of textbooks, classroom instructors, practitioners, models of good practice, and critics. In learning history, one is joining other historians, however humble one's position, as an apprentice in this intellectual activity. In learning mathematics one is acquiring a public language, developed over time and through social criticism and enquiry.

Furthermore, one deliberates within a moral framework, a set of assumptions about the life worth living, which one is born into rather than has invented. The values and assumptions within that framework are enshrined within the institutions one attends and within the style of relationship one enters into. The idea of the autonomous person as independent of or above moral frameworks is incoherent. Distinctions between what is and what is not important in life depend upon such frameworks, and those are learnt. To exit from one framework requires entry into another, although the transition is often gradual and beset with contradictions – a problem so often faced by religious people adapting to a secular society.

Again, the life worth living is within a particular set of social and economic relationships. Those who are ill-prepared for those relationships will suffer accordingly. There are riches beyond their reach, opportunities lost, resources unexplored. To lack the necessary social skills prevents one from benefiting from the conversations of others; bereft of a foundation in the arts one fails to enjoy the community's productions; deprived of social and political awareness one cannot shape the society which inescapably shapes oneself; lacking relevant vocational skills one cannot ensure a satisfying occupation or the necessary financial returns. Preparation for adult life, broadly conceived but including the necessary foundational knowledge and skills for finding a job or a career, though much derided by some who claim to speak on behalf of liberal education, is essential for personal development. To quote John Dewey (1916, pp.306–7):

> ❧ Culture has also tended, latterly, to be associated with a purely private refinement, a cultivation of certain states and attitudes of consciousness, separate from either social direction or service. It has been an escape from the former, and a solace for the necessity of the latter ...

but

❛ ... nothing could be more absurd than to try to educate individuals with an eye to only one line of activity. In the first place each individual has of necessity a variety of callings, in each of which he should be intelligently effective; and in the second place any one occupation loses its meaning and becomes a routine keeping busy at something in the degree in which it is isolated from other interests. No one is just an artist and nothing else, and in so far as he approximates that condition, he is so much the less developed human being; he is a kind of monstrosity. He must, at some period of his life, be a member of a family; he must have friends and companions; he must either support himself or be supported by others, and thus he has a business career. He is a member of some organised political unit and so on. We naturally *name* his vocation from that one of his callings which distinguishes him, rather than from one of those which he has in common with others. But we should not allow ourselves to be so subject to words as to ignore and virtually deny his other callings when it comes to a consideration of the vocational phases of education.

Finally, there is an ancient tradition bequeathed by the Greeks that the truly human life requires participation in the political life of the state. Participation was not just a right, it was an obligation. The reasons for this were many – to ensure delivery from tyrants, to protect one's self-interest, to promote the public well-being. But above all it was because such deliberations about what is worthwhile and about the political and moral framework through which we discover our own identities was a good in itself. It was an essential ingredient in the life worth living of the free individual.

The quality of life of each person cannot be disconnected from the quality of life of the political and social units to which each belongs. Personal formation disconnected from social formation in this broader sense is an impoverished one. A fortiori, education conceived simply as personal development without regard to economic usefulness or social relevance or political influence is also an impoverished one. And yet too often we suffer from a conception of education as academic excellence without reference to this wider social, political and economic dimension of being a person and of being one more abundantly.

Conclusion: Key issues

The difficulty we are tackling is that of reconciling an idea of education dominated by academic success with one of vocational preparation dominated by economic usefulness. The problem is a real one.

Defenders of liberal education are rude about vocational trainers; and vocational trainers blame the irrelevance of education for our economic and social problems. Young people, unable to succeed within the framework of liberal education, are branded failures and ineducable. Those who succeed in vocational pursuits are denied the status accorded to academic success. There is a hierarchy of values and academic excellence is at the top of that hierarchy. And no declarations by Ministers about equal status will alter that. The result is separate systems as though there are two quite different educational experiences for quite different people – the pursuit of knowledge for its own sake for some and the training in useful know-how for others.

The aim of this book is to challenge what I see to be the 'false dualisms' between academic and vocational, theory and practice, education and training, which fragment the educational system and impoverish the experience of everyone.

It has been necessary, therefore, to examine the base of any claim to educational value. Why are some people thought to be educated and others not? Often that claim lies in academic excellence, and defines that excellence in a range of intellectual achievements which only a minority can manage. However, although learning which leads to understanding and knowledge is central to education, it can, despite intellectual excellence, be narrow in scope, given the range of capacities that are part and parcel of what it is to be a person. These capacities are all dependent on learning, but the learning extends more widely than that normally associated with liberal education. It requires the acquisition of social skills, an awareness of one's responsibilities, virtues and dispositions which are constitutive of personal well-being, the ability to find value and pleasure in the world and people, confidence to explore what makes life worth living. All this stems from a consideration of what it means to be a person and to be regarded with the respect deserved by those who live distinctively human lives. Such considerations should be where we begin our educational thinking and curriculum planning.

Nonetheless, such a broader educational landscape does find a central place for the development of the intellect and for the importance, therefore, of those public forms of thought – history, science, mathematics, literary and aesthetic expression – through which experiences are refined and understood and through which values are explored. It is foolish to jump from the narrowness of the liberal tradition to its rejection.

Part of that wider notion of being educated, based on the idea of the *whole person* – as a doer as well as a thinker, a social person as well as an individual, responsible to others as well as to oneself, exploring what is a worthwhile form of life as well as being introduced to the best examples of it – includes preparation for the adult world. Being a grown up person includes earning a living, acting politically, contributing to the social life that shapes one's own personal well-being. To hold in contempt the useful knowledge and skills necessary to help one find fulfilment in that world is to ignore a vital aspect of being a person. Vocational preparation, as that is generously defined by Dewey, should therefore be part of, not in opposition to, the liberal ideal. Vocational training might or might not be educational; it depends on how one is trained – critically or narrowly, encouraged to understand the processes one is trained in or focused solely on the practice, questioning the values of the activity or concentrating on the efficiency of the action. When the YTS changed its commitment from personal development to personal effectiveness, it was not shifting from education to training, but taking the education out of training.

The implications of this ethical account of education, based as it is upon an analysis of what it is to be a person, puts into focus the poverty of the current debate on standards in our schools. Teachers feel aggrieved at seeing standards defined entirely in terms of academic excellence when they know that there is much more to being a person than that. Academic excellence so defined does little justice to the intellectual qualities necessary for exercising the range of capacities attributable to being a person. The broader concept of education which I am advocating entails a consideration of different standards against which one judges someone to be an educated person.

The purposes of education, therefore, the content of educational programmes, the standards by which educational progress is judged, the idea of the educated person itself are all permeated by feelings and judgments of value. Ultimately it all depends upon one's view of the life worth living. But there is no certain answer to these central questions of value. Education, therefore, cannot be a programme of learning that takes those values for granted. They are, through literature and drama, through science and religion, through art and history, through the very mode of teaching, the very stuff of the educational enterprise. To be a person is to explore and to find out for oneself what is of value. The liberal tradition, unlike the vocational one, has always made such considerations central – albeit by ignoring certain voices in the conversation that deserve to be heard.

Finally, however, this account raises important questions about the role of the state and of the teacher in determining the aims of education and the standards by which educational achievement is to be assessed. Where there is not consensus over the life worth living, then who has the authority to compel young people to learn certain things rather than others? How does one reach conclusions about the best that has been thought and said? After all, does not the very problem that I am addressing arise from the fact that too many people with a narrow conception of liberal education have been in a position of authority and power, able to define those aims and standards, and able to promote an idea of education which excludes so many?

6

Education and Knowledge

Learning

To educate is to get people to learn – an obvious statement, maybe, but one worth asserting. Why?

It is necessary to be reminded of the central *educative* function of schools, namely, to enable young people to learn what is valuable and significant. Such a statement focuses analysis upon what it *means* to learn and upon what is *important* to learn.

What it means to learn

People learn a wide range of things – a point which needs constantly to be borne in mind. They learn facts, concepts, principles, skills, attitudes, competences. They learn *how* to do things (for example, *how* to cook or *how* to ride a bicycle) as well as *that* something is the case (for example, *that* dinosaurs lived in the Jurassic period) or *to* behave appropriately (for example, *to* be kind or *to* work co-operatively), or *to* be someone (for example, a humble person or a good politician). The complexity of learning – the different sorts of things which are learnt – escapes simplistic learning theories. So, too, does it escape simplistic approaches to assessment – a point to be remembered by examining boards. But what the different kinds of learning have in common is that there is some change in how one comes to see, understand, appreciate or feel, and that such a change, if genuine learning, has to meet standards of success.

Learning, therefore, is not simply modification of behaviour or conditioning. It implies an achievement, a coming up to standard –

often gained after considerable struggle. One might say of a driver who constantly fails to reverse into a parking bay that he has not yet learnt how to drive. There are logical requirements to what counts as successful learning, determined partly by the purpose of that which one is trying to learn, and partly by the conventions which define what is appropriate and which one needs to internalise.

Just as learning cannot be identified with a change of behaviour, so it cannot be reduced to a change of belief. Those beliefs must meet standards of truth, accuracy, or validity. For example, not any gobbledygook counts as having learnt science. To learn science is to acquire and to internalise relevant concepts, forms of judgment and ways of enquiring. Not any change of belief counts as learning – only that which meets certain standards. Those do not arrive at birth. They have to be acquired.

Furthermore, 'learning' is different from 'development'. Young people develop physically without having to *learn* how to grow, although growing might be affected by what they learn (for example, about nutrition). Similarly there are changes to the mental structure of experience, as Piaget showed, which result from maturation rather than from learning. It would be wrong just to let learning happen as though concepts are grasped, skills acquired, facts understood simply from a process of development. These things are not innate, waiting 'to come out'. Of course, once language has been acquired and curiosity developed, then much learning will take place on an informal and experiential level. For that reason good teachers ensure the appropriate contexts for informal learning. But there are limits to how far learning progresses in its different forms without the careful, structured intervention of a teacher, aware, on the one hand, of the logical structure of that which is to be learnt and, on the other, of the psychological process whereby that subject matter is matched to the level and motivation of the learner.

Learning, therefore, is different from (i) modification of behaviour, (ii) acquisition of opinions irrespective of the truth of those opinions, and (iii) general development or maturation. Rather does it require the acquisition of ways of seeing or behaving, which reach certain standards. These standards are defined by the nature of that which is learnt. They are reflected in how one behaves *appropriately* or argues *intelligently* or understands *accurately* what is experienced. Central, therefore, to the idea of the educated person is that he or she has come to know, to understand, to appreciate and to behave in a way which reflects application of relevant standards.

This abstract account needs to be developed further through an analysis of what it means to have knowledge. That I shall do below.

Meanwhile, I return to the matter I outlined earlier, namely, the notion of *worthwhile* learning.

What is worth learning ?

To educate people is to get them to learn those things which make them educated persons – to acquire those personal qualities and attributes, characterised by intelligent knowing and doing and appreciating, which enhance the quality of life.

'Education', therefore, is an evaluative term in two senses. First, the learning must meet appropriate standards. For example, Jason has learnt the causes of the First World War, meaning that his account accords with the agreed evidence; Seb has learnt how to teach, meaning that his conduct meets professional standards. Second, however, that which is learnt and which meets those standards is *worth* learning. It enhances the quality of life.

The two notions of value must not be confused. It is possible to appraise what someone has done because the action meets appropriate standards, and yet to regard the activity itself as trivial. Music provides a good example. No one could doubt the sophistication with which discussions are held by devotees about the merits of 'rap' or 'soul'. Each kind of music embodies standards whereby it seeks to be judged good or bad. To learn 'rap' or 'soul' is to have internalised these standards and to apply them to one's own performance or to the appreciation of the performance of others. And yet such music does not find a place on the National Curriculum; achievement in these areas of potential learning are not regarded as educational; mastery of the standards implicit within 'rap' or 'soul' are not seen as the attributes of the educated person. Liberal education highlights not just the importance of meeting standards but also of selecting only certain standards as worth acquiring. Only certain musical traditions are believed to deserve our attention.

Deciding what is worth learning is an ethical question, and various kinds of argument have, as I explained in the last chapter, been deployed. But, as I argued, the idea of an educated person needs to attend carefully to what it means to be and to grow as a person. That, in turn, raises broader moral questions about the quality of life associated with being human and with living in a community of human beings. Hence, what is the knowledge which we think young people should acquire if they are to participate in and contribute to the sort of life which we think is worth living?

To fill in this picture, we need to attend to the wider forms of learning. In so doing I shall look at learning from a different angle. I have argued that learning is more than a modification of behaviour. There is an intellectual content – a conceptualisation of experience, the formation of principles of behaving, the gaining of skills which can be intelligently applied, the acquisition of modes of appreciation. In other words, learning entails acquiring a new way of knowing. Let us look at what this means.

Knowledge

Education aims to liberate from the immediate and the fashionable. It gives mastery through knowledge. The educated person, freed from ignorance, is less likely to be deceived by events or by people. Education opens up new horizons; it shows what can really be achieved in the arts, in writing, in scientific discovery. It offers ideals to be emulated. In that sense education, liberally conceived, is about the formation of the mind brought about through knowledge acquired. And the educated person is the one who has the knowledge foundation for recognising mental excellence in others and for pursuing it in him or herself.

Not all education is thus liberally conceived. Sometimes it is a matter of forming the consciousness of young people in a way that binds them, limits their horizons, prevents them from broader understandings, creates stereotypes, makes them conform, hides from them examples of excellence. The successful products of certain sorts of 'education' would not be widely regarded as educated persons.

There are several aspects of this mental formation.

There is the acquisition of the knowledge which makes the world intelligible. That knowledge must not be narrow because otherwise the learner will get a distorted or limited picture of the world. A well-trained and specialised mind may not be an educated one. This is what Peters (1966) referred to as 'cognitive perspective', seeing things from the many angles that different forms of knowledge make possible. Part, therefore, of the debate about liberal education concerns *balance* between different kinds of knowledge and understanding.

Furthermore, knowledge must to some degree be valued for its own sake – although it might also, thankfully, be useful as well. The person who was curious only because knowledge would help her further her own material interest would not, in this perspective, be regarded as educated. There has to be a curiosity, an interest in ideas, a concern for the truth in its different manifestations, a wish to solve problems. The intellectual life, in other words, is something valued and taken seriously.

Finally, not any way of acquiring knowledge will do. For example, to understand things historically is to be aware of the evidence for conclusions. It is to see things against a wider perspective of historical debate. It is not a matter of 'learning off' what has been dictated. It makes little sense to separate knowledge from the way of knowing, understanding from the process of gaining understanding. Educated persons have acquired their knowledge through processes of learning which treat learners as having, at least potentially, questioning and critical minds. The liberally educated person is the very antithesis of the indoctrinated or the conditioned one.

Thus, the pursuit of intellectual excellence – reflected in the breadth and balance of knowledge, in the delight and value found in knowing and in the mode of 'possessing' that knowledge – is what often characterises the idea of liberal education. Vocational training, by contrast, is conceived as narrowly focused, selective in pursuit of goals, lacking a wider vision, pursued for ulterior ends rather than for its own sake.

Such a view of education, therefore, attaches central importance to the acquisition of knowledge. But immediately there are difficulties, some of which were anticipated in the last chapter. Teachers want to promote other qualities than knowledge: character, attitude, creativity, imagination, moral disposition, appreciation of what is good and beautiful. Knowledge often appears a jejune concept, identified with facts that have been learnt, often by rote. It is something in books which has to be remembered. Often liberal education is identified with such a boring acquisition of knowledge – as in the case of the auto-didact who, to be educated, attempted to read systematically every book in the library, starting in the top left-hand corner with those beginning with 'A'.

That, however, is a distortion of what we mean by saying that we *know* something or somebody. Knowledge presupposes several things. First, it presupposes a set of beliefs about the world – a set of statements, if you like, which are considered to reflect the world as it really is. Second, 'knowledge' presupposes that the belief is a true one. Third, for this belief to rank as knowledge, even though true, it must be more than mere guesswork, hallucination, or fantasy. It is more than an isolated blob of 'knowledge'. It is understood within a framework of interconnected claims; it is seen to be true because of the reasons given. Such an analysis – knowledge as justified true belief – has its difficulties, but it is implicit in the whole educational enterprise – getting students to believe certain things in science, say, because they are claimed to be true and because those claims rest on good argument and experiment. For the learner to do more than believe, for the learner to *know* the laws and theories of science, he would have to grasp the reasons and to see their significance against a wider theoretical background. What is most important, however, is the implicit belief that education is concerned with generating true beliefs rather than false ones, with shedding the light of understanding where previously there was darkness, with correct accounts rather than misleading ones. It presupposes that there is a correct way of seeing the world and of explaining events within the world – and that there are criteria by which that correctness might be ascertained.

This is worth stating. There are many who attack liberal education – the promotion of certain kinds of knowledge rather than others – precisely because they wish to make 'knowledge' parasitic upon 'belief'; beliefs are sacrosanct and, if held with conviction and sincerity, to be regarded as good as anyone else's. But the tradition of liberal education I have in mind says the opposite – 'belief' is parasitic upon knowledge, upon the claim that some statements are either true or false and that we can have objective and public grounds for such a claim. Where we feel worried about those claims, where we feel that our beliefs go beyond the evidence, we express hesitation and doubt, and we say that we *think* something is the case, we do not know. Hence, education is concerned with helping the learner to distinguish between true and false belief, valid and invalid argument, correct and incorrect ways of proceeding, well-substantiated belief and mere opinion.

We need, however, to pursue this theme more deeply. Knowledge requires both a way of conceiving the world (a set of concepts, if you like, through which experience is organised) and a set of judgments by which these concepts are applied to a world existing independently. To have an idea or a concept is to have a way of shaping experience, of linking things together, of seeing relationships between otherwise disparate experiences. To learn biology, for example, enables the learner to connect up the otherwise quite distinct experiences of warm sunshine and growing vegetation. The theoretical perspective of photosynthesis shifts one's vision, provides an explanatory framework and opens up the possibility of yet further experience. To understand is to see these connections through which we make sense of the world and to have mastered the ways in which the resulting truth claims might be tested out.

The growth of knowledge lies in the acquisition of those concepts through which we have come to see the world and ourselves, and in the acquired capacity to apply those concepts correctly to new experiences. Therefore, knowledge, even if not explicitly recognised, is central to those other qualities which the teacher wished to identify with the educational enterprise – personal qualities, dispositions, attitudes, skills, values, sensitivities. Of course, all these go beyond knowledge itself, but they involve it. The morally educated person has acquired moral concepts through which he or she perceives the world and relationships in a distinctive way. Moral behaviour and sensitivity require a knowledge of how others feel. Creativity is impossible within a context of ignorance. Imagination requires the discipline of knowledge – of techniques and subject-matter.

Liberal education is concerned with the development of such conceptual schemes. It is concerned with the development of judgment – the ability to apply those concepts discriminately, precisely, correctly. It is, in other words, to develop the intellect in the sense of enabling people to acquire, to deepen and to apply a way of making sense of the world which is publicly available. It is central to the liberal tradition that there are structures of thought – specific intellectual disciplines – which are more basic than others and which give greater insight than others. It is also central to the liberal tradition that certain texts, constituting the 'canon', give greater insight than others – providing a knowledge, an understanding, a set of judgments which form the mind in a particular way. This structure of thought and this insight form the central qualities of the 'educated person'.

Different kinds of knowledge

The difficulty that many have with this thesis, and the reason why many reject the close association of the educational enterprise with the pursuit and the development of knowledge, is that it seems to omit much which teachers, parents and employers believe to be educationally desirable. And behind that rejection may lie a moral or, indeed, a political motive, for the emphasis upon knowledge excludes many as ineducable – those who, whatever their personal efforts, achieve so little academically.

To meet this difficulty, it is important to make distinctions between different kinds of knowledge. The first major distinction is that between commonsense, theoretical and practical knowledge; the second distinction is between different forms of knowledge.

Commonsense knowledge

First, we know *that* it is generally cold in winter, smoking injures health, 'spare the rod and spoil the child', leisure is necessary for mental well-being. There is a fund of understanding which one acquires simply from participating in a community and from picking up generally unquestioned beliefs. Such commonsense beliefs may be peculiar to particular groups – one group's commonsense may not be another's. Thus, it is *commonsense* to some, but not to others, that early selection is essential to the maintenance of academic standards. But there are certain kinds of knowledge that are shared broadly and which provide a common set of assumptions within which ordinary discourse and social relations can be conducted. Certainly, part of early education is to introduce children to this commonsense knowledge. And it is not to be despised. Often we say of someone who claims to be educated that he or she lacks commonsense – they simply do not see what is obvious to everyone else and they act foolishly as a result. Or they lack judgment, being unable to apply their theoretical knowledge to the practical world they inhabit. Indeed, that might be the result of too much emphasis upon academic success. They cannot discern when their theoretical understandings apply to the everyday world they share with others. Are not education theorists often accused of lacking commonsense? Seduced by theory, they are said to ignore the practical wisdom of teachers or parents or community. And 'back to basics' is, by contrast, defended as commonsense.

Commonsense can be more or less sophisticated. One can have a great deal of commonsense knowledge but little theoretical understanding and operate successfully in business or in practical affairs; one can be practically discerning even though unable to explain the basis of one's judgment. On the other hand, one can, as I have suggested, be theoretically sound without sharing the commonsense of those around or without having judgment in applying theory to ordinary situations. What characterises commonsense knowledge is not so much what is believed but the way it is believed – unquestioningly, without reference to reasons, as self-evident and uncontroversial, shared with the group with whom one identifies (see Pring 1977).

Theoretical knowledge

Education, therefore, seeking to develop a more intelligent and knowledgeable understanding of experience, goes beyond common-sense by raising questions where once these were not thought to be necessary, by asking for reasons where these were not given, by seeking foundations for beliefs which had been thought self-evident. Commonsense is limited and, as we observed, one group's common-sense may be seen by another as erroneous. Hence, the importance of questioning, studying, deepening the knowledge base, and respecting the intellectual journeys of others who have questioned and shown how answers to the questions might be found. It is that which academic studies open up to the young learner.

Here we need to make further distinctions. Such theoretical 'knowing that' takes different logical forms. There are theological forms of knowledge, mathematical, scientific, historical, aesthetic, moral, social, and so on. According to Hirst (1965), such forms of knowledge were logically distinct in that each was characterised, first, by those concepts through which experience was organised, second, by particular kinds of truth claims and distinctive ways in which those claims might be verified, and, third, by the mode of enquiry through which questions were pursued.

Thus, the biologist would look upon animate matter through a range of logically interconnected concepts such as 'organism', 'cell', 'protoplasm' and 'tissue'. To see things as a biologist, the learner would need to internalise such concepts, thereby to come to see the world differently. The learner would learn how to raise questions – to 'do biology'. He or she would learn how to test hypotheses – to verify or falsify what is claimed. Thus equipped, the biologist would be able to make connections which the person of commonsense could not make, and to contradict commonsense claims as a result of evidence or a more theoretical perspective. Of course, theoretical advances of one age become the commonsense of another. We now know that the world is round, moves in a sphere around the sun and rotates on its axis. But, though now commonsense knowledge, it is quite sophisticated, requiring the internalisation of geographical concepts which at some stage of one's life need to be learnt. One might make similar observations about other kinds of truth claim. Religion has its own distinctive concepts – God, sin, redemption, sacredness, sacrament – which interconnect to give a distinctive explanation of the world. These ways of seeing are developed by theologians, and ways of arguing, disputing evidence, verifying religious claims are agreed upon. Hence, education lies in getting the learner on the inside of these different forms of knowledge and in transforming commonsense into something more refined, grounded in evidence and reason, related to a theoretical perspective which goes beyond commonsense – and might undermine it.

Criticisms of the 'Hirst thesis' would be that it gave too simplified and tidy a picture of the logical structure of the different forms of knowledge and that no connection was made between these forms and the commonsense which the learners bring with them to school. Thus, for example, there are many different academic disciplines, each characterised by its own (often technical) concepts and modes of enquiry. The subject 'English' includes the study of language – its grammar and syntax – as well as the appreciation of literature – its style, structure and value. 'Mathematics' refers to different sub-disciplines. And new forms of knowledge constantly arise. Furthermore, only some of these 'forms of knowledge' are disconnected from the language and insights of 'commonsense'. The metaphor employed by Peters (1966) to describe education as 'an *initiation* into worthwhile activities' suggested a logical gulf between the understandings which the young learner brings to school and those which they *will* have, once initiated. But certainly in the humanities – in the exploration of what it is to be human, aided by the help of literature, history, social studies, geography and religion – that is not the case.

Nonetheless, the main thrust of Hirst's argument is surely correct, namely, that to grow in knowledge and understanding requires the acquisition of an ever more sophisticated set of concepts and modes of enquiry. Some of these concepts, as in the sciences, are interconnected through theoretical models which are far from commonsense. Even where that is not the case, as in the appreciation of literature, the different forms of enquiry are a refinement of, and a systematic approach to, thinking about matters of taste and value, which need to be learnt.

The importance of this for curriculum planning is clear. Standards which need to be internalised through learning are integral to forms of knowledge as these are reflected in the different ways of organising experience, of engaging in enquiry and of verifying the truth. Hence, as Bruner (1960) argued, curriculum planning requires the identification of the key ideas at the heart of those forms of knowledge which are important for the educated person to acquire. Forget the detail – the lists of facts. Identify instead the concepts and principles which are the most fruitful for subsequent learning and which are the chief structuring elements in that particular way of knowing. Such ideas or concepts provide the logical structure of the subject and need to be returned to again and again as learning progresses (a 'spiral curriculum'), something sadly forgotten in much of the National Curriculum.

Practical knowledge

School learning is dominated by 'knowledge that' – being able to state or write 'what is the case' in history or geography and other subjects. Therefore, the predominant mode of assessment has been the written examination. The acquisition of the knowledge which can thus be presented in written form – propositional knowledge – has come to define the educated person.

But there is a different kind of knowledge which cannot be reduced to propositions, namely, 'knowing how' or practical knowledge. One *knows how* to ride a bicycle without knowing the theory which explains balance; politicians *know how* to get policies accepted without being able to explain the secret of their success; business people *know how* to succeed without reading economic theory; children *know how* to manipulate adults though unaware of the psychology underpinning their behaviour. Furthermore, such practical knowledge, not being reducible to theoretical knowledge, cannot be gained simply from reading books or from studying theory. One learns practical knowledge from practising, albeit under guidance and subject to criticism. One learns *how* to be virtuous through following example and from practising the virtues; moral education, like so much education, is a kind of apprenticeship.

Why should such practical competence be called knowledge? First, it quite clearly requires, as in 'knowing that', a way of conceptualising experience, a set of ideas through which the experience is organised. The cyclist recognises the object before him as a bicycle; the politician discerns and discriminates on the basis of what he sees and understands. Second, practical, as with theoretical, knowledge must meet certain standards if the person is to claim that he *knows* or has *learnt* how to cycle or to run a business or to teach. Third, the person who *knows how* to do something exercises that knowledge in an intelligent way, responding to changed circumstances appropriately.

There is theory embedded in practice, but the practice cannot be reduced to theory. Hence, it is mistaken, for example, in the training of teachers to teach them how to be professionals simply by exposing them to theory – as though intelligent practice follows from the internalisation of theory. Those who are the best talkers about teaching are not necessarily the best teachers, and those who know how to teach may be unable to give a good account of their practical knowledge.

On the other hand, there is a connection between theory and practice. Assumptions embedded in practice about its value or about the social and physical environment in which one practises, can be made explicit and criticised in the light of commonsense or theoretical knowledge. Teachers can analyse their performance and that analysis will be better informed by what is known more generally about the motivation or social conditions of those being taught. Hence, one regrets the disdain shown for educational theory by some politicians and their advisers. Learning to teach is partly an apprenticeship, but not entirely. Such practical knowledge, though not reducible to theory, is enlightened by a theoretical perspective.

Practical knowledge, what the RSA referred to as 'capability', is much neglected in a liberal tradition which equates knowledge with 'knowing that' and which therefore distrusts anything which cannot be expressed in propositions and assessed in written form. And yet capability with a practical turn of mind – *knowing* how to live socially or enjoy relationships or work co-operatively or behave morally or act politically or weigh up practical problems – must surely be one mark of an educated person, a person who can live a fully human life.

Furthermore, it is, as Bruner (1960) observed, through this practical knowledge that the young learner most effectively comes to theory. The central ideas which structure theoretical knowledge are often known and represented in a practical form. Indeed, in the absence of such a practical mode of representation, the theoretical ideas get little purchase on the practical and commonsense world which the learner inhabits. Religious practice preceded theology; moral practice preceded ethics. It is not clear what sense can be made of ethics unless one had had to struggle with moral problems, or what sense one would make of theology without some intelligent involvement in religious practice. Science is a practical activity, though the practice of science is often neglected in the presentation of the theory which is the product of that practice. Thus, Bruner gives an example from classical mechanics – the grasp, in a practical or 'enactive' form, of the principle of leverage by the young child who plays on the see-saw, shifting balance and position to get the desired effect. Later that practical knowledge can be envisioned or represented 'iconically'. Later still the principles implicit in practice can be made explicit and represented symbolically – indeed, with a mathematical precision. Therefore, for Bruner the curriculum is a kind of 'spiral', a constant returning to the key ideas which structure the form of thought but which are returned to in a different mode of representation.

This brief account of different kinds of knowledge – commonsense, practical and theoretical and different forms of knowledge within the theoretical – does not solve our problem, namely, that of deciding what kinds of learning should be selected within a liberal tradition of education which also tries to redress the divide between liberal and vocational. But it does do two things. First, it alerts us to the mistake of reducing education to one kind of knowledge, namely, the propositional knowledge which is too often academic in the sense defined by the Oxford English Dictionary (1964) 'scholarly, (and by implication) abstract, unpractical, cold, merely logical'. There is a need to respect the practical knowledge and capability which, in their different forms, are essential for the quality of life. Second, whatever kinds of learning are selected for the education of the next generation they have a logical structure – a set of key ideas and distinctive modes of enquiry and verification – which guide the curriculum planning and define the standards of successful education.

Social relativism and the 'educated person'

There are two obvious difficulties in the account given about the relation of knowledge to the idea of an educated person. First, what, from the many different claims to knowledge, are to count as genuine ones and thus valid contenders for the education of the next generation? Second, who is to decide what knowledge is of most worth and essential to the idea of the educated person? I want here to tackle the first question and postpone the answer to the second to the next chapter.

The difficulty is this. There are many ways in which we could conceptualise things, and indeed we know that how we understand the world now is not the same as it has always been understood; and no doubt in the future people will come to see things differently. Moral appraisals have changed immensely even within our own lifetime. New artistic traditions replace old ones. Science develops not so much from the discovery of new facts as from the reorganisation of old ones. And there can be different scientific traditions. For example, in medicine there are Chinese traditions very different from the Western ones which 'see' and explain things differently.

Why, therefore, should some literary texts be seen as the ones which reflect the best that has been thought and said? Why should certain ways of conceptualising experience be preferred to others? There are many other possible claims to knowledge and valuing, but they sadly never get a look in. Only small groups of people have the power to define or to 'legitimate' what is the best or what counts as intellectual excellence or what are the preferred texts. And that is a cause of anxiety where those small groups are hand-picked by the Secretary of State for Education.

This criticism has deeper philosophical roots in the sociology of knowledge. The thesis was developed most effectively in a book edited by Michael Young in 1971, *Knowledge and Control*. Briefly the argument might be summarised as follows.

Knowledge is created by people at particular times and in particular places. It is (to employ a commonly used phrase) a 'social construct'. As such it has two features which should be noted.

First, the ways of looking at and understanding and appreciating the world (that is, the concepts we use) and the criteria whereby we apply those concepts to reality (that is, the basis upon which we regard certain judgments and arguments to be true) are relative to social groups, located in particular places and points of time and in positions of power to enforce their beliefs. The prevailing idea of an 'educated person' is something legitimated by those who, normally in positions of power within the universities, are able to say what counts as knowledge or what is 'the best that has been thought and said'. What is assumed to be quite objective and independent of personal whim or preference is in fact relative to those who are able to enforce their view of the world. Why else should such bodies as the Centre for Policy Studies infiltrate the political machinery of education in the way that they do?

Second, the construction of such ways of knowing are social events – interactions between individuals in which how one person or group sees things affects, and in turn is affected by, how others understand things.

It is a 'negotiation of meanings', but one controlled by those in positions of power.

To rephrase the thesis: we have no access to reality independently of the concepts and forms of judgment which we, living within a particular time and place and tradition, share with other people – those who share in a religious or moral tradition, or who are part of a wider cultural circle. There is no absolute (that is, not socially relative) truth and no essential (that is, as things really are) way of seeing things. And what ultimately prevails is as much the result of political influence and legitimation as it is of argument, experiment or reasoning. Indeed, the criteria for valid reasoning, good argument or valid experiment would themselves be a 'social construction'.

Should anyone find this argument too esoteric for the purposes of this book, they should reflect on the criticisms of how certain ideas of liberal education come to dominate. The advocates of a more vocationally oriented curriculum despair of the control which a particular liberal tradition holds over what count as standards. Academics and industrialists, who produced the 'Capability Manifesto', regretted the rejection of practical forms of knowledge by those who maintain the dominance of a particular form of academic excellence. Some forms of knowledge (for example, economics and sociology) struggled with difficulty to get a place on the curriculum. And within the forms of knowledge (for example, in history or in English) differences concerning the nature of the subject, which affects what the content of the curriculum should be, are angrily fought over.

I want to go so far with this account of knowledge, but not too far. It has done a service in pointing to the sociological and political story of how knowledge is developed and of how certain kinds of knowledge and value come to dominate as the socially important ones. It has made us question the dominance of certain ideas of educational standard and of the educated person. One must always look at the interests which the preservation of such ideas serves, for ideas of what is educationally worthwhile arise in particular social circumstances. They too are part of a continual argument about what is important in life. So much is this the case that it is important to ensure the right kind of institutional environment in which these ethical questions can be constantly explored – a point I shall develop in the next chapter. Indeed, a mark of an educated society – of a community of educated persons – is the recognition of the uncertainties which surround our claims to knowledge and the consequent openness to wider sources of criticism whereby those uncertainties might be resolved.

What then are the limits to sociological relativism? The following is a brief summary of the argument I have presented in more detail elsewhere (Pring 1972).

First, there are limits to how far one can talk about reality being socially constructed. The distinctions we make within our different social frameworks presuppose that there are distinguishable features of a reality existing independently of our private wishes or political machinations. Our different 'constructions of reality' presuppose that there is a world of material objects existing in space and time and interacting with each other in accordance with laws of cause and effect, and that some of those material objects are persons with the capacity to think, feel, communicate through language and take responsibility for what they do. Whatever the different ways in which social groups have come to think about reality there must be assumptions which enable us to explore and argue about the differences and to engage in the enterprise of scientific and humanistic studies. Hence, the development of knowledge is marked as much by argument, criticism, search for evidence, corroboration or falsification of claims made, as it is by social control and political legitimation. An educated society recognises that and institutionalises the possibility of open argument and criticism rather than forecloses it.

Second, differences in judgment which, in the face of uncertainties, are inevitable in any open society, do not entail the relativity of truth. My belief in God's existence, in the capacity of human beings to be responsible for their actions, in the irrelevance of business metaphors to describe education, in the ineffectiveness of present institutions to promote learning, in the danger to health of smoking – such beliefs are either true or false, correct or incorrect, valid or invalid. The very assertion of these beliefs, the possibility of arguing them and the confident behaviour which follows from them presuppose that there are standards of truth or correctness or validity, within those particular forms of discourse, against which my arguments and claims might be appraised. Belief (and how is it possible to live without commonsense beliefs in a material world, other people, moral demands, social realities?) presupposes the distinction between truth and falsity – that there are ways of talking about the world that correspond to how things are and that we have reasons for describing and evaluating things in the way we do. The educated person realises the uncertainties which lie behind the claims. But uncertainty does not entail there is nothing to be uncertain about.

In educating young people we are introducing them to those ideas and beliefs which, although not necessarily held with certainty, have survived, or indeed evolved from, the criticism which has been systematically pursued across the generations. In a free and open society such ideas and beliefs will change through criticism. To be educated is to be able to appreciate what has been achieved and to respect those achievements as the product of systematic and critical reflection, but to be aware that there can be few certainties – that the present state of knowledge is part of a more general 'conversation between the generations of mankind'.

Skills and competences

The liberal tradition of education has quite rightly emphasised the importance of knowledge, of freedom from ignorance, of acquaintance with forms of understanding through which one is able to think and act intelligently. But it is a criticism of such a tradition that, in stressing 'knowledge that', it has neglected practical knowledge, in particular the skills and the capabilities which enable one to cope with everyday practical demands and the economic requirements for getting a job. Business success requires not only thinkers but doers, and 'doing' requires specific skills. Even living fruitful and successful lives with other people, either in the intimacy of a home or in the wider community, requires capabilities and social skills which cannot be derived from theoretical study.

By contrast with the liberal tradition, therefore, the vocational one has emphasised the competences required to do a job effectively. Such competences are derived from an analysis of the job or the social situation which one seeks to be competent in. The emphasis, therefore, is upon the measurable outcomes of learning – the 'can dos' which relate to specific tasks.

Skill acquisition is surely important. And who could be against competent teachers, engineers or workers? But something bizarre is happening where all learning is organised around the concept of competence. In particular, it threatens the liberal idea of education.

Competence is related to the notion of skill. Thus one speaks of the skilled or competent teacher, footballer or politician. The NCVQ, in adopting this vocabulary, seeks to analyse the range of competences required to do particular tasks. The more sophisticated the job the greater the number of competences and the more difficult they are to learn. But at least they can be spelt out in terms of a list of observable 'can dos' related to an explicitly stated range of tasks. The hairdresser is competent to do a finite list of tasks – trimming curly hair, styling long thin hair, taping the hair at the nape of the neck. One difficulty, however, is the apparent non-transferability of the skills which make one competent at particular tasks. Hence, the reference to *core skills*. And much time and energy has been expended by national bodies in trying to spell out what these are. In general they refer to skills of communication, numeracy, problem solving and personal effectiveness.

It is necessary at this stage to question the notion of skill. The paradigm case of a skilled person is the craftsman who is able consistently to undertake a task which requires practical ability learnt from doing and perfected through repetition. Such practice meets certain standards. The skilled person recognises those standards and is able to criticise accordingly the outcomes of what he or another person does. It is possible to identify the skills required for particular jobs. When the nature of the job changes, those skills often become redundant. Cutlery grinders are a dying breed.

The advantage of the concept of skill for curriculum planners is that it is quite specific. Hence, one is trained in a skill. One perfects it from practice, undertaken more likely than not under the guidance and criticism of a master craftsman. The role of theory takes a back place because the skilled craftsman learns from doing; he knows *practically*; success requires no theoretical analysis of principles behind the practice. The skilled driver *feels* the strain on the engine, responds instantly to perceived danger, knows without thinking how and when to overtake. Similarly the competent teacher knows how to manage the class, gain control, ensure an orderly lesson, deal with the potential troublemaker. Such a teacher demonstrates a range of management skills obtained from constant practice. And often such a teacher will be chosen to act as mentor to a new teacher who needs to learn to be a competent teacher. The concept of skill, therefore, is an important one for those who wish to plan the curriculum, to control what is learnt and to say exactly what the outcomes should be on which the learner is to be assessed.

The disadvantage of attaching so much importance to skill is that the concept fails to do justice to the other mental qualities and cognitive achievements which are much more than skills – for example, the imagination through which the artist uses skills to particular effect, the theoretical insight behind the skilled construction of the bridge, the personal qualities which guide the skills of personal effectiveness, the judgment showing when and when not to apply a skill. Such mental qualities are not reducible to the finite list of 'can dos', to the list of competences, which those who wish to plan and control learning insist upon. Successful education requires more than the competent teacher. Skills which make one competent are necessary but not sufficient; teachers need to be more than good at a craft.

These difficulties emerge especially in the advocacy of communication and problem-solving skills. Certainly there are skills involved in communication which can be learnt from constant practice and from criticism of performance – for example, maintaining eye contact, raising the voice, using one's hands demonstratively, etc. All these are useful communication skills. No doubt, also, the concept might be stretched to cover the 'skill' of organising an argument, relating what one has to say to particular audiences or maintaining a certain rhythm in the presentation. But communication is much more than a skill. It involves sensitive understanding of the audience and an understanding of that which is to be communicated. Communication skill as an end in itself may produce the sophist but not the intelligent communicator. To communicate, one needs to have something worthwhile to say. Similarly with problem-solving skills, it is not clear what these are when abstracted from particular kinds of problems. Problem solving in mathematics is very different from problem solving in history.

Certainly, therefore, one needs to add to the range of achievements, which a liberal education requires, those practical skills essential for the tasks of everyday living, obtaining employment, working and living effectively with others, engaging in economic and political activity, communicating. However, it is a particular ploy of the vocational trainers to extend the concepts of skill and of competence to cover mental and personal qualities – judgment, imagination, understanding, shrewdness – which are very different from skills. But that is so to stretch the meaning of the concept that it no longer contains analytic value. The particular benefit of the use of skill and competence models of learning is precisely one of reducing all learning to lists of 'can dos', accessible through observation and thus easy to assess. But the mental and intellectual life is more complicated than that.

Mental powers and virtues

This brief mapping of the subject-matter of education, namely, the different kinds of knowledge at the heart of personal development leading to a desirable form of life, is still deficient for two reasons.

First, there is a danger of fragmenting the intellectual achievement into distinct forms of knowledge or practical competence. The curriculum correlate of that is the modular system in which the process of learning is broken down into brief and discrete periods of learning. The assessment correlate is the checklist, within the vocational tradition, of discrete competences. But it is, in my view, difficult to get away from the idea of mental powers – those of imagination or creativity or judgment or logical sharpness – which transcend subject boundaries and, indeed, put those subjects in perspective. Furthermore, the educated person is able to think and to address problems from a perspective which integrates these different subject-matters and which tempers the force of argument from one angle with a sense of proportion and a practical capability. The imagination is no doubt nurtured through the study of history or literature, and it will take on characteristics which are determined by the logical nature of those subjects. But it cannot be defined in terms of those subjects, even though constrained and disciplined by them. There is a danger, therefore, of ignoring the gradual formation of mature judgment, creative capability, lively imagination, self-reflection and evaluation, which takes time and the right conditions and a recognition that such powers cannot be reduced to the modules and assessment schedules of modern curriculum planners.

Second, and connected with these powers, are the virtues which are associated with the acquisition of those intellectual capacities both theoretical or practical. Central to the learning which I have been describing are dispositions or virtues – the seriousness with which the learner wants to get things right, the importance attached to truth, the concern over doing things to a high standard, the readiness to seek and to accept criticism, the openness to alternative views and values. Too often one witnesses the prototype of the educated person – one who is certainly clever and accomplished – who nonetheless lacks such virtues. There is a lack of seriousness, a refusal to face criticism, a lack of humility in the face of alternative explanations, the treatment of knowledge as a personal display. But dispositions which I wish to identify with the educated person can be learnt by anyone who is interested in finding out the truth, however limited the academic ability. Indeed, it is the virtue of seriousness which marks out the educated person – especially seriousness over the life worth living.

Curriculum consequences

The place of subjects

'Knowledge' comes packaged in discrete subjects, each characterised by its own logical structure. Such subjects have long been regarded as the building blocks of an education which forms the 'educated person'. And the educated person is he or she who succeeds academically in these different subjects. Only with those regarded as unable to benefit from a liberal education have alternative ways of organising the curriculum generally been explored – more vocational, practical and relevant.

I wish both to agree and to disagree with the importance attached to subjects. First, I wish to agree in that the subjects at their best offer that organisation of public knowledge, the product of scholarly research and study, which must be welcomed by all who address seriously questions about the physical or the social world or about the kind of life worth living. And there is no doubt that the knowledge represented by those subjects often needs to be acquired through systematic study of the concepts, the principles, the modes of enquiry – the logical structure, in other words – of a way of thinking. Those who have attacked liberal education as no more than the acquisition of arbitrary and socially constructed forms of knowledge, and who, in the name of child-centredness, have wanted education to arise out of the activities and interests of the child, are simply wrong. They have not attended to the nature of knowledge and to its centrality in the formation of the educated person.

On the other hand, I wish to disagree, because there is much more to the educated person than 'knowing that'. Such knowledge, impersonally packaged, has to become personally significant. It requires, too, a range of qualities and propensities which involve practical know-how and capability too often neglected in the pursuit of academic excellence. It requires, further, that seriousness about the quality of life worth living which, although enhanced by the intellectual 'tools' developed through the different forms of knowledge, is not reducible to them. Moral formation, surely part of the liberal ideal, requires knowledge certainly but not the knowledge confined to an academic tradition.

The arts and the humanities

It is a cause of some disquiet that, in alleviating the bureaucracy of the National Curriculum, the Government decided, following the Dearing recommendations, to make the arts and the humanities optional from the age of 14. To insist upon a compulsory core of mathematics, science and English is driven more by the perceived requirements of the economy than it is by any idea of liberal education or by considerations of the life worth living.

The main theme of this book, however, in addressing the liberal/vocational divide is that liberal education should enable the young person to see personal significance in that which is so often presented, quite impersonally, as a good in itself. In finding personal significance, the learner will quite rightly look for vocational relevance – after all, what can be more personally important than that which enables one to earn a living in an interesting and fulfilling way? But serious people will look for more than that and will value those studies and experiences which help them understand more clearly what it is to be human – which address perennial questions about values worth pursuing. And interest in such questions is not confined to the academically able.

When the school-leaving age was raised in 1972 from 15 to 16, there was considerable concern over what to do with those who normally would have left as soon as possible – those who were not able academically and who in the main were seen as educational failures. The problem, then, was this. How can we seriously address the aspiration of secondary education for *all*, irrespective of age, ability or aptitude, where we are deeply rooted in a tradition of liberal education which seems accessible only to an academic few?

The answer was partly sketched out in the 1967 Schools Council Working Paper, *The Raising of the School-leaving Age*, which boldly stated not just the central importance of the humanities to the education of all young people but also the nature of an education in the humanities – contrasting that, first, with the narrowness of vocational training and, second, with the too often impoverished treatment of the humanities within an academic tradition.

The humanities was that part of the curriculum where the teachers emphasised their 'common humanity with the pupils and their common uncertainty in the face of significant and personal problems'. They did so in the light of what others have said through the arts, literature, history, religion and so on. And teachers and learners could examine these together – the *objective* and external grounds for *intersubjective* exploration leading to *personal* resolution of those questions which were of deepest concern. The humanities – the poetry, the novel, the dance, the arts, history, social study, religious studies – were the 'objects' through which occurred the transaction between teacher and learner as they explored together those issues of profound personal and subjective importance: the use of violence, racism, sexual relations, social justice, etc. These different human studies were the selected public recordings of the best 'conversations' about those matters which concern all young people. They were the resources upon which the learners might draw in their deliberations. In that way the curriculum made *personally* significant that which was preserved in a public and impersonal form.

The classroom, therefore, is the community where these issues of deep personal concern might be explored, though in the light of what others have said and done who have preceded us. As Stenhouse (1967), the director of the Schools Council *The Humanities Curriculum Project*, argued,

❝ the essence of the classroom situation may best be captured by asserting that the group is prior to the individual, that individuals are well educated because they take part in groups and share experiences which have an educative quality.

It was the job of the teacher to assist in the sharing of those experiences in the light of those public conversations captured in the arts and in literature. And there would be a gradual realisation that, although that exploration could be more or less reasonable, could meet appropriate standards of enquiry, could withstand criticism, it always fell short of certainty. Furthermore, everyone, even those with limited academic abilities, can be educated in this sense – that is, enabled to think seriously and to deliberate morally about those values and beliefs which shape their lives and affect their choices, and to do so in the light of what others have said and written to illuminate these personal matters. The expertise of the teacher lies in the careful selection of the rich resources of our culture and to make them accessible to the learners in their deliberations.

Practical and relevant

The curriculum associated with the prevocational tradition – developed in Britain through *A Basis for Choice* and thence through such schemes as TVEI or BTEC, but anticipated philosophically by that great American educator, John Dewey – did not deny the value of the subjects in its version of a more vocationally oriented idea of liberal education. And certainly the humanities at their best were part of that tradition. For the purpose was to make the curriculum personally relevant – to enable the learners to see how the content of the curriculum related to their personal needs and yet also to the adult world which they were entering into. There was, therefore, stress upon the process of learning, upon negotiation of learning objectives and upon relevant personal qualities, so often ignored in curriculum thinking geared, in the academic tradition, to coverage of content and, in the vocational tradition, to skills and competences.

The questions which, therefore, began the curriculum thinking were: What needs to be learnt in the preparation of young people for personally fulfilling lives in a difficult and unpredictable future? What has to be learnt so that they might also meet the needs of the wider community of which they are members? And the answer to both must take into account the economic and social realities in which the learners have to live.

In answering such questions, teachers need to draw upon the resources of the academic disciplines, certainly, but the curriculum need not be organised around such disciplines, for practical and personal relevance becomes a further consideration. Such a curriculum, therefore, had to show the *relevance to vocational needs* both of the individual and of society; ensure *progression and coherence* from 14 into further and higher education or training; place greater emphasis upon *careers guidance and counselling* against a background of work experience ('knowing thyself' in relation to subsequent career choices was seen as a central, not peripheral, curriculum concern); attach importance to the *process of learning* or *learning styles*, especially to more practical modes of learning; emphasise technology, *especially information technology*, because of the way in which this transformed the processes of learning by giving ready access to information and other aids to further thinking; give priority to *personal exploration* in which the learners' ideas and concerns are taken seriously, drawing upon the humanities and creative arts through which these concerns are objectified and examined; develop, however, those skills, dispositions and confidence which make for *personal effectiveness*; insist upon the continued acquisition of *communication skills and practical numeracy*; create *community consciousness*; acquire the understanding necessary for *economic and political awareness*; emphasise the importance of *co-operative learning and team work*; promote *equal opportunities* in the choices made and the attitudes formed; and help with the formation of defensible *moral attitudes and beliefs* in a world bereft of moral certainties.

These became the principles which shaped a different idea of liberal education, one which, though respecting the knowledge protected through traditional academic disciplines and school subjects, nonetheless saw the importance also of making learning personally and socially relevant and broadened knowledge to embrace practical know-how and capability. Such different emphases and aims required a re-examination of the standards whereby achievement was judged and of the ways in which those achievements were to be assessed. In particular, it was argued that there should be greater emphasis upon continual and formative assessment, reflected in regular *profiling* of each student, thereby providing a more generous and positive picture of the achievements and qualities of the student. (These principles are developed at greater length in Crombie-White, Pring and Brockington 1995.)

Distinctive of the liberal tradition had been the view that education was primarily concerned with the 'perfection of the intellect', with the development of intelligence in its various disciplined forms (mathematical, scientific, historical, etc.). Such 'perfection of the intellect' could ignore the practical relevance of what is learnt or, indeed, reference to the world of work. The well-trained mind would, so it was held, later be turned to whatever life had in store. It was that separation of the theoretical from the practical, the intrinsically worthwhile from the useful, understanding from skills and personal qualities, 'knowing that' from 'knowing how', the intellectual virtues from the practical dispositions required in the non-academic world, which was challenged by the prevocational tradition. And that challenge was reflected in the renewed importance attached to 'relevance' – the relevance of what is learnt (and how it is learnt), first, to the felt needs of the learner, and, second, to the needs of society for which the learners were being prepared.

In challenging these dichotomies, the prevocational schemes, including those of TVEI, challenged, too, the underlying educational aims and values which too long had prevailed in schools and which some would argue were at the base of so many social and economic difficulties. Why cannot one be trained in an educationally respectable way? Why cannot one enter the halls of theory through the portals of practice? Why cannot intrinsic value be found in the useful and the relevant? Why cannot skills be seen as an ingredient in the development of knowledge and understanding?

7

School and Society

Educational outcomes are shaped not only by moral and philosophical ideas but also by the social structures and the framework of power within which those ideas are put into practice. Plato's educational aims for the Republic's guardians were not disconnected from the role they would play in an hierarchically structured society. A philosophy of education, and the attempt to reconcile a tradition of liberal education with vocational preparation, cannot escape broader issues in social and political philosophy concerning the responsibility of education for social improvement and concerning the legitimate powers of the state in determining what the aims of education should be.

This chapter examines the social ideas which are shaping arrangements for the provision of education and training – and which thereby transform the very aims of education themselves. In doing so, it first reviews some of the factors which are causing the changes in the provision of education and training and makes explicit the contradictory ideas which underpin these changes; second, it identifies at a deeper level the competing philosophies; third, it indicates the implication of these ideas for the exercise of social control; finally, it draws conclusions for the development of what I want to call a 'community of educated people'.

Social context

The first half of this book demonstrated the way in which social and economic needs affected the political agenda for education. In turn that agenda changed public awareness – so much so that there is frequently a wide divergence between what professional teachers aim to achieve and what some members of the public want the outcomes to be.

Such a divergence results in a struggle for the control of education and a questioning of the legitimacy of the control held, on the one hand, by the teachers over what is taught, and, on the other, by locally accountable politicians over how that teaching should be organised.

This is illustrated through the introduction of TVEI. In 1982 the Secretary of State at the DE announced this initiative in which public money would be put into schools from the DE rather than from the DES on the condition that the LEA supported curriculum programmes which met vocational criteria. If the LEAs were not to accept these criteria, then the quite substantial money would not be made available to their schools, and indeed new schools, outside the control of the LEAs, would be established. The political significance of this is that, in pursuit of objectives exclusively aimed at the improvement of work related skills, one government department attempted to change the educational agenda by bypassing those who were the traditional guardians of educational standards. TVEI represented a mode of central control over the curriculum of schools which had, since the 1944 Act, escaped central government. It did so to counter a tradition of liberal learning which was seen to militate against the vocational training required by the economy.

This centralisation, initiated by TVEI, was continued by the DE, through the agency of the MSC, in the funding and organisation of vocational training. The latest form of this *dirigiste* policy is the establishment of the TECs, the regional agencies through which government chose to fund vocational training. Such money was to be dispensed according to criteria laid down by a govenment department – no longer by local authorities responsive to the needs and demands of local employers. It was as though those at the centre knew best, and that the needs of the economy and of potential workers were too important to be left either to local communities and their representatives or to the teachers who, by experience and professional preparation, maintained a particular tradition of education and training. But the significance of this shift in social policy – from local accountability and professional responsibility – did not escape all government ministers. As Alan Clark, junior Minister of Employment, exclaimed:

> ❝ I am really *sick* of DE. I could only stay on if I were to be promoted to Minister of State and really *do* something – like winding up the whole MSC .... The MSC is a completely Socialist concept. Nanny State, with just a hint of Orwell. (Clark 1993)

In contrast with this centralisation (the Nanny State that Clark spoke of) there has been a much heralded move in the opposite direction towards the diminution of bureaucratic control, whether that be of central and local government or of the professional power of the teacher. Polytechnics, freed from the control of local government, reached the autonomous status of universities. Colleges of Further Education and Sixth Form Colleges received corporate status, with a new independence which, although requiring for the most part central funding, was subject to the vicissitudes of 'the market' and all that that entailed concerning customer satisfaction. LEAs had to devolve to their schools most of the money received for running costs, and thus schools, in an increasingly competitive world, could exercise control, through Local Management of Schools, over their own destiny. New kinds of school were created – grant maintained and city technology colleges – ostensibly to create the conditions of local choice unconstrained by administrators, politicians or professionals. As the Secretary of State said in the 1993 White Paper, *Choice and Diversity*, 'Parents know best the needs of their children – certainly better than educational theorists or administrators, better than our mostly excellent teachers.'

There are different levels at which one might understand these opposite tendencies, namely, centralised government control over details and yet transfer of choice and responsibility to the 'customer'. One might question, for example, the honesty of the Secretary of State's claim that 'parents know best' when what is taught in schools through the National Curriculum has been subject to an unprecedented scale of detailed legislation, or when ILEA was abolished, ostensibly in the interest of choice, despite the wish of the vast majority of parents for it to be retained. One might question, too, the honesty of the claim that university autonomy has been extended when the funding agency, traditionally acting as a buffer between central government and the institutions, became increasingly an agent of government policy for higher education. Indeed, there must always be the temptation of those in power to increase that power, as the Secretary of State has done, even when the opposite is proclaimed – and possibly believed in. Therefore, it is tempting to seek no deeper explanation for this centralisation than the ambitions and hubris of those who have been in power for a long time – a genuine belief in the diffusion of responsibility, sullied by a distrust of those to whom power would be diffused.

That would, however, be mistaken. There are competing ideas concerning the proper role of government and the place of other potential sources of power and influence.

On the one hand, there is the belief that government has a minimal role in which it simply provides the necessary conditions for individuals and their associations (e.g. voluntary bodies such as the Churches) to choose freely the sort of life they want to lead. On such a view, the government would have no right to promote particular values except those which are procedurally necessary for people to live together in harmony.

On the other hand, the distinction between procedural and substantive values becomes blurred. Quite clearly the central initiatives over vocational training and over the National Curriculum are justified by reference to the economic needs of the country as a whole in a very competitive world. A condition of freedom, so it is argued, is a well-trained and a well-educated public, and the obligation of government is to ensure that those conditions in terms of an appropriate curriculum prevail. Or, again, to ensure that everyone has the freedom to choose the standard of living he or she thinks desirable, access must be made available to all who might benefit from further periods of education and training; therefore, institutions are subject to government intervention to enable that to happen. Or, yet again, the Secretary of State, believing that the precondition of civil liberty and social cohesion is a shared set of moral values, and believing too that such values can be sustained only within a religious tradition, ensures through legislation that there should be a daily act of worship and that there should be religious education of a broadly Christian character. The boundary between the minimalist view of government, in which it no more than ensures the conditions for each to have access to an education and training, and a paternalistic view, in which it knows what is best and legislates the values to be promoted, becomes very grey.

It is necessary to pursue further this tension between apparently conflicting 'philosophies'. Perhaps that is best shown in the blueprint for education and training in the 1993 White Paper, *Choice and Diversity*, which provided a framework for the future of the educational system. It claimed to be a radical departure from earlier arrangements, and indeed it was. *Choice and Diversity* represented a coherent set of ideas, characterised by the use of key words that have their own distinctive and interconnected logic; and these ideas embody an idea of human motivation and human nature, of the common good, of the relation of the individual to society and of the purpose of education in promoting individual welfare and the common good. The White Paper set out a new framework for schools – no tinkering with the present arrangements, no focus on specific parts of the system only, but a utopian plan which would transform a system of education that was thought to be fundamentally flawed.

The key interconnected ideas, giving structure to the framework, were five: quality, diversity, choice, institutional autonomy and accountability.

Quality referred to the meeting of *standards* of performance by the pupils. These standards could be related to explicit *performance indicators* by which learning achievement might be measured and ranked. Experts or 'authorities' in standards were required to define those performances so that there could be a National Curriculum with explicit attainment targets pitched at progressively more difficult levels. These authorities were people chosen by the Secretary of State who personally would not presume to be an expert in all areas of learning. Quality, therefore, was identified with reaching preconceived outcomes, selected by a non-representative group of experts, which could be measured and made public. A system of *quality control* (testing) and *quality assurance* (inspecting) ensured that the consequent judgments of quality were made available to a wider public for their use.

It is important to note the social and political implications of this idea of quality. Quality and the related concept of standard could be captured in *performance indicators* and made unambiguously available in national measurements. The epistemological limitations of this view were questioned in the previous chapter, but, more importantly for my purposes, the definition of quality was thus removed from the arena of educational argument – in universities and in schools – in which 'standards' and 'quality' are constantly questioned and redefined. Rather was that process of defining standards put into the hands of politicians who may not be able to participate in those arguments. Furthermore, the ensuing definition of standards was couched, not in the language of thinking, arguing, reflecting, imagining, striving, conversing, but in the language of outcomes and thus of political control. Possibly the gravest challenge to the tradition of liberal education lies, not in the vocationalising of the curriculum, but in the subversion of the social and political conditions essential for the maintenance of that liberal tradition – in particular, the subversion of those institutional arrangements through which the definition of standards is part of the open and public conversation about values to which the young are being initiated.

Diversity referred to the range of provision arising from the freedom which schools had been given 'to take decisions reflecting their own priorities and circumstances in a way that was not possible a few years ago under the bureaucratic rule of local government'. It was also characterised by a system which contains, at the secondary level, local authority and grant maintained schools, city technology colleges, state supported and independent private schools, grammar and secondary modern schools, sixth form and further education colleges. All of these were to be supported from different modes and rates of public funding. In this way, quality was to be promoted by a range of provision to reflect different means by which that quality might be acquired – and, indeed, defined. Independent schools, not constrained by the National

Curriculum and the national assessments, and city technology colleges, having a special relationship with the business world which sponsored them, were to be able to spell out different criteria of quality – not subject to the control of the experts chosen by the Secretary of State for public sector institutions.

Choice referred to the opportunities provided by that diversity. Remember that to choose rationally there have to be several things to choose from which roughly serve the same purpose, and those things have to be accurately labelled so that the choice is an informed one. National assessments provide the labels, and parents choose. The justi-fication for providing choice was threefold. First, freedom to do what one wants is a prima facie good. Second, the customer knows best. Third, in so choosing, the customer keeps the providers on their toes – thereby enhancing the quality of provision.

Autonomy referred to the status of the providers of the service. They, the schools, should be responsible for providing the service, where 'responsible' entails deserving of blame when the quality of service is poor. The autonomous institution cannot pass the buck to someone else – the politicians or bureaucrats, competing schools or external circumstances. Autonomy entails moral responsibility. There are no others the schools can rely on to help them out of a mess. They live or die by their own decisions.

Accountability referred to two things: the obligation of the school to give an account of itself so that the recipient of the service might exer-cise choice more freely, and the openness of the school to be evaluated on the basis of that account. Hence, schools were obliged to publish details of their curriculum, attendance, truancy and test scores.

These key ideas of *Choice and Diversity* hung together in a coherent 'philosophy' of how schools, through which the next generation was to be prepared for adult life, should be run – and also how they should relate, on the one hand, to the state, and, on the other, to those who make use of them (namely, the children or the parents on behalf of the children). Schools were seen to be the providers of a *service*, which was both public and private. It was public in so far as everyone was obliged by law to make use of it. But it was private in that it was concerned with improving the prospects and personal well-being of each pupil. And the pupils themselves or their parents were therefore claimed to be in the most privileged position to judge that well-being. The parents, so claimed the White Paper, know best; they are the ones who can best judge what is good for them and their children – not the professional, not the administrator. Hence, the schools in effect were to relate to *cus-tomers*, all seeking their own good out of the *service*. Each individual, as recipient of the service, was to be 'in the driving seat', in contrast with the previous arrangement whereby the local authority determined the arrangements for each child and where the teacher, as the *professional*, determined what the children should do when they got to school.

Furthermore, if the recipients of a *service* (which is for their personal good) were to be 'in the driving seat', they needed to know the details of that service and whether it was successful; they needed to be able to hold the school to account for when it failed to live up to expectations and to 'exit' from the school if they were not satisfied. To hold the school to account required accurate and objective information – one could not otherwise make rational decisions about the well-being of one's children. And to exit from the school, where one was dissatisfied, requires diversity of provision – one must have something different to go to. The weight, then, is put on individual choice and on the provisions necessary for that choice to be a rational and realistic one.

In such a system of autonomous providers, each of which is to serve the personal needs of the recipients, regulations are required to ensure that the recipient gets a fair deal. And, indeed, that was seen to be the government's main job – the minimalist view of the role of the state. The government would set the framework within which schools could act autonomously. It would ensure that the recipients of the service could get the information necessary for making rational choices. It would promote the conditions, namely, diversity of provision, which made choice possible and which enabled the recipient to register a protest if dissatisfied. That would be the role of government – maximising individual choice and providing the framework for it to happen.

In fact, as I have noted above, the government was not consistent with its philosophy because, in providing a very detailed framework, it actually curtailed choice. It said to parents that their choice must include the attainment targets of the National Curriculum – although it was possible for them to avoid that if they were to go private (and the government made that possible by subsidising the private sector through the Assisted Places Scheme). Furthermore, one incentive for state intervention went beyond the requirements of minimalist government, namely, that of gearing the state system of education and training to international economic competition.

Nonetheless, individualism, choice, subservience of provider to the purchaser, government as the regulator of the process to ensure maximum choice and a fairness in operating it, the common good arising out of the aggregate of individual choices within a framework set by a benign government – that was the 'philosophy' enshrined within the White Paper. It not only affected practice through the regulations which arose from it; it affected how we think about practice through the ideas which it embodied.

To examine critically such a conception of educational provision and to make sense of the consistencies which are manifestly within it, it is necessary to make explicit the underlying political philosophies.

Social philosophies

There are difficulties in talking about competing social philosophies in education. First, as I have pointed out, those who make decisions, may do so for a variety of personal reasons, such as the enjoyment of power or the fear of pressure groups, which should not be dignified with the name of philosophy. Second, even where what is said might be reconstructed into a set of ideas, these may be fairly eclectic, drawing upon a range of positions which belong to different social traditions. Third, even these social traditions may have different strands and lack a certain coherence. Nonetheless, even where Secretaries of State are moved by hubris or by self interested pressure groups, words are used and reasons appealed to which are of philosophical interest. Politicians, like everyone else, live in a world of ideas through which they and others make sense of what they do. Therefore, in this section, I try to give some philosophical coherence to the ideas through which we make sense of the practical world of education and training described in Parts I and II.

Egalitarian socialism: importance of community

I want to make explicit a set of ideas which, particularly in the post-war years, inspired teachers, politicians and administrators and shaped the institutions of education and training, but which current developments are a reaction against. It is as though the social ideas which prevailed in the 1950s and 1960s are to blame for the ills which many attribute to the claimed decline in educational and training standards.

Certainly there was a dominant concern for greater equality in society, and this was best argued for in the work of Tawney's *Equality*, published in 1931. Tawney was appalled at the massive inequalities within society in terms of the distribution of wealth, living conditions, opportunities for health care and provision for education and training. Those inequalities were not morally justified and, in their gross form, needed to be eliminated. Especially was that important in education. Subsequently, the pursuit of a more equal society was a central part in a social philosophy which characterised the socialist ideal of society and the preparation of the next generation for that society – access to secondary education for all, the elimination of discrimination through selection for grammar school education, the pursuit of mixed ability teaching, and the public funding and maintenance of those progressing to higher education.

A criticism of this pursuit of equality has been that it is the philosophy of envy, the hostility of those who have less towards those who have more, and the promotion of sameness – something which can be achieved only at the expense of freedom of choice and of a quality of life which arises from the encouragement of differences. What is so good about sameness? And what objection should anyone have to the fact that some are better off, unless that 'better off' is at the unjustified expense of others? In other words, equality simply expresses a relation between individuals; it cannot be considered an end in itself. Rather should we pay attention to what we think everyone needs for living a valuable life, and the concept of equality becomes redundant. Indeed, the concern for equality as an educational aim has, it is argued, led to a lowering of standards – the subordination of the more able to the average and less able in pursuit of equal treatment.

This criticism might rightly be directed against certain people or educational authorities. Equality became for them an end in itself, rather than an expression of a relationship between individuals, the absence of which was right or wrong depending on the extent to which it promoted or inhibited the achievement of other desirable qualities. But those like Tawney who attached central importance to equality in education never saw it as an end in itself. The elimination of gross inequalities in wealth or educational opportunities or living conditions was a means to the kind of society which was desirable for other reasons. Part of the tradition I am outlining emphasised the importance of community and the relationships arising from a shared form of life and shared values. Too much inequality militated against that. As Tawney argued

> In spite of their varying characters and capacities, it is the fact that men possess in their common humanity a quality which is worth cultivating, and that a community is most likely to make the most of that quality if it takes it into account in planning its economic organisation and social institutions – if it stresses lightly differences of wealth and birth and social position, and establishes on firm foundations institutions which meet common needs and are a source of common enlightenment and common enjoyment. (p.15)

Equality was not an end in itself. But certain equalities were essential to the kind of community in which a desirable quality of life was available to everyone. That 'quality of life' needed to be spelt out, but it would include self-respect, and respect for each other, arising from the recognition that one's common humanity was more important than individual differences, whether these be of wealth or status or religion or race or talent. Furthermore, that recognition had to be embodied in the social and political institutions through which that common humanity might be promoted – schools, libraries, democratic processes, working conditions – and through which individual interests might be protected against those who, in possession of power and wealth, might pursue their own interests at the expense of others.

The socialist ideal, as represented by Tawney's seminal work, required more than a welfare state which would provide a minimum standard of health care, educational provision and living conditions for those unable or too foolish to provide for themselves. There was a more positive sense of community than that. And that was born of the recognition of the interdependence of everyone, not only in the provision of material goods, but also in the cultural and spiritual enrichment of a society upon which all needed to draw. Unless the community supported the arts, then the arts themselves would be impoverished. Unless the community encouraged a feeling of solidarity, then there would be the social dislocations arising from the fragmented interests and alienated individuals. The alternative conception of society, namely, of an aggregate of individuals cemented together by contracts entered into simply for the purpose of self protection, ignored the essentially interdependent nature of the way in which each and everyone survives and flourishes.

Hence, behind the socialist ideal is both a moral story about the quality of life worth living and an account of human nature, in particular, the degree to which individual character is shaped within a framework of social values. To express this crudely, the contrast between this socialist tradition and that which is critical of it might be stated as follows. On the one hand, there is a society, and individual welfare is intrinsically connected with it – values are learnt and motivations acquired from society. On the other hand, there is no society beyond the aggregate of individuals held loosely together by rules which ensure harmonious relationships between them.

Liberalism

By contrast a tradition of liberalism puts far more emphasis upon the autonomy of individuals to choose the sort of life they want to lead. Here one needs to make distinctions between those who see such freedom as an end in itself and those who value it through a distrust in the powers of government either to know better than the governed what is good for them or, if they do, to organise affairs more efficiently.

The classical statement of the liberal position is in Mill's *Essay on Liberty* (1859).

❧ The object of this essay is to assert one very simple principle, as entitled to govern absolutely the dealings of society with the individual in the way of compulsion and control ... That principle is, that the sole end for which mankind are warranted, individually or collectively, in interfering with the liberty of action of any of their number, is self-protection. That the only purpose for which power can rightfully be exercised over any member of a civilised community, against his will, is to prevent harm to others. (p.135)

There were extra reasons for enforcing this freedom where matters of opinion were concerned:

❧ the peculiar evil of silencing the expression of an opinion is that it is robbing the human race; posterity as well as the existing generation; those who dissent from the opinion, still more than those who hold it. If the opinion is right, they are deprived of the opportunity of exchanging error for truth: if wrong, they lose, what is almost as great a benefit, the clearer perception and livelier impression of the truth, produced by its collision with error. (p.143)

If society is an aggregate of individuals and if the choices of those individuals are of supreme importance, the onus of proof lies on the shoulders of those who wish to subordinate the individuals' wants to those dictated by the 'aggregate' – the community. The binding of the individual to the community is but a social contract, an implicit agreement whereby the individual sacrifices rights, but only in order to acquire the protection of the state thereby established.

Furthermore, that is worthwhile which the individual finds desirable or value in. The only constraint is that, in pursuing those desires, the individual should not prevent others from pursuing what they want to do. Society is no more than a collection of individuals who have agreed upon a set of regulations whereby each is able to maximise his or her own choices without interference from others. No one has the moral authority to say what those choices should be or that some are better than others or that certain quality of life is superior to another. A life of hedonistic pleasure is as good as a life of scholarship if that is what gives the individual most pleasure and satisfaction.

Such a brief account obviously cannot do justice to the complexity of the liberal position, especially to the distinctions which Mill argued for concerning different kinds of pleasure (see Mill 1861, chapter 2). But it is sufficient to provide the theme which makes sense of the insistence upon choice and diversity in the government's arrangements for education. It also shows the inconsistencies in the government's position, for a liberal philosophy which espouses choice and diversity can hardly support the centralised control of what has to be learnt. This explains the opposition amongst many conservatives to a *National* Curriculum. Real freedom of choice would allow schools to provide whatever curriculum they thought would meet the wishes of parents – for example, 100% astrology if that, by some quirk, is what they wanted for their children.

This liberal position has recently manifested itself in the advocacy of a more privatised system of education as indeed of other parts of the public service (see, for instance, Letwin 1988, *Privatising the World,* no less, and also Lawton's 1992 account of the extension of this neo-liberal philosophy into education). Others (see Tooley 1994) have wanted a more market driven public service. It is argued that the market is a useful metaphor because it reflects a set of relationships which have not prevailed in education but which should prevail if educational goals are to be realised. Thus the school, and the teachers in that school, provide a service to a set of individuals. As with any service, the recipients are the best judges of whether that service meets their needs or wants. There is always the chance that the service might be sloppy or off target or not meeting the *customer's* wants. There is a need, therefore, to provide a way in which the recipients can demonstrate dissatisfaction, mainly by taking their custom elsewhere. The argument, underlying the 1988 Educational Act and the White Paper, is that in the past the 'customers' of the educational service have not had the opportunity to protest in the most appropriate manner, unless they were rich enough to pay for private education. The learners got what they were given – the teachers and their employers were 'in the driving seat'. Under the new arrangements, that has changed. The recipients can object through availing themselves of the opportunities provided by open enrolment and grant maintained schools. The providers must meet the wishes of the clients, otherwise they will lose the income necessary to stay open. 'Market' is contrasted with top down planning; it represents consumer as against bureaucratic power.

The metaphor of the market, therefore, emphasises the importance of choice and the conditions for the exercise of rational choice. The 'perfect market' assumes that people will look after their own self-interest. And the common good is essentially the aggregate of the individual goods, achieved by everyone pursuing his own self-interest. Not all can succeed as well as the others. But in trying to beat the others, all will gain more of what is wanted. Imagine, for example, the archetypal market, a set of fruit and vegetable stalls. The customer is able to examine the different fruits, their quality and their prices. They can decide whether they want several cheap apples or one excellent one – or, indeed, given the prices, whether to buy oranges instead. Prices are kept down because otherwise the customer will purchase elsewhere;

but quality is kept up because otherwise the customer will not purchase at all. Fashions change for all sorts of reasons; the interest in bananas gives way to the interest in kiwi. Thus, since the customer knows best, the merchant has to be sensitive to changes in taste and fashion. Choice requires different items to choose from, but, to be rational in choice, the chooser needs basic information about those items: the cost and the quality.

These then seem to be the characteristics of educational processes picked out by the market metaphor. Education is a *commodity* which can be bought or sold like any other commodity. It is much in demand because of the 'positional good' it can purchase. Since people are motivated by self-interest, there will always be a demand for the commodity. Teachers are there simply to provide it and thus to provide a service that people, in the light of their understanding of their own interests, ask for. What is needed for people to be able to choose wisely or rationally is simply the right kind of information about the quality of the commodity and about the price one has to pay for it. The government's responsibility is to ensure the framework for these market forces to operate fairly: namely, (i) schools, so that no one will be prevented from receiving an education, (ii) choice of schools, so that they can act on their judgment about relative values of the services provided, (iii) accurate information about the schools, so that, in the light of their values and desires, parents or students can be rational in their choices

There is an extensive debate (see Bridges and McLaughlin 1994, for example) about the suitability of the 'market' as a metaphor for the educational system or of educational relationships, although it is important, even for the critics of 'educational markets' to bear in mind the weaknesses of the educational system which the introduction of the market metaphor served to draw our attention to. That debate concerns the assumption that market conditions are the most suitable mechanism for delivering an improved distribution of education for everyone, as though the pursuit of one's own positional good by some will benefit everyone – the schools improve their performance for everyone to attract potential purchasers. The total is more than the sum of the parts.

For the purpose of this book, however, namely, that of making sense of liberal education against the pressures to be vocationally relevant, I wish only to question the underlying idea of human nature. The most important defect in the market metaphor and the underlying educational philosophy is the assumption they make about human nature and the relation of the individual to others and to the state. The kind of educational arrangements one makes and the content of that education presuppose a view, a theoretical position, about what makes people tick and what is worthwhile pursuing. Behind all education is an idea of human nature, and that idea can be, and often is, an impoverished one. Those who think that people act only from self-interest will welcome a market system which regulates that pursuit of self-interest. And those who, sceptical of any objective arguments for deciding what is humanly desirable, will no doubt wish to leave questions of what is worthwhile to the customer or client, not to those who claim to be experts within an educational tradition.

Similarly at stake is the relation of the state and the wider community to individual improvement through education. If there is no such thing as society, only an aggregate of individuals, then the pursuit of positional good is more significant than the apprenticeship to the values and activities of one's wider community. Enterprise becomes an important virtue. Competition rather than co-operation provides the social and economic background to the formulation of educational aims and programmes. And the state becomes the regulator of the ensuing competitive activities.

Conservatism

By conservatism I refer not to the doctrines of a political party but to a set of beliefs, shared by both the left and the right in politics, concerning the way in which wisdom is embodied in social practices and institutions, over and above what is or can be articulated explicitly. That wisdom is the product of generations of practical living and also of change as a result of discussion and debate. It is not sacrosanct; it is always open to examination as a result of experience. But it is to be respected, even when not fully understood.

There is inevitably such a conservative tradition within the Conservative Party, but it contrasts markedly with the libertarian philosophy which I have just described. Such a tradition is well described by Gray (1993). It embodies a distrust of utopian planning, of the perfectibility of mankind, of powerful government coercing people into a particular mode of living. Certainly there would be limits upon compulsory education determining in detail the quality of life which pupils should be educated for. At the same time there is a distrust of the powers of the human reason to solve problems from scratch. One needs, therefore, to respect those values, traditions and institutions which have proven themselves in the past and which have ensured stability and social coherence through troubled times – even if, on the surface, they are not wholly reasonable.

❢ The task of government is to bolster those institutions and forms of life which, if they cannot confer happiness, nevertheless enable the natural sorrows of human life to be endured in a meaningful and dignified fashion ... though government is limited government, it has nothing in common with the minimalist, laissez-faire, night-watchman state advocated by libertarian doctrinaires ... It has also a responsibility to tend fragile and precious traditions, to protect and shelter the vulnerable and the defenceless, to enhance and enlarge opportunities for the disadvantaged, to promote the conservation and renewal of natural and human environment and to *assist in the renewal of civil society and the reproduction of the common culture without which pluralism and diversity become enmity and division.* (Gray 1993, p.50, italics mine)

Such a tradition is deeply rooted in British culture. Coleridge (1830), in *On the Constitution of the Church and State*, refers to the clerisy, a body of teachers endowed by the nation, 'charged with looking after the moral and cultural interests of the nation'. The interests of both permanence and progression depend on 'a continuing and progressive civilisation' but not

where this civilisation is not grounded in *cultivation*, in the harmonious development of those qualities and faculties that characterise our *humanity*. We must be men in order to be citizens. (p.xviii)

Liberal education is, quite rightly, concerned with *cultivation*. In that sense it must involve a 'clerisy' of some sort – people who inherit a tradition of thinking, valuing and appreciating, who are given the task of communicating that tradition to the next generation and who will resist those who seek to distort that tradition for personal ends or in the pursuit of power. Such a tradition will contain, through critical activity, the sources of its own progress and renewal, as it reflects new social and economic conditions, new ideas, new insights into society and those who are members of it.

To develop further this ideal, there is within such a community a tradition of public service, reflected in the ethical codes of professions and in the practice of central and local government, which prides itself in providing a service for the benefit of the client without reference to personal advantage or profit. Such a tradition encapsulates a set of beliefs about society, about individual strength and weakness and about the moral framework which should shape the relations between society and those individuals. Furthermore, as with any tradition, it can be undermined and weakened; it requires social support, indeed, education. It requires constant renewal and institutional recognition and protection. The spirit of public service, as with any moral set of practices, is gained through a sort of apprenticeship. Just as a child learns to respect others, or to protect the environment, or to care for truth, through the internalisation of such values as they are manifested in the community, especially that of the family, so do people acquire the sentiments of public service through the organisations and institutions to which they belong and which embody those feelings and values.

Social control

It is that tradition, the best of conservatism, shared by many on different sides of the political spectrum, which is now being undermined. It is being undermined by the 'utopian engineers'- those who believe, from the bunkers of their respective quangos, that they know best; those who overturn at a stroke those institutions, such as an independent inspectorate, which for over 100 years have accumulated a wisdom born of experience, teaching, assessing and evaluating; those who pressurise government to remove civil servants whose advice, within a tradition of public service, does not conform to the libertarian ideology.

But the undermining of that tradition goes deeper – to the language through which education is described, a different moral framework created and children's learning controlled. It is a language of inputs and outputs (not of transactions between teacher and learner or of explorations of value and meaning); it is a language of performance indicators and audits (not of professional responsibility and judgment), of commodities to be delivered (not of a conversation to be engaged in), of producers and consumers (not of teachers and learners), of skills and competences (not of understanding, appreciating, valuing, imagining). Under the new reality shaped by such language, where funding cuts are described as 'efficiency gains', an exhaustive and comprehensive system of curriculum outcomes is created – attainment targets, behaviours, competences – which embrace every aspect of learning from the cradle to the grave, all recorded in the National Record of Achievement. To quote from the new style HMI

❝ As public interest in *managerial efficiency* and *institutional effectiveness* has increased, there has been a general acknowledgement of the need to use *performance indicators* to monitor the higher education system ... some concrete information on the extent to which the *benefits expected from educational expenditure* are actually secured ... [an] approach finding most favour in 1989 and 1990 is the classification of performance indicators within an *input, output process model*. (HMI 1991)

In searching for indicators 'which allow institutions to assess their own *fitness for purpose*, the report suggests a range of reference points which enable an 'assessment of *achievement against a defined objective* – cost effective indicators', 'academic operations indicators' such as 'inputs' (e.g. application in relation to numbers or ratios per place), 'process' (e.g. value added) and 'output' (e.g. employer satisfaction).

There will be

❧ *enterprise audits* which evaluate teacher and learning styles and *annual school audits* where senior staff spend one day reviewing all aspects of a school's work. Many institutions are working to sharpen their quality assurance procedures by systematising the use of performance indicators and peer review.

This changed language affects profoundly the nature of the activity as it is perceived, and the nature of the relationships between those who engage in the activity. Education shifts from being an evaluative word, picking out as valuable that formation of the mind through an encounter with the best that has been thought and said – the value of which can be judged only against broad and often barely articulated criteria, not against specific and preconceived outputs. It becomes instead a description of a set of activities which lead to certain outcomes, those outcomes being worthwhile or not in so far as either the controller (the government, say) or the customer finds them so. The judgment of the teacher – the one already initiated into an educational tradition – is relegated to insignificance in a world of mechanical rationalism, captured within this superficial language.

Hence, as one Treasury official felt able to declare:

❧ We took a strong view that education could play a much better role in improving industrial performance. The service is inefficient, rather unproductive and does not concentrate scarce resources in the areas that matter most. The economic climate and imperatives are clear; the task is to adjust education to them. (Quoted in Ranson, 1984, p.223)

The effect of language upon the social organisation and control of education is little explored. Certainly it opens up the possibility of social control. Funding depends on the achievement of prespecified targets. Measurement is in terms of observable behaviours. The role of the professional judgment is minimised as the manifestations of 'quality' can be easily recorded and observed and examined by non-professionals. Hence, the performance indicators and the league tables hailed as an instrument for improving standards of education.

But more fundamentally language changes our understanding of that which is to be controlled. It shifts from the moral framework of liberal education to the business framework of vocational training. But education as I have described it in this book is not that sort of thing. It is about the formation of persons and the preparation for a life worth living. However hard one tries, one cannot avoid the moral language through which the exploration of one's humanity is conducted and which makes the language of business, ideal for social control, an impoverished one for education.

A community of educated persons

It is so easy to see liberal education simply in terms of a given curriculum. But that would be mistaken. The curriculum has to be developed. It reflects a community's idea of what is worthwhile. It embodies a view of the good life within the community. But the 'good life', and what counts as an 'educated person', are themselves at the heart of educational deliberation. Intrinsic to liberal education must be the social mechanism through which that exploration of uncertainty of what it means to be human, is developed. Not only are we concerned with developing thinking persons; we need to do that in a thinking way.

The significance of this must surely be apparent. In the absence of this shared deliberation, in the failure to recognise the evaluative but uncertain nature of a liberal agenda, then one is in danger of imposing the language of social control and direction. Others, with unwarranted certainty about the desirable outcomes of learning, will direct the educational enterprise.

Inevitably the shaping of the educational system, and the guidance to be given to schools and to teachers, suffer from uncertainties and disagreements endemic in a pluralist society. One can respond to their uncertainties by handing over responsibility for decision making to others – the government, the Secretary of State, or educational gurus. But in that lies no real solution. Uncertainties remain. The solution must be, therefore, the democratisation of problem solving and decision making.

Once that was tried. The Schools Council was established in 1964, very much the creation of Derek Morrell. In his Lectures to the College of Preceptors in 1966, entitled *Education and Change*, Morrell reflects upon that Council and what lay behind its foundation. He asked

> why educators, in all parts of the world, are finding it necessary to organise a response to change on a scale, and in a manner, which has no precedent ... Why can't curriculum modification follow the simpler pattern of partial and piecemeal change which we and other countries followed for so long?

His answer might be summarised in his own words as follows:

> The many reasons ... stem from the pace of change in modern society. Its rapidity, and the extraordinary difficulty which we face in defining its characteristics, and in communicating the implications of change throughout complex systems of human relationships, have destroyed or at least weakened the broad consensus on aims and methods which was taken for granted when our educational system took its present form.

Morrell pointed to the changes – economic, social and moral – which create a crisis of values. Old assumptions are challenged about the kind of knowledge which is worth teaching, the literature worth reading, the values worth pursuing, the gaps between liberal education and vocational training worth closing. And thus, he continues,

❦ Our educational crisis is fundamentally part of a general crisis of values. If education, and by implication the curriculum, is not thought of as contributing to a solution of this crisis of values, it can all too easily become an agent of the worst sort of conservatism.

By 'the worst sort of conservatism' he referred to that nostalgia for the past when consensus reigned – at least amongst those who had the power to impose their view of things upon the rest. Such conservatism offered past formulae for future solutions to different problems. It failed to recognise the seriousness of the challenge to received assumptions and values, and therefore offered technical answers but not the reappraisal of the values, beliefs and purposes themselves which shaped policy and governed action.

But there are no certainties, no consensus over what those values and beliefs should be. The questions therefore are: how might we develop a public system of education amidst such personal uncertainty? How can we, with confidence, pursue educational goals when there is little agreement over what those goals should be? The weight of such questions certainly must fall upon the shoulders of the teacher. As Morrell (1964), therefore, stated 'Teachers must themselves become problem solvers' but, he added, *'not only in their own schools but collectively'*. Teachers inevitably deliberate about the appropriateness of the different cultural resources – the selection of them for teaching purposes and the values to be attributed to them in the light of particular conceptions of the life worth living. Teachers, in other words, are part of a wider community of educated people, deliberating about and questioning the values which permeate their teaching in the light of their experience of the practice of educating. And since they can only share those deliberations with their pupils if they speak from personal conviction, they too need support.

Facing changes that have no precedent, where old solutions are inadequate guides to future action and where no one can be certain about the ends to be pursued – whether religious fulfilment, a secular heaven, or a socialist utopia – then teachers, as a basis for sharing these uncertainties with their children, need to share them with each other and to receive support in that sharing and in those deliberations, for, as Morrell argues (prescient that he was), an alternative

❦ Big Brother approach would not only fail to achieve its objectives: it would also be profoundly wrong to ask the teachers to adopt new objectives and procedures on any basis other than personal conviction.

But how might we support those personal convictions, bearing in mind that they should be educated ones – based on evidence, tentative, open to scrutiny, the result of deliberation? How might help be given to teachers whose maturity, says Morrell, 'lies in facing this uncertainty without anxiety and with conviction and confidence'?

That is the reason for a community of educated persons. In such a community, research and development must play a crucial role. Therefore, Morrell pleaded for a 'co-operative attack' on the problems to be solved.

❦ Jointly, we need to define the characteristics of change – relying, whenever possible, on objective data rather than on opinions unsupported by evidence. Jointly, we need to sponsor the research and development work necessary to respond to change. Jointly, we must evaluate the results of such work, using both judgment and measurement techniques ... Jointly, we need to recognise that freedom and order can no longer be reconciled through implicit acceptance of a broadly ranging and essentially static consensus on educational aims and methods.

To do that the democracy of this community of educated persons

❦ must also be locally organised bringing together teachers, dons, administrators and others for the study of common problems, some local and others national in their implications.

It is essential, therefore, in preserving a liberal tradition, to maintain independent centres of critical thinking, and of scholarship, which, whatever its specialisms, never neglects those central questions of value which affect all that we do, to which there are no certain answers but which are and have to be resolved in our everyday practice. Such centres of critical enquiry must never be in hock to government, of whatever political colour – and they must always be aware of the many ways in which they are in danger of becoming so.

This community will be centrally concerned with the quality of life which, if rightly pursued, will provide the educated people which society needs. But such a concern for the quality of life cannot be captured in the impoverished language borrowed from accountancy or business. Nor can it be discovered in the individual pursuit of personal good without reference to those previous efforts to define it, upon which present day deliberations are built. In that sense, education must be conservative – a reverence for the voices of the past – and teachers must be the custodians of cultural traditions against the inroads of narrow utilitarianism or government interference.

CONCLUSION

8

Liberal and Vocational Education

Introduction

There are two enemies that I have in mind in writing this book. The first are those who, in face of certain changes, retreat to a narrow concept of liberal education which leaves so many dispossessed. The other is those who, in trying to make education more relevant, betray the best that is preserved within the liberal tradition. The divide is, and no doubt always will be, between liberal education and vocational preparation. But it need not be.

In the second series of the Victor Cook Lectures (1994) I addressed two questions. First, what is the aim of education – liberal or vocational? For that is the dualistic way many think about current educational policies and practices. Second, where should be the place for education: 'monastery' or market place? For, once again, views seem to be so very divided.

I argued for an abandonment of those dualisms between education and training, between thinking and doing, between theory and practice, between the intrinsically worthwhile and the useful, which bedevils our deliberations on education. Surely, if we focus on what it means to become fully a person, and to render personal that which so often arrives in an impersonal form – if, in other words, we respect both the learner and those cultural resources upon which that learning must draw – then there seems no reason why the liberal should not be conceived as something vocationally useful and why the vocationally useful should not be taught in an educational and liberating way.

This book has been an attempt to enter into that argument in greater detail, to offer the background to the philosophical questions and at the same time to identify the philosophical issues more precisely. By way of conclusion, therefore, I wish to summarise what I said there, whilst extending the argument where that is warranted.

The liberal ideal

In his inaugural address in 1867, John Stuart Mill argued that universities should not be places of professional education as

> their object is not to make skilful lawyers, or physicians, or engineers, but capable and cultivated human beings.

Universities were places where knowledge was pursued, where the intelligence was perfected, where that culture was acquired which

> each generation purposely gives to those who are to be its successors, in order to qualify them for at least keeping up, and if possible for raising, the level of improvement which has been attained.

They were not places to provide professional skills or vocational preparation. It was assumed that education was about 'improvement', not about being useful. But it was also assumed that the educated and the cultivated person would thereby be useful. Mill argued that

> men are men before they are lawyers and if you make them capable and sensible men, they will make themselves capable and sensible lawyers ... what professional men should carry away with them from an University is not professional knowledge, but that which should direct the use of their professional knowledge, and bring the light of general culture to illuminate the technicalities of a special pursuit.

A common thread in the different interpretations of liberal education has been the central significance given to the cultivation of reason and to those studies which enhanced the capacity to know, to understand, to pursue the truth. For that reason, liberal education was based firmly on the nature of knowledge, learnt not as a set of inert and discrete ideas but as disciplines of active thinking, internalised and interconnecting with each other. And this idea of liberal education has dominated the formation of our educational institutions, at every level and in every shape, and the content of the learning promoted by them.

Such a liberal ideal might be characterised in the following way.

First, its chief aim is to develop the intellect – to improve the capacity to think and to understand, and indeed (in the area of the arts) to appreciate what is worthy of appreciation. 'Improvement' is the word, but the improvement concerns not character or behaviour, but appreciation of what is true – or, indeed, in Arnold's (1869) words, the best that has been thought and said.

Second, that development of the intellect depends on the nature of knowledge – that which is the true object of the intellect. To be educated is to be initiated into those intellectual disciplines (the scientific, mathematical, historical, aesthetic, religious, philosophical, poetic) which constitute what it means to be acquainted with a true account of things. Such disciplines are the extensions of right reason, the ways of getting at the truth. Intellectual excellence requires a grasp of the basic concepts, a mastery of the essential skills, an acquisition of the techniques of enquiry, the development of the moral habits, within these fundamental ways through which we come to see and understand the world. Hence, the 'liberal curriculum' is an aggregate of those subjects through which the next generation acquires these different forms of knowledge.

Third, the point or the value of the apprenticeship into the intellectual traditions requires little further justification than reference to their own intrinsic value. The cultivation of the intellect is intrinsically worthwhile, although such intellectual excellence should also be socially useful as the cultivation of the intellect leads to the improvement of society. Indeed, to answer the question 'Why is it worthwhile?' would require already an initiation into these intellectual disciplines, because they are the tools through which one is able to reflect, to think, to address that sort of question. How can one think intelligently about the life worth living unless one has some historical perspective, or unless through science one has a basic understanding of the physical world, or unless one has been introduced through literature to images of human nature?

Fourth, the formation of the intellect is a demanding task. It cannot, in the main, happen incidentally. 'Learning from experience', or 'learning from interest', attractive though these student-centred phrases sound, will not provide the insights that intellectual excellence requires. Such excellence requires teachers, people already acquainted with the best that has been thought and said. And they need space and time set apart, free from the distractions of the immediate and the relevant. They need, in other words, schools and universities separated from the world of business and usefulness. Indeed, schools ideally should be like monasteries, rather than market places. Oakeshott describes it in his essay 'Education: the Engagement and its Frustration',

> In short, 'School' is 'monastic' in respect of being a place apart where excellences may be heard because the din of worldly laxities and partialities is silenced or abated. (1972, p.69)

And why does it have to be a world apart? Because, as he explains in another essay,

❝ Liberal education is a difficult engagement .... It is a somewhat unexpected invitation to disentangle oneself from the here and now of current happenings and engagements, to detach oneself from the urgencies of the local and the contemporary, to explore and enjoy a release from having to consider *things* in terms of their contingent features, *beliefs* in terms of their applications to contingent situations and *persons* in terms of their contingent usefulness ...

Fifth, the control and the direction of the teaching must lie in the hands of those who are authorities within the subjects themselves – certainly not government or industry or the community at large, but the scholars who, in the main, work in universities. And if schools are to address the problems of change within that liberal tradition – to relate intellectual excellence to social improvement – the school teachers too must be regarded as authorities within the development of liberal learning.

Liberal education so conceived has been likened by Oakeshott (1972) to a transaction between teacher and learner, in which the learner is introduced to the conversation which takes place between the generations of mankind in which the learner listens to the voices of poetry, of history, of philosophy, of science. We live in a world of ideas. And education is the initiation into that world. It has no purpose other than to let people into that conversation and to enjoy it.

This ideal has, as this book has demonstrated, its critics. It writes off too many young people. They fail the initiation test. Their voices are not allowed into the conversation, and the voices *they* listen to are not considered to be worth hearing. It is as though the liberal education is but for the few. Furthermore, the liberal tradition, in focusing upon the world of ideas, ignores the world of practice – the world of industry, of commerce, of earning a living. There has been a disdain for the practical intelligence – indeed, for the technological and the useful.

Vocationalising the liberal ideal

There are two responses to these criticisms. The first is that of having two sorts of education, preserving the liberal ideal for the few, and offering a vocational alternative for the many. The second is to dilute the liberal education with a vocational emphasis.

But there are important differences between the vocational on the one hand and the liberal on the other. In general, vocational preparation signifies the acquisition of skills, qualities, attitudes and knowledge that are judged to be important for entry into the world of work – either because the economy needs them (for example, trained mechanics or physicians) or because the learner would otherwise be ill prepared to find employment within it. Such vocational preparation can be pitched at different levels of generality. The science syllabus might be skewed towards the industrial application of science; communication skills might be incorporated into 'core skills' because that is what employers want; bee-keeping and rural science might be taught in the country comprehensive school. But, whatever the level of generality, there is this in common, namely, *the shaping of the transaction between teacher and learner by considerations other than those which are internal to the intellectual disciplines themselves.*

The following seem to be the characteristics of vocational preparation.

The aim is, not intellectual excellence for its own sake, but competence at work – or competence in the tasks which adults have to perform not only at work but also at home and in the community. Preparation for citizenship, or for parenting, are but extensions of vocational preparation. The dominant idea is that of 'competence'.

The content of the education and training programme is not derived from the intellectual disciplines, or from the best that has been thought and said, but from an analysis of the work to be done. People in industry say what skills are needed to run a business or to be an electrical engineer or to supervise staff, and the training programme is geared to produce those skills. There is an emphasis upon the 'can do' statements, on practical competence, as an object to be achieved through learning.

The value of what is learnt is not justified by reference to intrinsic worth or, indeed, to social improvement, but to the usefulness of it. This usefulness might apply to the economy as a whole or to the economic well-being of the learner or to the community at large. Consequently, a different set of virtues characterises vocational preparation – enterprise rather than disinterested pursuit of the truth, entrepreneurship rather than love of ideas.

The best place for this useful learning is not away from the busy world of commerce and industry, nor away from the practical problems that the young person will face after school and university. To prepare for adult life is best done through a kind of apprenticeship in which the young learner is engaged practically in the adult world, though of course under supervision and with a systematic introduction to the skills and competences required. No one doubts the need for systematic learning and thus for periods set apart. But those are dictated by the learning needs, not by a liberal ideal separating the learner from the distractions of the practical world of economic reality. Implicit in the vocational learning, therefore, is a view about how learning best takes place – practically, relevantly, with useful and specific goals in mind. On the whole, people learn by 'doing', although preferably under critical supervision. Thus, the BTEC and the new GNVQ are practical though demanding, assignment-led rather than based on intellectual disciplines, drawing upon the resources of the community rather than remaining aloof.

Finally, such a view of learning – its aims, its content, its value and its location – cannot be left in the hands of the academics. After all, it is argued, they and their ideal of liberal education have been responsible for economic neglect and for the impoverished idea of education in which the majority is excluded and in which important areas of experience play no part. Therefore, education and training must be under wider control. 'Authorities' over what should be learnt, and over what counts as successful learning, must include those from industry who know best what learning is useful and what research should receive public support. They must include the government which has broader interests to serve, and which ultimately pays the bill.

Vocational preparation, therefore, uses the language of usefulness, fitness for purpose, effective means to an end. It cherishes different values. It respects different personal and social qualities. It requires a different process of control and accountability.

Such modifications of the liberal ideal – justification of educational activities in terms of extrinsic utility rather than intrinsic worth, educational content reflecting economic relevance rather than intellectual excellence, assessment and control in the hands of employers rather than academics, education in the work place rather than in places set apart – are sometimes confined to the less able for whom training rather than continued education is deemed more appropriate. But increasingly it affects the idea of liberal education itself, challenging the values for which it stands. And this is best illustrated, as we have seen, by the changing language of education – the shift from the metaphor of 'conversation' to one of 'business audit' – and by the emphasis upon preconceived and measurable objectives, often expressed in terms of competences.

Such a vocational way of thinking and speaking may, on occasion, be intended only for the less able, even though they might be the majority, leaving a wider chasm still between the education of some and the training of others. But this vocationalising of education now permeates the idea of liberal learning itself.

Re-examination of the liberal ideal

There is a mistaken tendency to define education by contrasting it with what is seen to be opposite and incompatible. 'Liberal' is contrasted with vocational as if the vocational, *properly taught*, cannot itself be liberating – a way into those forms of knowledge through which a person is freed from ignorance, and opened to new imaginings, new possibilities: the craftsman who finds aesthetic delight in the object of his craft, the technician who sees the science behind the artefact, the reflective teacher making theoretical sense of practice.

Indeed, behind the liberal/vocational divide is another false dichotomy, namely, that between theory and practice. Theory is portrayed as the world of abstractions, of deep understanding, of the accumulated wisdom set down in books, of liberation from the 'here and now'. Practice, on the other hand, is identified with 'doing' *rather* than 'thinking', with the acquisition of skills rather than knowledge, with low level knowledge rather than with understanding. Intelligent 'knowing how' is ignored, the practical way to theoretical understanding dismissed, the wisdom behind intelligent doing unrecognised. Because of the dichotomy of theory from practice, of thinking from doing, science teaching, rather than be contaminated with the label 'vocational', enters into a mode of symbolic representation which loses the vast majority of young people – cuts them off, at an early age, from an understanding of the physical world in which they live. 'Real science' is for the able; craft is for the rest; the science within the craft goes unrecognised, and for that both the able and the less able suffer.

There is another false dualism. Certainly, the concepts of 'education' and 'training' do not mean the same – education indicates a relatively broad and critical understanding of things, whereas training suggests the preparation for a relatively specific task or job. But, despite the different meanings, one and the same activity could be both educational and training. Thus, one can be trained as a doctor, as an electrician, as a bus driver, or as a pharmacist, but that training can be such that the experience is educational. For example, the student teacher can be trained to plan the lessons, to manage the class, and to display the children's work. But the training can be so conducted that the student is educated *through* it – in becoming critical of what is happening, in understanding the activity, and in coming to see it in a wider educational context. Competence as a goal might be limiting. But it need not be. Indeed, without a certain degree of competence in playing the piano, one might be denied the chance of appreciating the finer points of a musical score, or, without some competence as a politician, one's political theorising might miss the mark. Furthermore, a critical stance requires very often the practical competence – as, for example, in the understanding of the use of technology. Skills training is not the opposite to understanding, but very often a precondition of it.

This acknowledgement of false dichotomies goes only part way to closing the liberal/vocational divide. Once more we must return to the aim of education. The liberal ideal picked out intellectual excellence. But 'helping children to become human' or enabling them to develop as persons needs more than that. It includes, of course, the perfection of the intellect – after all, what is more distinctively human than the capacity to think and to act intelligently, and what is best that has been thought and said other than what cultivates the intellect in its many different manifestations, practical as well as theoretical? But being human, and becoming more so, is the privilege of everyone. Each person, whatever his or her individual capacities and talents, is engaged in thinking and doing, in feeling and appreciating, in forming relationships and in shaping the future. All this can be engaged in more or less intelligently, more or less sensitively, more or less imaginatively. So long as there are thoughts to be developed, relationships to be formed, activities to be engaged in, feelings to be refined, then there is room for education. But that is possible only if the those thoughts, feelings, relationships and aspirations are taken seriously – not contemptuously rejected as of no concern to the tradition of liberal education. And that requires bringing the educational ideal to the vocational interests of the young people, educating them through their perception of relevance, helping them to make sense of their social and economic context, enabling them to be intelligent and questioning in their preparation for the world of work.

Dewey's defence of vocational education was as follows:

> A vocation means nothing but a direction of life activities as renders them perceptibly significant to a person because of the consequences they accomplish, and also useful to his associates. The opposite of a career is neither leisure nor culture, but aimlessness, capriciousness, the absence of cumulative achievement in experience, on the personal side, and idle play, a parasitic dependence on the others on the social side. Occupation is a concrete term for continuity. (p.307)

For any young person, assistance with how to live one's life, in which the sort of job one does plays such a significant part, is the most important of all educational experiences – clarifying the style of life judged worth living, identifying the training and work that will enable one to live that life, questioning the ends or values embodied within it, acquiring the necessary skills and competences.

A philosophy of education needs a more generous notion of what it is to be human than what has too often been captured within a liberal ideal. In the absence of such a notion, many young people have been dismissed as ineducable. A focus upon intellectual excellence has ignored the wider personal qualities, informed by thought, feeling and various forms of awareness, which need nurturing, even if this must be for many in the context of the practical and the useful.

The vocational alternative has, however, missed the point entirely, substituting a narrow form of training for a generous concept of education, transforming learning into an acquisition of measurable behaviours, reducing understanding and knowledge to a list of competences, turning educators into technicians.

The resulting danger is a two-track system. But this ignores the intuitive sense of so many teachers that education, helping young people to become human, is not like that. Certainly that education must be rooted in an educational tradition as that is captured in litera-ture, in history, in the human and physical sciences, in philosophy, in poetry – in the voices that make up the conversation between the generations of mankind that Oakeshott spoke about. But that education must also establish a continuity of experience with the young people themselves as they sort out their future employment or establish the quality of life which for them is worth living. It is the dismissal of those thoughts and feelings as of no educational significance which leads to the alienation of so many young people. Education is not for them.

The educated person

'Education' picks out those activities which form the educated person, and our concept of the educated person, contestable though it is, refers to those qualities and accomplishments which we value highly in people. 'Educated' is a commendation, granted by virtue of certain achievements. But those achievements have a cognitive core; they entail some sort of learning and the development of understanding. However, the nature of that understanding, and the selection of the achievements thought worthwhile, depend on wider ethical questions concerning the kind of life worth living and the kind of society which we think is desirable to live in. Moreover, just as the economic base of society changes, so will change the list of accomplishments which we see the educated person to need if he or she is to live intelligently within that society and to make a significant contribution to it. The liberal ideal of education needs constantly to be re-examined as our moral ideas develop concerning what it is to be a person and indeed how that person might adapt intelligently to changing economic and social conditions. And the question that I have been addressing concerns the extent to which such an ideal needs to incorporate the idea of vocational preparation. One danger of its failing to do so is that the vocational tradition – its language, its dominant concern for utility, its indifference to moral·deliberation and to philosophical speculation, its reduction of successful learning to the efficient achievement of someone else's goals, its equation of personal development with personal effectiveness – nudges out the liberal ideal, impoverishing the aims of education. That, as I have shown, is reflected in the new importance attached to the language of the market.

On the other hand, it is a common mistake – and one encouraged by certain interpretations of the liberal ideal – to perceive the educated person on the basis of purely personal accomplishments without reference to the greater social good to which that person contributes (or from which he or she takes away). But intellectual excellence needs to be related also to social improvement. That requires reference to the context of education within which the aims of education are to be achieved. It requires, too, reference to the kind of society which one believes to be appropriate for fulfilling those moral goals. Questions about the aims of education may be a matter of ethics, but they shade quickly into the area of social philosophy. One cannot disassociate the quality of life from broader questions about the institutional framework within which that education is to take place.

Furthermore, concern for the quality of life cannot ignore the kind of occupation to be pursued, the practical talents and intelligence to be acquired, the capability to be striven for of engaging creatively and imaginatively in the practical world, an awareness to be gained of the social and economic context in which one acts and lives, the moral framework to be sought of the relationships which one enters into – the very stuff of the prevocational curriculum described in chapters 3, 4 and 6. Vocational preparation in that broader sense must surely be part of a re-examined idea of liberal education.

Such an idea must have appeal to everyone, not the privileged possession of the few. Everyone, in his or her different way, and no doubt at different levels, is capable of thinking intelligently and sensitively, of having hopes and aspirations, of entering into relationships, and of having a sense of achievement and of personal worth. Teaching is first and foremost an attempt to achieve that in young people, and to do so through the mediation of a diverse and rich culture that we have inherited. But such a mediation must address those practical questions, concerning the preparation for the future, which are uppermost in the minds of the young, and which are not unrelated to the economic context into which they are entering. In that sense, there is a need to vocationalise the liberal ideal – to question the dualisms between thinking and doing, between theory and practice, between the world of education and the world of work, between education and training, which for too long have impoverished the educational experience of many.

Coleridge (1830) spoke of that inner awareness which was potentially present in all people, though it needed habits of reflection and imagination if it were to be developed:

> You have been bred in a land abounding with men able in the arts, learning and knowledge manifold. But there is one art of which every man should be master, the art of reflection. If you are not a thinking man, to what extent are you a man at all?

The principal of the American high school was right to be suspicious of education because it so often produced the educated physicians, the trained nurses, the high school and college graduates but not the 'thinking man'.

But I have also pointed to the dangers of an impoverished tradition of vocational training transforming education into something which is educationally indefensible, importing inappropriate metaphors through which that transaction between teacher and learner is described, valued, controlled and owned.

The community of educated people

This is the phrase used by Stenhouse (1967) in his book, *Culture and Education*. It refers to all those who seriously address important matters in life and do so in the light of the cultural resources bequeathed by previous generations. For, in those matters of supreme personal and social importance, there are no certainties. But one can have confidence and commitment in one's uncertainty if one submits what one believes to the critical scrutiny of others and if one examines them in the light of the deliberations which have taken place in literature, science, history, philosophy, theology and the arts. That is the essence of the humanities – a place where, in the words of the School Council's Working Paper, *The Raising of the School-Leaving Age*, 'teachers emphasise their common humanity with the pupils and their common uncertainty in the face of significant and personal problems'.

But such a community exists not only at the level of the classroom. The classroom teacher draws upon the resources of the much wider community of scholars and critics and artists and scientists both past and present. How else might one select that which will help the young learner to make sense of life and to find the ideals to follow? How else might he or she intelligently decide upon the kind of life which is worth living?

It is important therefore to create the conditions, if education is to remain essentially liberal, for the protection of that community from those who would deny the spirit of deliberation and of criticism, and who want to redirect the 'educated' conversation to political or economic ends. The Schools Council was one such institutional attempt, but that has been abolished. The great advisory councils established after the 1944 Act were a further guarantee of wide deliberation about aims as well as about means, but they too have been closed down. The universities are in theory the autonomous protectors of free thought and independent criticism, but their autonomy is increasingly encroached upon in the pursuit of greater 'efficiency gains' and vocational relevance. Teachers are central to that conversation in which the young learner is introduced to the voices of poetry and music and science and religion, but are increasingly reduced to 'delivering' someone else's (the government's) curriculum.

Conclusion

Liberal education is under threat from several angles – the political distortion of government, the vocationalising of its aims, the shifting language through which it is described and the narrowness of a vision of what it means to educate someone which excludes so many. It would be wrong, therefore, to seek to protect the 'liberal ideal' simply by resisting the inroads of vocationalism. Vocational relevance has an important place. It requires us, in respecting the aspirations and learning needs of the many, to broaden that liberal ideal. It encourages us to reconsider the place of practical intelligence, of personal development, of social and community relevance. It brings to our attention a range of skills, understandings and qualities which an educated person in this day and age should acquire.

In trying to reconcile different traditions of liberal education and vocational preparation – each characterised by different aims, values, curriculum content, institutional arrangement and authorities – we need to ask more fundamental moral questions about what it is to live

fully human lives and what the connection is between personal development and the wider social framework in which that development might
take place.

Our different notions of an 'educated person' embody judgments
about the qualities and knowledge of skills worth acquiring. But rarely
are these judgments made explicit or examined critically. The consequence is that, too often, liberal education promotes 'the unexamined
life', failing to address the perennial questions about the nature of the
life worth living – and, more importantly, failing to engage young
people in those questions. How dare those who, in 'reforming' the
National Curriculum, make humanities and the arts optional from the
age of 14 onwards?

This broader ideal of liberal education has to take everyone seriously,
even those who may not be academically able. Everyone, in his or her
own way, is capable of what Coleridge refers to as 'the art of reflection'.
And teachers, with proper support and with the richness of various
forms of cultural achievement as their resource, are capable of engaging
in that transaction with young people through which they, in their different ways, might explore the issues in literature, history, the arts, the
sciences which are of profound personal and social importance. But this
is possible only if we constantly remind ourselves of the ethical base of
our educational plans and purposes; otherwise 'education' is reduced
to impersonal knowledge, coverage of curriculum content, the achievement of other people's objectives, inert ideas.

To ensure that these moral questions are not suppressed by those,
including government, who wish to subvert education to their own
political or vocational ends, the ideals of this more generous concept of
liberal education need to be preserved within a 'community of educated
persons'. Such a community includes academics, artists, writers, scientists certainly who maintain and advance those cultural resources upon
which teaching must draw. But it includes, too, members of the community, including employers, who quite rightly question the relevance of
those resources to the economic and social world in which young people need to earn a living and find a quality of life. Above all, it includes
teachers who mediate the inherited culture to the personal aspirations
and needs of young people – who ensure that, whatever the differences
in cleverness or good fortune or background amongst those young people, their common humanity is recognised and their capacity 'to
become human' is enhanced.

Glossary of Acronyms

ABC   *A Basis for Choice*, published by FEU in 1979
A Level   Advanced Level of the GCE examination
APU   Assessment of Performance Unit, established at the DES in 1974
AS Level Advanced Supplementary Level of the GCE examination

BEC   Business Examination Council, which merged with TEC to form
          BTEC
BTEC   Business and Technician Examination Council

CBI   Confederation of British Industries
CGLI   City and Guilds of London Institute
CLEA   Council of Local Education Authorities
CPVE   Certificate of Pre-Vocational Education
CSE   Certificate of Secondary Education, started in 1964, succeeded by
          GCSE
CTC   City Technology College(s), established under 1988 Education Act

DE   Department of Employment
DfE   Department for Education
DES   Department of Education and Science, changed to DfE in 1990
DTI   Department of Trade and Industry

FAS   Funding Agency for Schools, established in 1993 to fund GMS
FE   Further Education
FEFC   Further Education Funding Council
FEU   Further Education Unit, established to advise FE on curriculum, etc

GCSE   General Certificate of Secondary Education, which succeeded
          GCE O Level
GCE   General Certificate of Education
GMS   Grant Maintained School(s), established by the 1988 Education Act
GNVQ   General National Vocational Qualification

HE   Higher Education
HMI   Her Majesty's Inspectorate
HND   Higher National Diploma of the BTEC

IB   International Baccalaureate
ILEA   Inner London Education Authority
IPPR   Institute for Public Policy Research

LEA   London Education Authority

MSC   Manpower Services Commission within the DE, later became TEED

NCC   National Curriculum Council, later merged with SEAC to become
             SCAA
NCVQ   National Council for Vocational Qualifications (NVQ and GNVQ)
NRA   National Record of Achievement
NVQ   National Vocational Qualification

OFSTED   Office for Standards in Education
O Level Ordinary Level of GCE, succeeded by GCSE
OND   Ordinary National Diploma of BTEC

RE   Religious Education
RSA   Royal Society for the Encouragement of Arts, Manufacture and
             Commerce

SAT   Standard Assessment Task
SCAA   Schools Curriculum and Assessment Authority
SEAC   School Examinations and Assessment Council, succeeded by SCAA

TEC   Technician Examination Council, later merged with BEC into BTEC
TEC   Training and Enterprise Council
TEED   Training Enterprise and Education Department
TGAT   Task Group on Assessment and Testing
TUC   Trades Union Congress
TVEI   Technical and Vocational Education Initiative

UBI   Understanding British Industry, an offshoot of CBI
UCAS   Universities and Colleges Admission Service

YTS   Youth Training Scheme

References

ALBSU (1993) in Dearing Interim Report (1993), London: SCAA.

Arnold, M. (1869) *Culture and Anarchy*, edition, Cambridge University Press, 1963.

Barnett, C. (1986) *The Audit of War*, London: Macmillan.

Bentham, J. (1789) *Introduction to the Principles of Morals and Legislation*, in Warnock, M., editor (1962) *Utilitarianism*, London: Collins.

Bowles, S. and Gintis, H. (1976) *Schooling in Capitalist America*, London: Routledge and Kegan Paul.

Bridges, D. and McLaughlin, T., editors (1994) *Education and the Market Place*, London: Falmer Press.

Bruner, J. (1960) *The Process of Education*, Boston: Harvard University Press.

Bullock Report (1974) *A Language for Life*, London: HMSO.

CBI (1989) *Towards a Skills Revolution*, London: Confederation of British Industries.

CBI (1993) *A Credit to Your Career: Routes for Success*, London: Confederation of British Industries.

Clark, A. (1993) *Diaries*, London: Weidenfeld and Nicholson.

Cockcroft Report (1982) *Mathematics Counts*, London: HMSO.

Coleridge, S.T. (1830) *On the Constitution of the Church and State*, edited by Barrell, J. (1972) London: J M Dent.

Cox, C.B. and Dyson, A.E., editors (1969a) *Fight for Education: A Black Paper*, London: Critical Society Quarterly.

Cox, C.B. and Dyson, A.E., editors (1969b) *Black Paper Two*, London: Critical Society Quarterly.

Cox, C.B. and Boyson, R., editors (1977) *Black Papers*, London: Temple Smith.

Crombie-White, R., Pring, R.A., Brockington, D. (1995) *14–19 Education and Training: Implementing a Unified System of Learning*, London: RSA.

Dearing Report (1993) Interim Report, London: SCAA.

Dearing Report (1994) *Final Report: The National Curriculum and its Assessment*, London: SCAA.

Dewey, J. (1916) *Democracy and Education*, New York: Free Press.

Elton Report (1991) *Discipline in Schools*, London: HMSO.

Engineering Council (1993) *A Review of Engineering Education*.

FEU (1979) *A Basis for Choice*, London: DES.

FEU (1992) *A Basis for Credit? A Paper for Discussion*, London: FEU.

Finegold, D. and Soskice, D. (1988) 'The failure of training in Britain', in *Oxford Review of Economic Policy*, 4(3).

Gleeson, D., editor (1987) *TVEI and Secondary Education*, Open University Press.

Gray, J. (1993) *Beyond the New Right*, London: Routledge.

Hadow Report (1926) *The Education of the Adolescent,* London: HMSO

Hansard (1978–8) *Parliamentary Debates: Commons, 123,* 771.

Hargreaves, D. (1982) *The Challenge for the Comprehensive School,* London: Routledge and Kegan Paul.

Harrison, G. (1987) Unpublished evaluation report, Department of Employment.

Hartley, D. (1987) 'The convergence of learner centred pedagogy in primary and further education in Scotland 1965 to 1985', in *British Journal of Educational Studies, 35*(2).

Hayward, G. (1995) *Getting to Grips with GNVQs,* London: Kogan Page.

Higginson Report (1988) *Advancing A Levels,* London: HMSO.

Hirst, P.H. (1965) 'Liberal Education and the Nature of Knowledge', in Archambault, R.D., *Philosophical Analysis and Education,* London: Routledge and Kegan Paul.

HMI (1988) *Curriculum Matters,* London: HMSO.

HMI (1988) *Records of Achievement: an Evaluation,* London: HMSO.

HMI (1991) *Higher Education in the Polytechnics and the Colleges,* London: HMSO.

HMI (1993) Annual Report, London: OFSTED.

ILEA (1979) *Improving Secondary Schools,* London: Inner London Education Authority.

Jessup, G. (1991) *Outcomes: NVQs and the Emerging Model of Education and Training,* London: Falmer Press.

Lawton, D. (1989) *Education, Culture and the National Curriculum,* London: Hodder and Stoughton.

Lawton, D. (1992) *Education and Politics in the 1990s: Conflict or Consensus?* London: Falmer Press.

Leavis, F.R. (1948) *The Great Tradition,* London.

Letwin, O. (1988) *Privatising the World,* London: Cassell.

Mill, J.S. (1859) *On Liberty,* in Warnock, M., editor (1972) *Utilitarianism,* London: Collins.

Mill, J.S. (1861) *Utilitarianism,* in Warnock, M., editor (1972) *Utilitarianism,* London: Collins.

Mill, J.S. (1867) Inaugural Lecture at the University of St Andrews, in Cavanagh, F.A., editor (1931) *James and John Stuart Mill on Education,* Cambridge University Press.

Morrell, D. (1966) *Education and Change,* The Annual Joseph Payne Memorial Lectures, 1965-66, London: College of Preceptors.

National Commission for Education (1993) *Learning to Succeed,* London: Heinemann.

NCC (1990) *Education for Citizenship,* London: NCC.

NCC (1991) *Core Skills 16–19,* London: NCC.

NCVQ (1994) Response to Alan Smithers, London: NCVQ.

Newman, J.H.(1852) *The Idea of a University,* London: Longmans, Green and Co. (1919 edition).

Newsom Report (1963) *Half Our Future,* Report of the Central Advisory Council for Education, London: HMSO.

Oakeshott, M. (1972) 'Education: the Engagement and its Frustration', in Fuller, T. (ed) *Michael Oakeshott and Education,* Yale University Press.

O'Hear, A. (1987) 'The Importance of Traditional Learning', in *British Journal of Educational Studies*, 35(2).

Oxford English Dictionary (1964).

Peters, R.S. (1966) *Ethics and Education*, London: Geo. Allen and Unwin.

Plowden Report (1967) *Children and Their Primary Schools*, Report of the Central Advisory Council for Education, London: HMSO.

Postlethwaite, N. (1988) 'English last in Science', in *Guardian*, 1/3/88.

Prais, S.J. and Wagner, K. (1983) *Schooling Standards in Britain and Germany*, NIESR.

Pring, R.A. (1972) "Knowledge out of control' *Education for Teaching*, autumn.

Pring, R.A. (1977) 'Commonsense and education', in *Journal of Philosophy of Education*, Vol.11.

Pring, R.A. (1992) 'Standards and quality in education', in *British Journal of Educational Studies*, 40(1).

Pring, R.A. (1994) 'The Aim of Education: Liberal or Vocational?' and 'The context of Education: Monastery or Market Place?', The Victor Cook Memorial Lectures 1993-1994, in Haldane, J., editor, *Education, Values and the State*, University of St. Andrews.

Ranson, S. (1984) 'Towards a Tertiary Tripartism', in Broadfoot, P. (ed) *Selection, Certification and Control*, London: Falmer Press.

Robbins Report (1963) *Higher Education*, London: HMSO

RSA (1984) *Newsletter.*

Schools Council (1967) *The Raising of the School-Leaving Age*, London: HMSO.

Schools Council (1968) *Enquiry 1*, London: HMSO.

Smithers, A. (1994) *All Our Futures: Britain's Education Revolution*, Despatches Report for Channel 4.

Spencer, H. (1861) 'What knowledge is of most worth?' in *Essays on Education*, London: Dent, 1911.

Spens Report (1938) *Secondary Education with Special Reference to Grammar Schools and Technical High Schools*, London: HMSO.

Stenhouse, L. (1967) *Culture and Education*, London: Nelson.

Strom, M. (1981) 'Facing history and ourselves', *Moral Education Forum*, summer.

Taylor Report (1979) *A New Partnership for Our Schools*, London: HMSO.

Tawney, R.H. (1931) *Equality*, London: Geo. Allen and Unwin

Tooley, J. (1994) 'In defence of markets in educational provision', in Bridges and McLaughlin, op.cit.

Tyler, R. (1949) *Basic Principles of Curriculum and Instruction*, University of Chicago Press.

White, R. (1980) *Absent with Cause*, London: Routledge and Kegan Paul.

White, R. and Brockington, D. (1978) *In and Out of School*, London: Routledge and Kegan Paul.

Wiener, M. (1985) *English Culture and the Decline of the Industrial Spirit 1850–1980*, Harmondsworth: Penguin.

Wilson, P.S. (1967) 'In defence of bingo', in *British Journal of Educational Studies*, 15.

Young, M.F.D (1971) *Knowledge and Control*, London: Collier-Macmillan.

Government Papers referred to, in chronological order

DES/HMI (1977) *Curriculum 11 to 16*, London: HMSO

DES (1977) *Education in Schools: a Consultative Document*, London: HMSO

DES (1979) *A Framework for the School Curriculum*, London: HMSO

DE (1981) *A New Training Initiative: A Programme for Action*, London: HMSO

DES (1981) *The School Curriculum*, London: HMSO

DE and DES (1984) *Training for Jobs*, London: HMSO

DES (1984) *Examinations at 17+*, London: HMSO

DES (1984) *Record of Achievement, a Statement of Policy*, London: HMSO

DE and DES (1985) *Education and Training for Young People*, London: HMSO

DE and DES (1985) *Working Together: Education and Training*, London: HMSO

DES (1985) *Better Schools*, London: HMSO

DTI (1988) *White Paper*

DES (1991a) *Education and Training for the 21st Century*, London: HMSO

DES (1991b) *The Parent's Charter*, London: DES.

DFE (1993) *Choice and Diversity*, London: HMSO

DE (1994) *Competitiveness: Helping Businesses to Win*, London: HMSO

Index